PONTEACH, OR THE SAVAGES OF AMERICA

Pontiac, or Ponteach, was a Native American leader who made war upon the British in what became known as Pontiac's Rebellion (1763 to 1766). One of the earliest accounts of Pontiac is a play, written in 1766 by the famous frontier soldier Robert Rogers of the Rangers. *Ponteach, or the Savages of America* is one of the only early dramatic works composed by an author with personal knowledge of the Indigenous nations of North America. Important both as a literary work and as a historical document, *Ponteach* interrogates eighteenth-century Europe's widespread ideological constructions of Indigenous peoples as either innocent and noble savages, or monstrous and violent Others.

Presented for the first time in a fully annotated edition, *Ponteach* takes on questions of nationalism, religion, race, cultural identity, gender, and sexuality; the play offers a unique perspective on the rebellion and on the emergence of Canadian and American identities. Tiffany Potter's edition is supplemented by an introduction that critically and contextually frames the play, as well as by important appendices, including Rogers' ethnographic accounts of the Great Lakes nations.

TIFFANY POTTER teaches in the Department of English at the University of British Columbia.

ROBERT ROGERS

Ponteach, or the Savages of America

A Tragedy

Edited by Tiffany Potter

UNIVERSITY OF TORONTO PRESS
Toronto Buffalo London

© University of Toronto Press Incorporated 2010
Toronto Buffalo London
www.utppublishing.com
Printed in Canada

ISBN 978-0-8020-9895-5 (cloth)
ISBN 978-0-8020-9597-8 (paper)

Printed on acid-free, 100% post-consumer recycled paper with vegetable-based inks.

Library and Archives Canada Cataloguing in Publication

Rogers, Robert, 1731–1795
Ponteach, or the savages of America: a tragedy / Robert Rogers;
edited by Tiffany Potter.

Includes bibliographical references and index.
ISBN 978-0-8020-9895-5 (bound).   ISBN 978-0-8020-9597-8 (pbk.)

1. Pontiac's Conspiracy, 1763–1765 – Drama.   I. Potter, Tiffany, 1967–   II. Title.

PS829.R6P6 2010   812'.1   C2010-904476-2

This book has been published with the help of a grant from the Canadian Federation for the Humanities and Social Sciences, through the Aid to Scholarly Publications Programme, using funds provided by the Social Sciences and Humanities Research Council of Canada.

The University of Toronto Press acknowledges the financial assistance to its publishing programm of the Canada Council for the Arts and the Ontario Arts Council.

 Canada Council   Conseil des Arts
for the Arts   du Canada

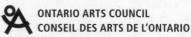 ONTARIO ARTS COUNCIL
CONSEIL DES ARTS DE L'ONTARIO

University of Toronto Press acknowledges the financial support of the Government of Canada through the Canada Book Fund for its publishing activities.

For my parents, Leslie and Fern Potter

CONTENTS

ILLUSTRATIONS ·

ACKNOWLEDGMENTS

Every edition has one author, one editor, and a large number of hands unseen in the final product. I hope to acknowledge here the many contributions, institutional and personal, that have helped to bring Rogers' play farther into the light. First, I am grateful to the students in my courses on eighteenth-century drama and on gender and indigeneity at the University of British Columbia; many of my students have offered fascinating comments on and engagements with *Ponteach* in the classroom and in their papers, and they have come up with several of the important questions I attempt to address in this volume. In particular, I wish to acknowledge the excellent work of Niki Parassidis, Kimberley Read, Carly Ryan, and Nancy Street, students in my 2008 majors' seminar, each of whom contributed an original annotation to this edition. I would also like to thank Peter Sabor, who first sold me on the pleasures of scholarly editing, and David Oakleaf, whose gift of a copy of Mary Rowlandson's narrative started me in such an exciting direction.

For their help in confirming the continuity of the print run of Rogers' play, I offer thanks to the librarians at Mount Allison University; McGill University; the Toronto Reference Library; Boston Public Library; the John Hay Library, Brown University; the Special Collections Research Center at the University of Chicago Library; the Rare Book and Special Collections Division at the Library of Congress; Houghton Library, Harvard University; the Huntington Library; the University of Virginia; the Rare Book and Manuscript Library, University of Illinois at Urbana-Champaign; the Lilly Library, Indiana University; Special Collections at Michigan State University; Special Collections at the University of Vermont, the Beinecke Rare Book and Manuscript Library, Yale University; the British Library; and the Trustees at the National Library of Scotland. For permission to reproduce the illustrations in this volume, I thank the New York Public Library, McGill University Library, the Clements Library at the University of Michigan, and the Ohio Historical Society. For research on the Ogden family, I am grateful to the scholars and volunteers at Fairfield Museum and History Center in Fairfield, Connecticut.

Editing forgotten plays is to some degree a labour of love, but the love is certainly helped along by good funding. This edition emerged from a larger three-year investigative project on gender and indigeneity funded by a Standard Research Grant from the Social Sciences and Humanities Research Council of Canada. I am most grateful to SSHRC for their support of literary and historical scholarship in Canada. I also wish to acknowledge the support of the Department of English at the University of British Columbia for funding conference travel related to this project.

At the University of Toronto Press, I wish to thank my editor, Richard Ratzlaff, and the two exceptionally engaged and informed anonymous readers. Their criticisms and suggestions have added enormously to this volume; errors, of course, remain my own.

And finally, as ever, I thank most of all my family for their support in everything that I do. I owe my start to my parents, Les and Fern Potter, and I am grateful every day for my brilliant husband Ken Madden and our equally brilliant daughter Sloane. They remind me every day in exactly the right ways how much and how little my work matters.

Vancouver, British Columbia
2010

A NOTE ON THE TEXT
AND PUBLICATION HISTORY

This edition is based upon the first and only printing of *Ponteach*, published in London by J. Millan in 1766. ESTC currently lists twenty-nine extant copies held by public institutions. To prepare this edition I reviewed the single copies held by McGill University and the Toronto Public Library, as well as a digital version of the British Library copy, all of which appear to be from the same print run. In correspondence with the extremely helpful librarians at the other holding institutions I have confirmed that all surviving copies share the same typographical errors, page breaks, and graphic additions and hence seem to be from the same print run. McGill University provided the copy text for this edition.

Because I believe that a scholarly edition of a largely unavailable text should resemble the original as much as possible (to allow for all types of analysis, including comparisons of non-standard spellings and syntax), this edition replicates the McGill copy as closely as I can manage. I have maintained old spellings and the eighteenth-century conventions in the capitalization of nouns (insofar as Rogers' printers follow them). I have altered only obvious typographical errors, indicating these emendations and the original forms in the notes.

Ponteach was 'printed for the Author; and Sold by J. Millan, opposite the *Admiralty,* Whitehall' (title page). John Millan was one of the best known of the Whitehall booksellers, printing and selling books for some fifty years until his death in 1784. After his death, the new owners of the shop, Thomas and John Egerton, repeatedly mention in their advertisements of collections for sale that they are 'successors to Mr. Millan.' Millan seems to have printed more historical, military, and non-fictional material than literary texts, notably an annual volume titled *Millan's Universal Register of Court and City Offices* which recorded the names of members of groups from the Royal Society to physicians authorized to practice in London. Millan published all three of Rogers' books, all in small octavo dress. The *Journals of Robert Rogers* sold

for 5s, and *Concise Account of North America* for 4s (published concurrently). *Ponteach* sold for 2s 6d, less than for Rogers' other publications, but
slightly more than typical for plays printed at the time. By comparison, in
1766 Thomas Francklin's *The Earl of Warwick: A Tragedy* (which was staged
and went to multiple editions) sold for 1s 6d, and the second edition of popular
playwright Arthur Murray's farce *The Citizen* sold for 2s 1d. Poet George
Cocking's *The Conquest of Canada or the Siege of Quebec* sold in its first edition in 1766 for 1s 6d. It is unclear how many copies of *Ponteach* were sold.

PONTEACH, OR THE SAVAGES OF AMERICA

INTRODUCTION:
STAGING SAVAGERY AND
FICTIONALIZING COLONIALISM
IN ROBERT ROGERS'
PONTEACH: A TRAGEDY

Robert Rogers' 1766 *Ponteach: or the Savages of America. A Tragedy* is the first play published in Britain about specifically North American subject matter by an author born in the American colonies.[1] Though the play has been read as functionally about England rather than North America, merely an 'obvious political allegory ... through which Rogers provides a loyalist critique of revolutionary rhetoric' (Tanner and Krasner 7, 5), I find it impossible to conclude anything other than that *Ponteach* is inescapably *about* colonial America and its self-construction. The play's aggressive efforts to remove Ponteach from realms of mere metaphor humanize him to a specific purpose: only a fully human, complex Indigenous character can communicate the tragedy of the dehumanizing colonial relationship that Rogers reports.

Rogers is best known to history as the great military leader of Rogers' Rangers, the most successful fighting unit in the French and Indian War of 1754–63. His fame is also partly the result of good self-promotion: he was first the author of an influential *Concise Account of North America* (which included a reasonably accurate and nation-specific sixty-page description of the 'Customs, Manners, &c. of the Indians,' reprinted here as Appendix A), and an autobiographical account of his American military experiences, sold

---

1 Though, of course, the political entity of the United States of America did not exist per se in 1766, Rogers was born in the colonies, and so is widely referred to as an early American writer, though his works were published in London. His case offers an excellent example of the transatlantic nature of colonial culture at this time, where texts circulated around Britain and the East Coast of America rather than being necessarily English or American. Published in January 1766, *Ponteach* is the second play published by a North American-born writer, after Thomas Godfrey's *The Prince of Parthia*, which appeared late in 1765 (though it had been written in 1759). Godfrey's play is an exoticized Orientalist imagining, leaving *Ponteach* as the first English-language play about explicitly North American experience.

as *The Journals of Major Robert Rogers* (which included a summary of the successful strategies he employed in training his troops and directing their tactics in battle). *Ponteach*[2] is less well known, receiving only a one-page mention in John Cuneo's 300-page standard biography of Rogers. While Rogers' historical documents are widely referenced and discussed, his play has been almost ignored critically, arguably because the play is widely perceived to be only adequate as art.[3] The play's importance, though, is not that it was very nearly the first published American play, or even in its entertainment value, as it was never staged[4] and is not well appreciated as a literary text. Its value is as a representation of a political speech act, and though it did not actually receive a production, it attempts to render for the first time for the English-speaking stage a knowledgeable representation of one of the Indigenous cultures of North America.[5] More importantly, it asserts for that culture a humanity that transcends eighteenth-century Europe's often-accepted ideological constructions of innocent noble savages or monstrous and violent mimics of almost-humanity. As Stephen Greenblatt suggests, until the late twentieth century, there was a long-standing tradition of writing and reading Indians as transparent: 'either as Hobbesian pagans in a state of

---

2 Not to be confused with another soldier's later dramatic effort, General Alexander Maycomb's 1838 *Pontiac, or the Seige of Detroit*.

3 Robert E. Morsberger, for example, sets up his discussion by asserting that 'Except for a few scenes, the play has almost no artistic value, but parts of it are most interesting in connection with Rogers' attempts to get support and authority for his project to seek the Northwest Passage' (246). For the record, I disagree: given the operatic nature of the tradition of heroic drama in which the play clearly locates itself, I find *Ponteach* to be perhaps not Dryden, but certainly entertaining and informative, two criteria for successful theatre by most eighteenth-century criteria.

4 The record is unclear, but most scholars agree that *Ponteach* was never staged. Tanner and Krasner assert without documentation that it ran in London for one night only. Montrose J. Moses argued in 1918 that there might have been one amateur production. The play was, however, reimagined as a musical presentation in 1977. In *Ponteach: A Melodrama for Narrator and Piano*, Lejaren Hiller uses speeches by Ponteach and other characters to exemplify character types in historical conflict, including the Trader, the Hunter, the Colonel, the Governor, and the Priest. The music is based on the Ojibwa war song 'Scarlet is its Head,' with allusions to other Ojibwa and Ottawa music, and recognizable British melodies such as 'The British Grenadiers' and 'Do You Know the Muffin Man.'

5 Outside of the English-speaking stage, there are other examples of knowledgeable theatrical engagements with both North and South American Indigenous cultures. In colonial Spanish America, for example, early miracle plays and even some Golden Age Spanish tragedies were translated and performed in Native languages, and Native performances such as the Mayan *Rabinal Achi* could be performed in ways that offered a response. See Dennis Tedlock's *Rabinal Achi: A Mayan Drama of War and Sacrifice*.

nature, condemned to lives that are solitary, nasty, brutish, and short, or as mute, naïve, miserable victims, condemned only to deception and enslavement.' He suggests that modern criticism gives 'the encounter between Europeans and American peoples a remarkable specificity and historical contingency. The Indians have lost the transparency of allegory, gaining instead the density of historical subjects struggling to come to terms with figures from a perplexingly different culture' (viii). Rogers' play makes a very early gesture towards exactly this epistemological shift in its rendering of the Ottawa war chief Pontiac as Ponteach, a complex, articulate human being driven to acts of violence and war both by his own excess ambition and a continuum of personal snubs and cultural encroachments that threaten his family and his community.

Rogers seems to have been moved to the dramatic arts by a review of his *Concise Account* in *Critical Review*, which noted that 'the picture which Mr. Rogers has exhibited of the emperor Ponteack is new and curious, and his character would appear to vast advantage in the hands of a great dramatic genius' (November 1765). Perhaps in response to such encouragement, Rogers wrote a dramatized version of the most notable individual figure in the broader historical and ethnographic accounts he had published, fictionalizing Pontiac extensively, most blatantly in giving him two sons,[6] and having the two sons fight over women, eventually leading to both their deaths.

Rogers had completed only a basic public school education in New Hampshire, however, and the play's formal structure and relatively accomplished blank verse leave some doubt as to whether his was the only hand involved in its production. Allan Nevins and Howard Peckham both suggest that Rogers must have had the assistance of another, more conventionally educated figure, and Rogers' personal secretary Nathaniel Potter is the most logical candidate for co-author or editor. Potter had been educated at New Jersey College (Princeton). Nevins calls Potter 'educated and rather clever, but disreputable'

---

6 Though Pontiac was old enough to have adult sons by the time of Pontiac's Rebellion in 1763, there is no indication in the historical record that any sons were present. The record on Pontiac's descendents is unclear. Peckham's still-standard 1947 biography of Pontiac notes that Pontiac 'definitely' had two sons in 1769, but their names are not known. He suggests that 'one of them was probably Shegenaba, who gained some prominence in 1775' by returning captive Ezekiel Field. Another source names Kasahda and Nebahkohum as sons of Pontiac. None of these men are named in documents pertaining to the rebellion, and none seem to have taken on leadership roles in the Ottawa communities. One of Pontiac's (much younger) wives, Kan-tuck-ee-gun was living at Maumee as late at 1815, with one son, Otussa. Another of Peckham's sources, though, identifies a Tuss-saw as Pontiac's nephew in 1825. Shortly thereafter the same source lists Tuss-saw as Pontiac's grandson, who was dictating a biography of Pontiac. The notes from this dictation have not been found (Peckham 316–17).

and provides manuscript evidence that British Superintendent of Indian Affairs Sir William Johnson asserted in 1767 that Potter 'had been hired because Rogers was so illiterate as to require someone to do business for him' (102). Though the evidence of Rogers' own journals and letters seems to contradict Johnson's assessment, there is little suggestion of rhetorical flourish either. Francis Parkman is correct in the summary that 'his books and unpublished letters bear witness that his style as a writer was not contemptible' (1: 162–3). Potter and Rogers had a falling out around 1767, but this would not seem to preclude collaboration on *Ponteach*. John Cuneo also nominates John Campbell as a possible collaborator (174–7). Campbell was a prolific and competent writer who had also been commissioned by Lord Bute to write a justification of the Peace of Paris, which would have given him a certain amount of detailed knowledge of America, though he had never been there. No author was listed on the title page of the printed text of the play, and though it was uniformly attributed to Rogers upon publication (Nevins 101), some form of collaborative endeavour seems likely.

Even with growing interest in North America and 'Indians' by the 1760s, even with the English cult of sensibility in full swing, and even amid the beginnings of the vogue for melodrama on the English stage, *Ponteach* was ill-received. All evidence indicates that it was never staged, and Rogers' decision to have actually occur onstage two unprovoked murders and scalpings (by English hunters), several violent deaths, an attempted rape by a priest, and an extended scene of torture (initially including an innocent woman and her breast-feeding child) was something that, according to *The Gentleman's Magazine* could be viewed or read only with 'abhorrence' and 'disgust' (February 1766). *Monthly Review* was particularly personal in its criticism, calling *Ponteach* 'One of the most absurd productions we have ever seen,' and noting that in 'turning bard and writing a tragedy Rogers makes just as good a figure as would a Grub-street rhymester at the head of our author's corps of North American rangers' (January 1766). Contemporary reviews of all of Rogers' publications are reprinted in this volume in Appendix C.

In addition to the artistic shortfalls such reviews pointed out, there were some odd historical inaccuracies as well that should be noted. The most significant of these is perhaps the apparently completely fictional story of Ponteach's two sons, Philip and Chekitan, but a second set of historical inaccuracies comes in the representation of the role of the Mohawks in Pontiac's Rebellion. As Rogers' own *Concise Account* acknowledges, the Mohawks and the Five Nations maintained ongoing hostilities with the Great Lakes Nations. Not only were they not traditional allies, but the Mohawks were a part of the long-standing Covenant Chain that established peaceful relations between the Five

Nations and the British, and were at no point part of the rebellion (though the westernmost of the Five Nations, the Senecas, had a vital role). One step beyond this broad slippage lies *Ponteach*'s representation of Hendrick, styled 'Emperor of the Mohawks' in the *dramatis personae*. The Mohawk leader Theyanoguin was known to the English as Hendrick, but he had been killed in battle in 1755 in the French and Indian War, long before the events of Rogers' play. In a play that seems in so many ways desperate for the appearance of accuracy, and that offers so much lightly veiled political commentary, such errors might seem surprising, but in fact there are both internal and external reasons for Rogers' depiction of Hendrick and the Mohawks. The first is fairly simple: the likely involvement of one or both of Nathaniel Potter and John Campbell in the composition of the play. Either man would have known that the tragic subplot of the second-generation Ottawas and Mohawks might appeal to the tastes of mid-eighteenth-century audiences (particularly in the language of sensibility and the elements of the melodramatic), and the star-crossed lovers plot requires families or nations in conflict. Other issues of marketing might also have overwhelmed desires for accuracy: the Mohawks were the Indigenous nation best known to most Londoners, and with their loyalty to the British in the war, they were widely depicted as heroic figures in Britain. A character named Hendrick, in particular, might have been considered to have sure appeal to audiences, given the recognizability of the Mohawk 'Hendricks' of the two previous generations. Londoners might have been expected to recall the famous Mohawk 'King Hendrick' who was one of the 'Four Indian Kings' whose visit created a sensation in London in 1711. English audiences could imagine such a man, because they or their parents might have seen him or his portraits. Adding further complexity is the subsequent slippage in the identity of 'Hendrick' in historical accounts. As Barbara Sivertsen has shown, there were actually two different Mohawk sachems who were called Hendrick Peters by Europeans. The two have been conflated by generations of historians, but as Dean Snow has documented, the sachem known to the Mohawks as Tejonihokarawa was a member of the Wolf Clan born around 1660, while the Hendrick Peters also known as Theyanoguin was a member of the Bear Clan born in 1692.

While such inaccuracies preclude *Ponteach* from being read as a conventionally historical depiction of Pontiac's Rebellion, the play offers a different kind of insight into Anglo-Indian relationships, allowing a more individuated and human understanding of the types of perceptions and interactions that contributed to what was in many ways the last great stand of the North American Indigenous nations against the westward expansion of colonial settlements. The play at no point asserts absolute historical accuracy, and these sorts of departures from documentable history tend to serve either artistic purposes (as in the presumed audience appeal of a love plot in Chekitan) or political ones (as in the fictionalization of real men to make more explicit what Rogers perceives to be their errors).

HISTORICAL CONTEXT

Running from the spring of 1763 until the final formal treaty was signed at Fort Ontario on 25 July 1766, the conflict most commonly known as Pontiac's Rebellion covered a geography from Pennsylvania to Illinois and included more than a dozen different tribes from the Illinois, Ohio, and Great Lakes regions, as well as the Senecas, the Keepers of the Western Gate of the Iroquois Five Nations (though the remaining groups of the Five Nations, including the Mohawks, maintained the Covenant Chain, which affirmed their allegiance to the British). Eighteenth-century estimates suggested that some 2,000 settlers and soldiers had been killed or captured by the end of 1763, though modern historians of the conflict are sceptical: as Gregory Evans Dowd points out, the most-cited source for this number is Deputy Indian Superintendent George Croghan, but Croghan was in London when he made the estimate, and the 'public and personal papers that he would have had at his disposal do not bring the number anywhere near that high' (142). Howard Peckham documents a plausible calculation of deaths, with some 450 soldiers killed in the conflict (239), and William R. Nester provides a similarly reasonable calculation of approximately 200 Native warriors killed (279). Regardless of the final numbers of dead on both sides, the conflict was long, wide-ranging, and bloody, fostering tremendous suffering in both settler and Indigenous communities.

As in any war, the origins of Pontiac's Rebellion are complex and at times contradictory. The long-standing conflict between Britain and France had most recently been activated in the Seven Years' War, which was fought on European, North American, African, and Asian soil. With reference to the specific events of North America, the conflict is most often called the French and Indian War. Hostilities in the French and Indian War ended for the most part with the September 1760 signing of the Capitulation of Montreal, though it was the February 1763 Treaty of Paris that formally ended the Seven Years' War and all of its subsidiaries, calling for a 'Christian, universal, and perpetual peace, as well by sea as by land, and a sincere and constant friendship shall be re established between their Britannick, Most Christian, Catholick, and Most Faithful Majesties, and between their heirs and successors, kingdoms, dominions, provinces, countries, subjects, and vassals, of what quality or condition soever they be, without exception of places or of persons.' Under the Treaty of Paris, nearly all of the territory previously controlled by the French was ceded to Britain, giving Britain control of all but a very small part of the American territory east of the Mississippi. As George Croghan reported to Sir William Johnson at the time, however, various Indigenous leaders asserted that 'the French had no right to give up their Country to the English' (quoted in Dowd 112). This sentiment alone might or might not have led to armed conflict, but, as Rogers' play points out, the relationship between the Indians and the British was very different from that fostered by the French in previous generations.

The relatively small numbers of French settlers had developed interdependent and widely amicable, if not necessarily egalitarian, alliances and trading and domestic relationships with many of the Great Lakes Nations, including intermarriage. After 1763, British policy instead generally addressed French and Indians as equally conquered peoples. Instead of leaving existing French forts as the generally small trading outposts they had been, the British rebuilt many of them (including the mammoth Fort Pitt), convincing the Indians that the British intended to take over their territory exclusively and permanently. Though the western expansionism implied by such fortifications is one obvious motivation for Pontiac's Rebellion, population pressures were much less important to Pontiac's Ottawas and the other Great Lakes Nations (Hurons, Ojibwas, and Potawatomis) than to the Shawnees, Delawares, Mingos, and Wyandots of the Ohio region, which faced constant pressure from the Thirteen Colonies. Still, though the Great Lakes and Illinois Nations had yet to face substantial pressures of colonial expansion, the experiences of the Ohio Nations made clear that the British plan was distinct from that of the French. Differences in administrative attitudes and policies soon became another common complaint and source of racial tension.

Among the British leaders of the North American colonies after 1763, Sir Jeffrey Amherst is perhaps the most emblematic face of the new modes of governance. Amherst was the governor general of British North America from 1760 to 1763, and he made no secret of his distaste for the Indigenous inhabitants of his newly claimed territory, and this was made most explicitly manifest in his decision to cut back on the long-standing tradition of gift-giving. In most of the Indigenous cultures of America, the giving or exchange of gifts functioned as a gesture of respect and communalism. The French had incorporated this tradition into their trading relationships, and regularly made gifts of European goods such as hunting weapons, gunpowder, blankets, clothing, and alcohol (as well as tobacco) to local sachems, who then distributed the goods in their communities as evidence of their status and their ability to negotiate benefits from the French. Though Superintendent of Indian Affairs Sir William Johnson and many of Amherst's officers in the field pointed out the enormous cultural significance of gifts among the North American nations, and advised against the policy change, [7] Amherst read the tradition as mere bribery at best and extortion at worst. He reasoned that 'we must deal more sparingly for the future, for the now tranquil state of the country and the good regulations you have put the trade under, I can see very little reason for bribing the Indians or buying their good behavior, since they have no enemy to molest them, but, on the contrary, every encouragement & protection they can desire for their trade' (quoted in Nester 51). To add potential injury to insult, Amherst also reduced the amount of gunpowder that could be traded. This had a doubled negative effect: at the most practical level, scarcity of powder made hunting and thus the sustenance of communities more difficult; this in turn contributed to a larger sense that the Indians were being weakened and disarmed in order to render them vulnerable to future attack.

Though the conflict is named after Ottawa sachem Pontiac, it was the Senecas who sent the first round of war belts, calling the Great Lakes Nations and others to uprising in 1761. Seneca support for war and later for Pontiac was not unanimous, however. Because the Senecas were a part of the Iroquois Five Nations, the sending of war belts constituted a break in the Covenant Chain, the long-standing agreement between the Iroquois confederacy and the British. For this and other reasons, this first round of discontent could not bring the different nations to unified action, but by 1763 two things had changed: the consequences of the handover of territory from the French to the British became undeniable, and a religiously based movement towards Indian nationalism gained great momentum.

In the early 1760s, word spread quickly among Great Lakes Nations of the dream vision of Neolin, known as the Delaware Prophet (of the Wolf Clan of the Delaware Nation). Rogers' play touches relatively briefly on the specific rhetoric of Neolin, but his historical importance, especially to Pontiac's role in the conflict, is great. The earliest recorded account of the Delaware Prophet comes in 1761 from a Pennsylvania fur trader named James Kenny, not long after the first of the visions, which Neolin asserted had begun in 1760. The version of Neolin's vision most closely associated with Pontiac, though, is the contemporary document, the *Journal of Pontiac's Conspiracy*, a French-language account of the Siege of Detroit written in the form of a journal. The *Journal* is generally attributed to Robert Navarre, a notary and interpreter at Detroit, who had access to both the garrison and Pontiac's

---

7 Johnson wrote to Amherst in 1763 that the withdrawal of gifts would be read to signify 'contempt, dislike, and an Inclination to reduce them so low as to facilitate Designs of extirpating them' (cited in Dowd 71).

camp during the conflict.[8] Navarre's account of Neolin's vision is reprinted in Appendix B of this volume.

Neolin claimed a dream in which the Master of Life demanded several changes to traditional practices of worship and domestic life. The account of Neolin's dream begins with the dreamer's quest to meet the Master of Life. After eight days of travel, the dreamer is directed to the Master of Life by a woman and then a man dressed in white. The Master of Life tells him, 'Because I love you, ye must do what I say and love, and not do what I hate.' In Pontiac's telling, the Master of Life rejects drinking 'to the point of madness,' infighting, polygyny, and adultery, and medicine dances seeking the Manitou, whom he calls 'an evil spirit who prompts you to nothing but wrong, and who listens to you out of ignorance of me.' He admonishes the dreamer for dependence on English weapons and trade goods: 'if ye were not evil, as ye are, ye could surely do without them. Ye could live as ye did live before knowing them ... I do not forbid you to permit among you the children of your Father;[9] I love them. They know me and pray to me, and I supply their wants and all they give to you. But as to those who come to trouble your lands, – drive them out, make war upon them. I do not love them at all; ... Send them back to the lands which I have created for them and let them stay there' (Navarre 28–30).

The Delaware Prophet conveyed his vision of the Master of Life to several groups across a surprisingly wide geography, but Pontiac was his most influential follower. Navarre's account reports that the 'adventure was soon noised about among the people of the whole village who came to hear the message of the Master of Life, and then went to carry it to the neighbouring villages. The members of these villages came to see the pretended traveller, and the news was spread from village to village and finally reached Pontiac' (32). Richard Middleton documents some of Pontiac's subsequent role in spreading Neolin's vision: 'according to Menominee tradition, he visited the Milwaukee some time in the fall of 1762 or the early spring of 1763 for a grand council, where he introduced the Wisconsin peoples to Neolin's vision' (66). Such introductions culminated in his repetition of the story at the critical war council of Hurons, Ojibwas, Ottawas, and Potawatomis near Detroit on 27 April 1763,

---

8 For the evidence on attribution, see the preface to the Burton edition of the *Journal*, pages 7–8. The Burton edition also includes reproductions of handwriting samples from the original manuscript and from other documents by Navarre. For a discussion of the limitations of the document as a historical source, see Dowd, 6.

9 The French. Earlier readers, including Peckham, have widely read Neolin's vision as anti-European ('twisted' by either Pontiac or the presumptive recorder Navarre to favour French over English), but Dowd makes a persuasive case for a differentiation between French and English (96–9).

where, Navarre records 'they listened to him as to an oracle, and told him
that he had only to speak and they were all ready to do what he demanded of
them' (32).

The war council depicted in Act III scene iii of *Ponteach* may allude to this
specific gathering, where a character named 'The Wolf' echoes Neolin's criticism of the abandoning of old ways in favour of European ones:

> Our great Forefathers, ere these Strangers came,
> Liv'd by Chace, with Nature's Gifts content,
>
> ...
>
> ...if some daring Foe
> Provok'd their Wrath, they bent the hostile Bow,
> Nor waited his Approach, but rush'd with Speed,
> Fearless of Hunger, Thirst, Fatigue, or Death.
> But we their soften'd Sons, a puny Race,
> Are weak in Youth, fear Dangers where they're not
>
> ...
>
> And would you stop it, you must resolve to conquer,
> Destroy their Forts and Bulwarks, burn their Towns
> And keep them at a greater Distance from us.

Given Pontiac's importance in spreading Neolin's word – and the huge persuasive effect that Pontiac's telling of Neolin's story is purported to have had
in the 27 April war council – it might seem odd that this speech comes directly from a character named 'The Wolf' rather than from Ponteach himself
in the play. With the play's intended English audience, however, to have Pontiac speak of a Prophet's dream vision might risk making Ponteach seem religiously misguided and thus less heroic. Instead, Pontiac has his own dream
of the elk, which is never called anything but a 'Dream' by anyone but the
untrustworthy Catholic priest, who at one point calls it a 'Vision' (III ii).[10]
Ponteach, then, rewrites Pontiac's apparently genuine belief in Neolin's vision as an 'article of faith' (Navarre 32) as the more conventional dramatic
device of the misinterpreted dream, alluding to the importance of Neolin,

---

10 I have used the words 'dream' and 'vision' with reference to Neolin throughout this discussion because they are the ones used in the standard translation of Navarre that I cite and are
standard in discussions of Neolin ('reverie' and 'rêve' in Navarre's original French). Dowd
notes that Neolin was purported to have had his first vision while seated before a fire (101).
Thus it seems important to recognize that that 'dream' may not offer exactly the correct
impression, and that it may more appropriately be seen as a shamanic vision.

perhaps, but declining to locate Rogers' hero as a follower of a human man who could be misperceived a charlatan.

Largely based on historian Francis Parkman's 1851 volume *The Conspiracy of Pontiac*, there has long been a sense that Pontiac was a singular leader in the war that bears his name. In fact, though Pontiac certainly led the attacks on Fort Detroit, and certainly did meet with war sachems from other tribes several times in the early 1760s, the evidence does not support a single individual leading the rebellion or creating a coordinated multi-centred plan of attack on British forts. Instead, the attack on and siege of Fort Detroit seems to have inspired other tribes and alliances to act. The timeline is perhaps the most concise way to make this clear. On 7 May 1763, Pontiac made his first attempt on Fort Detroit, as he attended a scheduled council. With him, he brought some 300 men carrying hidden weapons, but an informant had given away his plan, and the attempt was aborted. On 9 May, Pontiac and his allied warriors laid siege to the fort, indicating their seriousness by killing as many British settlers outside the fort as could be found, including women and children. While the Siege of Detroit went on, messengers were sent out to spread word of the action, fostering several smaller – ultimately more successful – rebellions: on 16 May, Wyandots took Fort Sandusky (which had only been built in 1761, under great protest from the Wyandots), killing several British traders and all of the soldiers except the commander. On 25 May, Potawatomis took Michigan's Fort St Joseph, and two days later Miamis took Fort Miami in Indiana, led by Cold Foot, who had attended Pontiac's war councils. Another fort in what is now Indiana, Fort Ouiatenon, was taken on the first of June by the tribes of the Illinois country, an unusual case, in that there were no deaths, and Nester and others argue that the local tribes took the fort not out of animosity towards the British, but because they feared retaliation from the Ottawas if they failed to do so (91). The next day, Michigan's Fort Michilimackinac was taken by a group of Ojibwa and Sauk warriors. This is the famous trick attack where warriors staged a game of lacrosse, drawing an audience of the fort's soldiers. A ball was apparently accidentally knocked through the open gates, and the warriors rushed after it, grabbed weapons that had been hidden under the blankets of Indian women spectators and traders, and attacked the soldiers, killing approximately half and later torturing some survivors to death. Pennsylvania's Fort Venango and Fort Le Boeuf were taken on 16 and 18 June respectively by Senecas, and Fort Presque Isle was attacked on 19 June, falling to a band of Ojibwas, Ottawas, Senecas, and Wyandots two days later. A second siege was begun when Fort Pitt in western Pennsylvania was attacked by Delawares and others on 22 June. Fort Pitt was large and extremely well fortified, with walls twenty feet high and sixty feet thick at their base, protected by sixteen cannons, and so could not be taken in a single attack; it was held under active siege until 1 August, when nearly all of the warriors suddenly disappeared from the perimeter of Fort Pitt to meet the forces of Colonel Henry Bouquet at Bushy Run. It was a costly battle for both sides, but Bouquet's troops officially relieved Fort Pitt on 20 August.

The siege at Detroit continued throughout, receiving word of these victories, much as we see in the very condensed timeline of Rogers' play. The first attempt to liberate Detroit came on 31 July, when a surprise attack failed, and British soldiers were trapped on a bridge, leaving twenty-three soldiers dead and thirty-eight wounded in what came to be known as the Battle of Bloody Run (the creek ran red with blood).[11] As significant as this victory was for Pontiac, however, Fort Detroit still could not be taken, and enthusiasm for what had become a stalemate collapsed. As Rogers' play depicts, several of the groups that had held Detroit (including Ottawas, Chippewas, Potawatomis, Mississaugas, Hurons, and Wyandots) abandoned the siege through the harvest season of late summer and fall, and some negotiated peace with the British. It was not until 31 October, though, that Pontiac abandoned the siege, negotiating a truce with Henry Gladwin and promising to ask other nations to bury the hatchet as well.

Though violent hostilities became rare by the winter of 1763–64, it still remained to negotiate formal peace agreements. In the summer of 1764, Sir William Johnson negotiated a treaty at Fort Niagara with the Iroquois (most of whom had remained neutral in the war in any case), bringing the Senecas back into the Covenant Chain. That August, Colonel John Bradstreet negotiated a treaty with the Ohios at Presque Isle (though it was later rescinded by Major General Thomas Gage, who had by then replaced Amherst as the leader of British forces in North America), and at Fort Detroit, conducting a treaty with several Ottawa and Ojibwa leaders in September 1764. A second treaty with the Ohios was begun by Bouquet in October 1764 and completed by Johnson in July 1765. Pontiac agreed to a treaty with Johnson at Oswego in New York on 25 July 1766.

In the end, there was no clear victor in Pontiac's Rebellion. The allied Indigenous nations failed to drive out the British, but the British failed to realize their sense of the Indians as a conquered people. Fatigue and negotiated treaties replaced triumphant victories as the markers of the end of the conflict, and ultimately many circumstances returned to the way they had been under the French before the brief intervention of Amherst's attempts at conquest and control. Separate from the local treaties and peace agreements that developed

---

11 See Nester, 136.

between 1763 and 1766 came the English Crown's attempt to resolve the conflict. News of the Indian victories in the spring and summer of 1763 contributed to the Royal Proclamation of 1763, which first declared, 'whereas it is just and reasonable, and essential to our Interest, and the Security of our Colonies, that the several Nations or Tribes of Indians with whom We are connected, and who live under our Protection, should not be molested or disturbed in the Possession of such Parts of Our Dominions and Territories as, not having been ceded to or purchased by Us, are reserved to them, or any of them, as their Hunting Grounds,' and then designated Indian Territory as all land west of the Appalachians to the Mississippi River: 'And We do further declare it to be Our Royal Will and Pleasure, for the present as aforesaid, to reserve under our Sovereignty, Protection, and Dominion, for the use of the said Indians, all the Lands and Territories not included within the Limits of Our said Three new Governments, or within the Limits of the Territory granted to the Hudson's Bay Company, as also all the Lands and Territories lying to the Westward of the Sources of the Rivers which fall into the Sea from the West and North West as aforesaid.' This effort at segregation failed, of course, and colonists continued to press westward. Their resentment at being constrained by Britain was one of the many factors that contributed to the American Revolution.[12]

ROBERT ROGERS

Robert Rogers was born in early November of 1731 in Methuen, Massachusetts.[13] He is best known, of course, as the leader of Rogers' Rangers, one of the most successful fighting units in the French and Indian War. His earlier life, though, was marked by accusations of misconduct as a result of what Parkman calls 'his vain, restless, and grasping spirit, and more than doubtful honesty' (1: 163). There were several legal skirmishes, but most dangerously, he was tried in New Hampshire in February of 1755 for counterfeiting, a potentially capital offence. Though four of the sixteen men tried in the conspiracy were jailed, Rogers was first held over for further investigation, and then released, apparently as a result of handing over twenty-four men he had recruited as soldiers for Massachusetts to the service of New Hampshire instead (Nevins

---

12 See Dixon, 246, and Calloway, 90–1, for fuller discussion of this implication of Pontiac's War.

13 I follow the standard placing of Rogers' birth at Methuen, Massachusetts, as listed by the *Dictionary of Canadian Biography* and biographers John Cuneo and Allan Nevins, though the *Dictionary of National Biography* locates Rogers' birth at Dunbarton, New Hampshire.

42).[14] This manoeuvre was protested by Major Joseph Frye, who had paid him to recruit the men for Massachusetts, but Rogers was never prosecuted.

Later in 1755, as a young captain, he was given command of a regiment under Major-General William Johnson, who would later become Superintendent of the Indian Department, and whose knowledge of and respect for Indigenous traditions and cultures may be reflected in Rogers' *Ponteach*. Much of Rogers' work for Johnson and his other superior officers involved scouting and reconnaissance, and this experience (and the associated battles) perhaps qualified Rogers to prepare for the Army 'Rogers' Ranging Rules,' a list of twenty-eight military tactics suited to forest conditions, later published in his *Journals of Major Robert Rogers* (1765). Rogers invented neither the Rangers (there were three other Ranger companies in 1756, and one as early as 1744 in Nova Scotia), nor the battle techniques he described (some of which had been used by other companies serving in North America), but he systematized and distributed them, and thus they are widely associated with his name. Rogers was made major of the Rangers in His Majesty's Service in 1758.

Rogers and his Rangers became known for both great bravery and great hardiness, and stories such as those of the two Battles on Snowshoes contributed to their status. Named because the snowshoes worn by Rogers' men were both unusual and critical to the fight, there were two Battles on Snowshoes, in January 1757 and March 1758. In the first, Rogers' men were pinned down and vastly outnumbered, but, according to the account of Private Thomas Brown (taken captive in the battle), 'we Killed more of the Enemy than we were in number' (quoted in Cuneo 48). In fact, later historians have suggested that Rogers took seventy-four men into battle, with some twenty being killed or captured, while the French forces had perhaps thirty-seven casualties. Despite the defeat, Rogers was praised for preventing a worse outcome. As Captain Abercrombie put it, 'You cannot imagine how all ranks of people here are pleased with your conduct and your mens [sic] behaviour' (quoted in Cuneo 51). The second Battle on Snowshoes, in March 1758, was also a defeat, but was even more spectacular in its myth. Rogers' men leaped from hiding places along a river near an enemy camp to attack a group of about 100 Indians and French soldiers; the enemy retreated, and the Rangers gave chase, only to discover that this had only been an advance party from a much larger group. Only

---

14 In his firmly laudatory biography of Rogers, Nevins summarizes Rogers' testimony: 'The general impression to be gained from the answers of Rogers to their questions is that he had been temporarily led astray, in part by native dishonesty, in part by a rural want of judgment, but had early forsaken his evil course in alarm' (41n). Given later accusations against Rogers of treason and fraud, this seems overly optimistic.

fifty-four of the original 181 soldiers returned to Fort Edward. This battle also gave rise to the famous legend of Rogers' defying death (and gravity) by sliding 400 feet down the side of an almost-vertical slope to the frozen surface of Lake George. While there is no proof of this event, the rockface he supposedly went down has become known as 'Rogers Rock.' Shortly after these events, Rogers was promoted to major. A widely read account of a more successful battle in March 1759 appeared in the *Gentleman's Magazine*, and is reprinted in this volume as Appendix D.

In his most famous battle (depicted in the 1940 Spencer Tracy film *Northwest Passage*), Rogers led six Ranger companies under General Amherst to fight alongside James Wolfe in Quebec in 1759. In this conflict, Rogers and his men were sent by Amherst to confront the Abenaki community of Odanak (St Francis), members of which had attacked English settlers to the south. In his letter of orders, Amherst reminded Rogers of 'the barbarities that have been committed by the enemy's Indian scoundrels on every occasion, where they had an opportunity of showing their infamous cruelties on the King's subjects, which they have done without mercy' (Rogers, *Journals* 105). The sunrise attack was a success, and the village was burned to the ground, though Rogers' claims in his *Journals* to have killed over 200 Abenakis may be overstated. Rogers was also present at the 1760 capitulation of Montreal, and he was sent from there by Amherst to claim Fort Detroit from the French. It was on this mission that Rogers claims in his *Concise Account* to have first met Pontiac, who purportedly facilitated Rogers' journey through at times hostile territory.[15] This meeting will be discussed further below, but the *Concise Account* notes, 'At our second meeting he gave me the pipe of peace, and both of us by turns smoked with it; and he assured me he had made peace with me and my detachment; that I might pass thro' his country unmolested, and relieve the French garrison; and that he would protect me and my party from any insults that might be offered or intended by the Indians' (see pages 180–1, this volume).

After the end of the French and Indian War, Rogers took posts with regular divisions in South Carolina and New York, and went on half-pay after the New York companies were disbanded. During Pontiac's Rebellion, Rogers served under Captain James Dalyell in the efforts to counter Pontiac's Siege of Detroit. Dalyell's party reached Fort Detroit by the Detroit River on 28 July 1763, and managed to enter the fort at dawn. Dalyell advocated a quick attack,

---

15 Though the narrative in *Concise Account* is fairly detailed, it is worth noting that Rogers makes no mention of Pontiac in the *Journals* written at the time of the journey, though he does describe a meeting and smoking of the calumet with 'a party of Ottawa Indians just arrived from Detroit' (Rogers, *Journals* 155).

but the French habitants appear to have sent word to Pontiac, who had recently moved his main camp to a location some two miles from the fort, keeping the fort and town surrounded at all times. The Battle of Bloody Run took place on 31 July. Dalyell was killed in action, but Rogers survived to endure the siege until its end.

Rogers' administrative talents were unfortunately not in the league of his military ones: he had failed to make sufficiently detailed agreements for payment of expenses for his Rangers, and many costs had been paid out of pocket. He struggled to gain reimbursement for his expenditures, but made several bad (and possibly illicit) financial decisions in the early 1760s, including pressing litigation about his family lands in Merrimac and a fruitless claim to 25,000 acres on Lake George. Even his own father-in-law sued him for debt. Near the end of the French and Indian War, Rogers was suspected of illegal trading with the same Indian nations his military units were supposed to regulate, earning the wrath of Sir William Johnson. In January 1764, he resigned his commission suddenly and headed to New York, where he was briefly arrested for debt.

In early spring 1765, he travelled to London to seek some sort of fortune: a military promotion (now unlikely in America because of the disapproval of Johnson and others for his ethics and tactics outside of battle); an administrative position in one of the colonies; or funding for his next venture, a search for the Northwest Passage. There was an appetite in London for tales of battle in America, and Rogers was a very minor celebrity in his first season in London, mentioned in *The Gentleman's Magazine*, *Monthly Review*, and *The Critical Review* in 1765 and 1766. *Monthly Review* for January 1766, for example, asserted that 'Few of our readers are unacquainted with the name, or ignorant of the exploits of Major Rogers, who with so much reputation headed the provincial corps called Rangers during the whole course of our late successful wars in America.'

It was during this period that he began his publishing ventures. He published his *Journals of Major Robert Rogers* and *A Concise Account of North America* in London in October of 1765, and both received wide acclaim. The *Journals* offer short, generally factual first-hand accounts of his military excursions from September 1755 to February 1761, written, Rogers asserts 'not with silence and leisure, but among deserts, rocks, and mountains, amidst the hurries, disorders, and noise of war, and under that depression of spirits which is the natural consequence of exhausting fatigue' (iii–iv). They also reproduce correspondence and letters of order from Amherst and other leaders. *Concise Account* is the more entertaining book, a work of highly descriptive historical geography. It is generally typical of this genre in the later eighteenth century, but is notable particularly for its last section, a sixty-page overview of the

'Customs, Manners, &c. of the Indians.' This too is a typical element of such a document, but Rogers' stands out in the detail of its depiction and the fact that he distinguishes customs and traditions among several of the Great Lakes and Five Nations, rather than describing 'Indians' as a homogeneous group. Not least because its material so consistently illuminates the circumstances of *Ponteach*, this section of *Concise Account* is reprinted as an appendix to this volume, as are contemporary reviews of the publication from *Monthly Review* and *Critical Review*.

For a time Rogers was also named as the author of *The Diary of the Siege of Detroit,* published in 1860 by Franklin B. Hough, but the attribution of this document and the one that follows it in Hough's collection ('A Narrative of the Principal Events of the Siege. By Major Robert Rogers') have long been disputed. John Cuneo cites the *Diary* as a misattribution in his biography of Rogers, for example, and David Dixon's *Never Come to Peace Again* explains, 'Since Rogers did not arrive at the beleaguered post until later in the siege, the information contained in this portion of the diary clearly came from someone other than the famed ranger. Indeed, Rogers's account of these events was lifted directly from a letter written by Lieutenant James McDonald to Colonel Henry Bouquet on July 12, 1763' (299n25). Though Hough's title page and introduction are unclear on exactly what documents are attributed to Rogers on what provenance, the Clements Library at the University of Michigan lists the original manuscript diary given in the volume as 'Diary of the Siege of Detroit' under the authorship of Jehu Hay, a lieutenant at Fort Detroit beginning in 1762 and throughout the siege, who eventually became the last lieutenant-governor of Detroit.[16]

Much more confidently attributable to Rogers (at least in substantial part) is *Ponteach*. Rogers' final publication – also written during his period in London – failed to find a stage for its depiction of the dishonour, violence, and passion of the North American front. Rogers was more successful in his other London endeavours, though. On orders from the king, he was appointed commandant at Michilimackinac, one of the most important and westernmost of British forts in America. Early in 1766, Rogers took up the post and sent men on exploratory journeys seeking the Northwest Passage, but they were unsuccessful (most

---

16 Hay was born in Chester, Pennsylvania. In 1774, Governor Haldimand sent him to Illinois
    country to report on conditions there. In 1776, likely because of his experience and the fact
    that he spoke a Huron language, he was appointed deputy Native American agent and major
    of the Detroit militia. In 1778, he was captured in Vincennes and taken as a prisoner of war
    to Virginia, and was exchanged in New York in 1781. Hay was appointed Detroit's last
    lieutenant-governor in 1782, and died in office 2 August 1785 (Thwaites and Kellogg 130).

notable among them Jonathan Carver, whose partly ghost-written journal of his attempt to find the passage became one of the best-known eighteenth-century accounts of North American Indians). Despite his royal preferment, however, Rogers was still disliked by Johnson and General Thomas Gage, the commander of British Forces in America who had replaced Amherst. In his efforts to create an effective administrative and trade system, Rogers continued his relationships with Indigenous nations who were friendly with the British, and developed amicable relationships with local habitants. He went too far, though, when in 1767 he created a plan to allow Michilimackinac and its regions to become a semi-independent 'Civil Government' administered by a governor and council, reporting directly to the Privy Council and the king in London. Not least in response to such actions, Gage maligned Rogers at every opportunity, including accusations of war profiteering, gambling, and profligacy. While the various accusations are unproven, the hostility of the relationship was clear, so when Rogers eventually offended his assistant Nathaniel Potter, Potter took an easy revenge by accusing Rogers of secretly planning to turn to the French if his governance plan was rejected. Such a circumstance seems unlikely, given that the French had no standing to speak of in North America, but the accusation was enough. Rogers was tried for treason in Montreal in 1768; he was acquitted of all charges, but was not reinstated to his post at Michilimackinac.

In 1769, Rogers returned to England, hoping for assistance with his debts and repayment of what he felt he was owed, either through the friendship of the king or through the courts. Neither was particularly successful, and Rogers spent extended periods in debtors' prison. He sued Gage for false imprisonment over the events in Montreal, and the suit was settled out of court: Rogers was returned to a major's half-pay in exchange for dropping his claim. Rogers also fought for the British in the American Revolution (after having his offer of service to the Continentals rejected by a suspicious George Washington), and returned yet again to Britain at the end of the war. Rogers' last years were spent in London, still in and out of debtors' prison and with a reputation for drunkenness. He died on 18 May 1795.

PONTIAC

In reading Rogers' *Ponteach*, it is essential to keep in mind the distinctions between the fictionalized character of Ponteach and the historical figure Pontiac. The Ottawa war chief Pontiac was a smart man opposed to the British taking control of territory in the Great Lakes region; that much is certain.

Beyond that, though, his character and historical significance have long been in dispute. The earliest detailed depiction of Pontiac comes from Navarre's *Journal of Pontiac's Conspiracy*. The *Journal* recognizes Pontiac's leadership at the siege of Detroit, but opens with this characterization: 'Pontiac, great chief of all the Ottawas, Chippewas, Pottawattamies, and all the nations of the lakes and rivers of the north, was a proud, vindictive, war-like and easily offended man' (16). Most other information that we have on Pontiac from contemporary sources survives in the communications of British military leaders who are understandably hostile. Rogers' *Concise Account* reports that Pontiac describes himself as 'the King and Lord of the country [Rogers] was in' and demonstrates what Rogers calls 'great strength of judgment, and a thirst after knowledge' (see page 181 this volume). The most famous account of Pontiac, though, comes in Francis Parkman's rather hagiographic *The Conspiracy of Pontiac and the Indian War after the Conquest of Canada* (1870 [1851]), which imagines Pontiac as a great man, a brilliant tactician, and a noble single-handed leader of a vast, complex conspiracy designed to heroically protect an ultimately doomed people. In perhaps his most famous summary line, Parkman asserts that (despite Pontiac's belonging to a race that Parkman assumed marked him as inherently inferior and 'thorough[ly] savage'), 'The American forest never produced a man more shrewd, politic, and ambitious' (1: 183, 166). Howard Peckham's 1947 biography is still the most scholarly overview of Pontiac's life, and Gregory Evans Dowd's *War under Heaven: Pontiac, the Indian Nations and the British Empire* (2002) and Richard Middleton's *Pontiac's War: Its Causes, Courses, and Consequences* (2007) offer the most effectively detailed analyses of Pontiac's place in the complex historical circumstances of the 1750s and 1760s.

One major note of conflict comes in the question of the singularity of Pontiac's leadership in the rebellion that bears his name. The most common sense currently is that Pontiac did send war belts and call to council the nations involved in the attack on Detroit, that he likely planned and led those attacks, and that he was the public face of the conflict in the eyes of the British. But rather than individually orchestrating a multi-centred attack, Pontiac more likely sent messengers to other communities to convey the news of the attack, which may have motivated other nations to take up their own arms, leading to a cascade effect. As Richard White has documented, Algonquian societies like the Ottawas did not have a single chief or king in the way that the British imagined (*Middle Ground* 37), but rather had less conventionally formal systems of leadership organized around an *ogema*, or 'most respected man,' who would lead a grouping of extended families. *Ogemas* might come together to deal with the concerns of a community or collection of communities, but they did not impose their wills upon their villages.[17] On a larger scale, as Peckham documents, there was no king or 'principal chief' presiding over the Great Lakes Nations (22). Ojibwas, Ottawas, and Potawatomis were all Algonquian-speaking, and they traded and intermarried in what Dowd calls 'a fellowship,' in which they called themselves collectively Anishinabeg (the plural form of Anishinabe), but that identity 'implies strong senses of commonality and identity, not of political and social unity' (9).

With those ethnographic caveats and scholarly contradictions in mind, a brief biography is challenging, but perhaps possible despite the lack of first-hand sources from within the Ottawa communities. Pontiac was born circa 1720, but there is no substantive documentation of his life before he came to British attention in the early 1760s. The *Dictionary of Canadian Biography* speculates that Pontiac might have been among the sixty Ottawas and Ojibwas taken to Montreal to fight the English in 1745; that he might have been involved in the 1747 conspiracy of Orontony, a rebellion near Sandusky, Ohio, over a rapid increase in the prices of goods; that he might have participated in the French and Ottawa attack on the village of Pickawillany in 1752; that he might have been one of the 800–1,000 Indigenous men to help to defeat Edward Braddock's forces at Fort Duquesne in 1755; and that he was likely one of the thirty warriors from Pontiac's village at Detroit who served Montcalm at Montreal and Fort William Henry. None of these possibilities can be confirmed. It is not until 1757 that the first printed record of Pontiac appears: Sir William Johnson's French-language copy of a speech made by 'Pontiague, Outava chief' at Fort Dequesne.[18]

After the 1760 Capitulation of Montreal, Rogers began his journey to Detroit, and this is where Rogers and Pontiac appear to have met. Though some scholars find Rogers' version of the encounter to be unreliable,[19] it offers an intriguing vision of Pontiac and his response to the arrival of the British to the lands around Detroit. The report is included in the *Concise Account* (see pages 180–2 this volume). Whether the incident is exactixely historically accurate or a self-aggrandizing semi-fiction on Rogers' part, it offers insight into what the

---

17 For a concise overview of Ottawa and Ashinabeg leadership traditions that White pursues in detail, see Dowd, 9–17.

18 As Peckham records, the document survives only in a bibliographical summary, as the original was burned in a fire at the New York state capitol in 1911 (48n).

19 See Dowd, 55–6, for example. Such scepticism is most firmly based in the fact that though Rogers' *Concise Account* describes in some detail a meeting with Pontiac, his *Journals* do not mention Pontiac at all, though they do cover the relevant time period.

highly knowledgeable Rogers would have thought was a plausible portrait of Pontiac as smart, powerful, and ambitious:

> He attended me constantly after this interview till I arrived at Detroit, and while I remained in the country, and was the means of preserving the detachment from the fury of the Indians, who had assembled at the mouth of the strait with an intent to cut us off … He assured me, that he was inclined to live peaceably with the English while they used him as he deserved, and to encourage their settling in his country; but intimated, that, if they treated him with neglect, he should shut up the way, and exclude them from it; in short, his whole conversation sufficiently indicated that he was far from considering himself as a conquered Prince, and that he expected to be treated with the respect and honour due to a King or Emperor, by all who came into his country, or treated with him.

On 27 April 1763, Pontiac called a council to urge Anishinabeg leaders to act to drive out the British, who now claimed the Great Lakes lands as their own. The record of this council comes from the *Journal of Pontiac's Conspiracy*, which reports that Pontiac and the Ottawas met with Potawatomis, led by Ninivois, and Hurons led by Takay (but not those led by Teata, who had rejected the war belt); a total of some 460 warriors were present. The first element of Pontiac's argument for war seems to have been the highly dubious claim that he had received war belts from the 'Great Father' the king of France, asking that he attack the English in preparation for an imminent French return. The *Journal* records that Pontiac 'also spoke of pretended insults which he and his nation had received from the Commandant and the English officers' (20). Finally, Pontiac related the vision of Neolin, the Delaware (Wolf) Prophet, and the demand from the Master of Life that Indian nations rise up to rid their lands of the English.

After this successful council, Pontiac led a party into Fort Detroit on 1 May to assess its defences under the guise of dancing the calumet. Fort Commandant Gladwin had been warned about pending trouble, and he initially refused to let Pontiac and his men in; an appeal to interpreter Pierre La Butte was successful, and both the dance and the spying went as planned. Pontiac then called another council for 5 May at the camp of the Potawatomis. The *Journal* reports this speech, ostensibly verbatim, and it is reprinted here in Appendix B. He repeats his assertion that the French king seeks their assistance and that the English are disrespectful and trade in cheap goods at high cost. He argues, 'It is important for us, my brothers, that we exterminate from our lands this nation which seeks only to destroy us … I have sent wampum belts and messengers to our brothers, the Chippewas of Saginaw, and to our brothers, the Ottawas of Michillimackinac, and to those of the Thames River to join us. They will not be slow in coming, but while we wait let us strike anyway. There is no more time to lose' (196, this volume). The plan was to have Pontiac lead sixty warriors into Fort Detroit with weapons hidden under their blankets, and to have women and children in the fort with hidden weapons as well. Once again Gladwin had been warned, though by whom is still a matter of speculation. All of the garrison's soldiers were armed, and Pontiac never gave the signal for attack. The Siege of Detroit began on 9 May, with upwards of 900 warriors on the site at the height of the conflict, with Pontiac controlling the French habitants' entry and exit from the fort, blocking English movement and preventing the restocking of the fort by blockading river access. By 12 May, Pontiac felt successful enough in the siege to coerce the Huron clans who had so far refused to join the action: Teata and Baby agreed under Pontiac's threats to enter the conflict.

On 25 May, senior members of the habitant community met with Pontiac with the reasonable complaints that their people had been injured, their livestock killed, and some homes burned. They pointed out that supposed requests for voluntary contributions of food to support the allied Indians had at times come with hatchets raised. Pontiac's response is recorded in the *Journal of Pontiac's Conspiracy*: he argues that he fights partly on behalf of the French, who have signed away their legacy – 'a thing they could not do to us' – and whom Pontiac and his people had protected from other attacks in the past. By the end of the meeting, the habitants had agreed to allow Native women to begin to plant corn on their lands. Pontiac's reputation for rhetorical brilliance does not seem to be misplaced.

The groups maintaining the siege were not always in agreement, however, and several smaller conflicts eventually led to the withdrawal of support by several nations. On 30 May, a group of English captives taken from a ship were tortured to death, to the shock of some members of the camp. In the following weeks, the Potawatomis and some of the Hurons negotiated peace agreements and exchanged prisoners with the English. On 19 June, Kioncha-mek, son of the leader of the Chippewas (and perhaps the idea for Ponteach's fictional sons) met in council with Pontiac and other leaders, only to chastize him for unnecessary violence: 'Like you, we have undertaken to chase the English out of our territory and we have succeeded. And we did it without glutting ourselves with their blood after we had taken them, as you have done.' The Eries and Delawares are reported to have expressed similar concerns as well as a frustration at the abuse of the habitants, 'our brothers, the French' (*Journal* 172, 174).

Having lost the support of several Indian groups, Pontiac turned to the French. On 2 July, he summoned the heads of all of the local French families and attempted to persuade them to fight. He outlined the victories of the rebellion and listed the forts that had been burned or taken, asserting again, 'when I began this war it was for your interests as well as ours.' He argued that in a siege ostensible neutrality was the same as supporting the British, and so 'there is only one way open today: either remain French as we are, or altogether English as they are. If you are French, accept this war-belt for yourselves, or your young men, and join us; if you are English we declare war upon you' (*Journal* 194). A senior member of the French delegation actually produced a copy of the Capitulation of Montreal and argued that – because they were French – they were forbidden to fight the English, but a group of young men leaped up to accept the war belt. The meeting ended unhappily on both sides, and it was the next day that one of the young men took the war belt back to his father, who returned it to Pontiac with the warning that 'those who have told thee that they are going to assist thee in capturing the Fort will be the first to run away.' Pontiac accepted the war belt and did not again press the habitants to enter the fray (*Journal* 196).

The skirmishes continued, including the Indian victory at the Battle of Bloody Run on 31 July, but as the harvest season and then winter approached, most of the Ottawa and Ojibwa supporters trickled away. In late October, a letter arrived from the French Major de Villiers, addressed, as Peckham reports to the 'French Children,' advising them that the English and French kings had been inspired by the Master of Life to make peace, and that the hatchet should be buried (236). With no hope of either French or Indian support continuing through the winter, Pontiac lifted the siege.

Though Pontiac was more the instigator of the rebellion than its architect, he ironically gained great prominence in no small part due to the length of the Siege at Detroit, a result of the relative failure of the initial plan of attack compared with the utter devastation of the smaller forts that fell in May and June. After lifting the siege in October, Pontiac travelled to Illinois country, where he continued to encourage active resistance against the British. Because of the profile he had earned in the Siege of Detroit, and because he successfully turned that profile to his advantage in Illinois, Pontiac continued a face (if not a force) to be reckoned with. Sir William Johnson negotiated a formal peace with Pontiac at Oswego, New York, on 25 July 1766. This high profile was as dangerous as it was flattering, however, as Pontiac became embroiled in a series of conflicts with other Indigenous leaders, which led to his expulsion from the Ottawa community on the Maumee River in 1768, and possibly to his death at the hands of a Peoria man on 20 April 1769.

EIGHTEENTH-CENTURY THEATRE

Ponteach does not appear ever to have been staged, and as the reviews in Appendix C demonstrate, the play was not well received when it appeared as a printed text. The *Gentleman's Magazine* in particular objected to Rogers' characterization ('All the personages of the play may be considered as devils incarnate, mutually employed in tormenting one another; as their character excite no kindness, their distress moves no pity'), the dialogue ('it cannot be read without disgust; *damning* and *sinking*, and calling *bitch*'), and its shocking content ('who but would turn with abhorrence and disgust, from a scene in which *Indian* savages are represented as tossing the scalps of murdered *Englishmen* from one to the other'). Though the response was negative, however, it is clear that Rogers (and his likely collaborator/s) wrote the play in a style that aimed to meet the tastes of contemporary English audiences. The English-style courtship scenes between Chekitan and Monelia, for example, are highly conventional, echoing everything from the touching but doomed romance of Shakespeare's *Romeo and Juliet* to the grand assertions of integrity and purity of Sir Richard Steele's *The Conscious Lovers* (1722). Such scenes might well have pleased the typical theatergoer more than they did critical reviewers, and that these are not the scenes noted in the negative reviews might well suggest that they succeeded at least in some degree in touching their intended audience. Similarly, the untrustworthy French priest is a stock figure of English theatre, though his villainy seems both politically specific to North America and much more broadly pandering to anti-French and anti-Catholic sentiments at the end of the Seven Years' War.

Among such fairly straightforward appeasements of contemporary taste, Rogers also offers a more unexpected appeal to the theatrical fashion of musicalization. *Ponteach* offers us a war song and dance at the close of Act III. The song is in quatrains made up of closed heroic couplets, and sung to the tune of 'Over the Hills and Far Away,' a popular tune that had already been used on stage in George Farquhar's 1706 *The Recruiting Officer* and John Gay's 1728 runaway hit (and repertory regular) *The Beggar's Opera*. Farquhar was the first to alter the song's original lyrics of courtship into a soldier's song, though his version emphasized the joys of escaping the domestic ('By getting rid of brats and wives / That scold and bawl both night and day') in favour of public glory ('Courage, boys, 'tis one to ten, / But we return all gentlemen').[20] Rogers

---

20 The Farquhar version that Rogers revises emphasizes the potential for individual success once away from the social strictures of England:

rewrites the lyrics again to redirect the song from its associations with Englishmen going into battle to a depiction of Indians going to battle against the
English. In a gesture that will be repeated several times in several ways in *Ponteach*, Rogers makes political points by depicting an aspect of English culture
put into flux by the colonial context, and then turned against its English
originators.

Though to modern readers such a scene seems obviously out of place in the
midst of a tragedy, there were several successful precedents that might have
tempted Rogers. In terms of musical interludes in general, Shakespeare's *The
Tempest* was staged throughout the eighteenth century, and its Act IV masque
scene provides perhaps the most immediately identifiable example of interpolated
song and dance. Other examples are less expected: in 1664 William Davenant's
spectacular revision of Shakespeare's tragedy *Macbeth* (widely derided by later
critics) included songs and dances, ranging from the formally operatic to the
more popular, as well as elaborate costumes and mechanically assisted flying
witches. The vogue for musical elements is also clear in the mid-eighteenth-
century genre of the afterpiece (a shorter play designed to run after the main play
and perhaps a musical interlude). Fully half of the afterpieces published in the
period employ some form of music or dancing. Rogers is thus not necessarily
wrong in his understanding of the tastes of his audience, but it is ironic that it is
his efforts to please that result in some of the weaker elements of the play.

One element of popular taste that Rogers' play could not avoid, given its
historical origins, was that 'box-office receipts suggest that audiences preferred
new comedy to new tragedy' (Staves 87). *The Revels History* documents that
only about 100 new tragedies were staged in the latter half of the eighteenth
century (Davies 6: 153). Few were particularly successful, and even fewer are
read today. The Licensing Act of 1737 had made staging new tragedies or

---

Our 'prentice Tom may now refuse
To wipe his scoundrel Master's Shoes,
For now he's free to sing and play
Over the Hills and far away.
...

Courage, boys, 'tis one to ten,
But we return all gentlemen
All gentlemen as well as they,
Over the hills and far away.
Over the Hills and O'er the Main,
To Flanders, Portugal and Spain,
The queen commands and we'll obey ˙
Over the Hills and far away.

serious political plays more difficult, and 'whole seasons passed in the 1740s, 1750s, and 1760s without a new tragedy appearing' (Bevis 201).[21] New tragedies that were staged were often derivatives of classical Roman narratives or plays that located themselves in the exoticized Orient. The earlier vogue for domestic tragedy did not make a substantive reappearance as a genre, though as we will see, the domestic was an important part of the revisionist Shakespeare productions that were extremely popular. The tragedies aimed broadly at high nobility and heroic scope, but there were no new major schools or styles until perhaps the semi-tragic melodrama around the 1770s. Even much better known writers had trouble having tragedies produced around mid-century, as is most notably demonstrated in the well-documented experiences of Samuel Johnson and Tobias Smollett in attempting to find stages for *Irene* and *The Regicide, or, James the First of Scotland* respectively. This audience preference, combined with the expense of producing a new stage tragedy, made it substantially less likely that Rogers' play would be as successful as his other publications.

Perhaps because there is no identifiably conventional tragic style of the 1760s, and because few new plays were being produced in American theatres,[22] *Ponteach*'s tragedy hearkens back to an earlier time. The play echoes the Restoration genre of blank verse heroic tragedy in the modes of John Dryden's *All for Love* and Thomas Otway's *Venice Preserved* in several ways: in the epic nature of the conflict, involving the fate of empires; in the love-versus-honour choice on which the second-generation subplot turns; in the public versus private demands faced by Ponteach; and in the elevated styles and long speeches. Julie Ellison narrows this generic category even more closely, arguing for republican tragedy, making *Ponteach* into a Roman play in the shadow of Addison's *Cato*. In Roman plays, Ellison argues, 'weeping men – especially

---

21 The 1760s in particular were not a pinnacle in the history of theatrical tragedy. Richard Bevis writes off the entire decade thus: 'Few tragedies of the 1760s repay study' (207).

22 If conservatism of form was fairly typical of the English stage, it was nearly universal on the American stage in the colonial period. Relatively few purpose-built theatres existed: Odai Johnson and William J. Burling's documentary history of the colonial America stage lists twenty-four purpose-built theatres in America before 1776: three in Annapolis, five in Charleston, five in New York, three in Philadelphia, three in Williamsburg, and one each in Baltimore, Norfolk, Halifax NC, Newport RI, and Petersburg VA. Though productions occurred in other venues such as schools, assemblies, and great rooms, the choices tended firmly to the tried and true. The most performed play in colonial America was Shakespeare's *Romeo and Juliet* with thirty-five productions, followed by George Farquhar's *The Beaux' Strategem*, Shakespeare's *Richard III*, and John Gay's *The Beggar's Opera*. With the exception of John Home's 1756 Scottish heroic *Douglas*, none of the ten most-produced plays were written after George Lillo's 1731 *The London Merchant*.

the indifferent republican's tenderhearted son – circle around stoic Romans framed by an imperial, international setting. The Roman republic configures tensions between political decision and indecision, cultural centrality and marginality, law and tears. These texts foreground the need for impersonal law while accompanying its stern tones with the outcry of deep-feeling masculine subjectivity' (16). Though the play clearly alludes to the values of republican drama, it is a problematic fit with some of the conventions of the form. A typical summary of the genre notes that 'these dramas present exemplary heroes who embody civic virtue and celebrate republican love of liberty and sacrifice of private desire for the public good. (Occasionally, as in *Cato*, the protagonists may die, but they do so in order not to compromise their exemplary virtue. Secondary characters, especially women, may also perish)' (Staves 89). As the next section of this discussion will argue, Ponteach is not an exemplary hero, and he is driven as much by his private ambition as by any desire for public good. Since her argument is based on the definition of Roman drama embodied by Addison's *Cato*, Ellison asserts that Ponteach's (historically accurate and thus required) survival to the end of the play is an exception to 'the habits of republican drama' because he cannot commit battlefield suicide. Regardless of which specific elements of Roman drama one chooses to consider, though, *Ponteach* clearly engages not only the long-standing character and structural codes for heroic drama and its offshoots, but also the old-style forms of verse tragedy.[23]

Though the genre of *Ponteach* seems very much of the early eighteenth century, for many readers its language echoes Shakespeare, whose work would almost necessarily be an influence for a less-experienced playwright. Shakespeare's plays were among the most produced and most popular of the day. As Charles Beecher Hogan documents, approximately one-sixth of all plays staged in London in the eighteenth century were by Shakespeare (2: 715), and in colonial America, *Romeo and Juliet* was the most-performed play and *Richard III* was the third most popular. The second most popular play was George Farquhar's *The Beaux' Strategem*, from which Rogers borrows the tune to 'Over the Hills and Far Away.' These plays were not all identical to the Shakespeare that we know today: many were cut down, edited

---

23 Of course, there is no safe way to generalize about staged Roman tragedy in classical times. No play survives of the genre in which we can be absolutely certain what happens at the end. Instead, theories of Roman tragedy also consider historical narratives that attempt to represent historical events dramatically; such narratives were never intended for the stage. Even in Lucan's version of the Cato narrative in *Civil War*, only ten of twelve projected books were completed. Later Cato stories that include his battlefield suicide are likely descended from Plutarch's narrative (a Roman author, writing in Greek, likely consolidating earlier, now non-extant sources), some 200 years after the death of the historical Cato the Younger.

for specific emphases, or even entirely rewritten (perhaps most notoriously in Nahum Tate's happy-ending *King Lear*). Particularly between the 1740s and 1760s, 'the new alterations of Shakespeare which prosper ... present a domestic Shakespeare who is at the same time eminently patriotic, identified at once with virtuous family life, vigorous trade, and British glory' (Dobson 187). As Jean Marsden points out, by the later century, 'managers, actors, and playwrights actively sought to evoke the experience of sympathy, and, increasingly, audiences came to the theater expecting not only to be spectators of distress but to be able to identify personally with the distresses they witnessed' (29). And so the combination of high heroics and human identification that I will argue is so central to the political implication of *Ponteach* also links to Rogers' attempt to meet contemporary audience desires and contemporary ideas of great dramatic art, embodied in the 'bardolatry' (Hudson 'Vexed' 44) of Shakespeare in the eighteenth century. Throughout the play there is evidence of Shakespeare's influence: the *Romeo and Juliet* qualities of the lovers from opposing tribes in Chekitan and Monelia; in Ponteach's *King Lear*-like speeches near the end of the play, and in the plot of a parent betrayed by an overambitious and immoral child; in Ponteach's occasional associations with Othello's efforts to negotiate a foreign system that both grants him status and constantly holds over him the threat of denying that status. These are only the first of many examples of the importance of Shakespeare to Rogers' notion of playwriting, dramatic language, the tragic, and the heroic, but they will suffice to demonstrate the debt.

Among all of these disparate authorial and generic models and audience expectations, the most direct literary precursor of Ponteach still seems not to be Lear or Othello or Cato, but Oroonoko, the African prince created by Aphra Behn in 1688 and brought most famously to the stage by Thomas Southerne in 1695. Oroonoko is a prince, tricked into slavery by the slick language and bald-faced lies of an English captain. Though he is later treated well and has his status recognized by his English owner (within the framework of slavery, of course), he is driven by the pregnancy of his wife Imoinda[24] to lead a rebellion to attempt to free the next generation of slaves. The rebellion is unsuccessful, partly because those fighting for him lack his noble bravery, and partly because he mitigates his actions because he is unwilling to kill the English randomly. In Behn's version, Oroonoko fulfils the request of his pregnant wife that he kill her (rather than see her ravaged by the English and their child left a slave); he is then captured, tortured, and dismembered by the English. In Southerne's version, Imoinda kills herself when Oroonoko cannot do it; Oroonoko then

---

24 In the Behn version of the story, Imoinda is also of African descent; Southerne is the first of a series of playwrights to make her white.

kills the corrupt governor and stabs himself, and the final word is delivered by the representative good Englishman, Blanford:

> I hope there is a place of happiness
> In the next world for such exalted virtue.
> Pagan or unbeliever, yet he lived
> To all he knew. And if he went astray
> There's mercy still above to set him right.
> But Christians guided by the heavenly ray
> Have no excuse if we mistake our way. (V v)

The nobility of the leader of a rebellion, the blank verse form (at least in Southerne's tragic main plot), the dangers of taking the English at face value (and of using their language), and the problematization of Christianity all recur in the most famous plays of the eighteenth century on African and American Indian rebellion.[25] There are obvious differences too, but since the Oroonoko narrative was widely referenced in the eighteenth-century anti-slavery movement, with new dramatic adaptations in 1759, 1760, and 1788,[26] its potential as a source text is substantial. Further, the use of *Oroonoko* as a touchstone in the larger debate on race, humanity, and power provides evidence for the possibility of a Rogers' seeking some sort of public political effect from *Ponteach* beyond what he certainly also hoped would be profitable dramatic biography.

PONTEACH, OR THE SAVAGES OF AMERICA: A TRAGEDY

While *Ponteach* clearly tries to appeal to the trends and values of eighteenth-century theatre, it does so from a uniquely historicized position. Rogers' personal observation of the conflicts between Indigenous and colonial cultures, and his individual interactions with the historical Pontiac, provide a foundation

---

25 Richard White asserts in the *Encyclopedia of North American Indians* that 'Robert Rogers' *Ponteach* made Pontiac the most famous Indian of the eighteenth century' (496).

26 Parallels among the mid-eighteenth-century Oroonoko adaptations and *Ponteach* abound. They all raise questions about English ideas of race, difference, and humanity. In John Hawkesworth's 1759 *Oroonoko*, evil lieutenant-governor tries to rape Imoinda, with some of the same symbolic implications as the Priest's attempted rape of Monelia. A rape is planned but not carried out in Francis Gentleman's *Oroonoko* (1760), and both are clear in their anti-slavery tenor. John Ferriar's adaptation, *The Prince of Angola* (1788), is the most blunt. In his preface, Ferriar announces that his goal is to shock white people out of their insensitivity to the evils of slavery: 'We talk of the destruction of millions, with as little emotion, and as little accuracy of comprehension, as of the distances of the Planets'(i).

for a distinctly atypical dramatic representation of race, heroism, and violence. Rogers' play is highly unusual for the time in its sympathetic portrayal of Ponteach and the circumstances faced by his people. *Ponteach* offers detailed criticisms of colonial policy and very lightly veiled attacks on individual his- torical figures, such as Fort Detroit commandant Major Henry Gladwin's apparent embodiment in the acid-tongued Governor Sharp. A critique of de-humanization and cultural eradication can only be powerful, however, if the objects of cultural construction and destruction are established as undeniably human to begin with, rather than accepted as mere ciphers or passive tools for paeans to European enlightenment. As Linda Colley points out, 'From the be-ginning of settlement through to the Revolution of 1776 and beyond, the people called Indians were integral to how men and women in early modern Britain perceived that part of their empire that was America' (*Captives* 140) and, equal-ly importantly, that this triangulation of identities was critical in the construction of contemporary ideas of nation and the national identity of the Briton.

Throughout *Ponteach*, ideas of identity, especially in terms of race, are con-stituted through language, often specifically through discourses of gender. This allows established power hierarchies to be taken as given, insofar as that which is feminized is devalued, even at times rendered less than human. The gendered fluidity given to racial difference by several of the play's characters shifts male to female and equates Algonquian identities with weakness and failure. Though such parallels were not likely foremost in Rogers' own mind, the play offers intriguing insights into the relationship between race and gender in the ongoing development of the identity of colonial America.[27]

The depiction of Indigenous characters in Rogers' play replicates – perhaps consciously, perhaps not – the convention that widely accepted European con-structions of gender function as one of the naturalized foundations for the lin-guistic and social construction of racial difference. This construction of race, in turn, is the foundation for inappropriate and perhaps dangerous political and social policy in Rogers' understanding of colonial conflict. The agonies on all sides created by Pontiac's Rebellion are written here not as collateral damage from military might, but as the inescapable outcome of policy based upon a badly constructed and misperceived identity. Rogers recognizes remarkably early that the futures of several nations are grounded in language, performance, and negotiated fictions. In the early days of not-yet-America, *Ponteach* reaches conclusions very similar to those that were not explicitly articulated until much later by modern historians like Robert Berkhofer and Richard White: much

---

27 For an exceptionally useful overview of the role of American Indians in the perceptions and shifts of the identities of Britons in Britain and in America, see Colley, 137–202.

conflict was the perhaps unavoidable result of 'the stories these various peoples invented about each other. Both sides had no choice but to respond to the version of themselves the other side invented, and in responding they blurred the line between invention and actuality, between the people who existed in the minds of others and those who acted on their own behalf, between objects and subjects' (White, 'Fictions' 64). The importance of fictions of the Other in times of conflict had, of course, been recognized and dramatized from at least Shakespeare's history plays onward (and with particular relevance in *Othello*, for example, and Southerne's *Oroonoko*). Not least because of his first-hand experience in such conflicts, however, Rogers' staging of the performative nature of racialized identity adds another element: in *Ponteach*, Rogers seeks first to establish the authority inherent in his personal knowledge of North America and its people,[28] and to then problematize what he sees as the dangerous misreadings of constructed racial identities by others with less knowledge but more social, political, and economic standing.

Rogers' dramatization conveys to a broad English audience the political complexity of the Seven Years' War in America, given Ponteach's assertion that though the French had been defeated (whom Pontiac had supported in the war and who had supplied the Ottawas with weapons to fight the English), the Indigenous people had not been conquered, and they still claimed sovereignty over the land and independence from the Europeans:[29] 'Think you, because you have subdu'd the *French*, / That *Indians* too are now become your Slaves? / This Country's mine, and here I reign as King' (I iii). Rogers' fictionalization of Pontiac and his rebellion is set after the meeting described in *Concise Account*, in which the Ottawa sachem responded to exactly the sort of gestures of disrespect Rogers warns against in his historical account and that he renders so explicitly in the first act of his play.

More importantly, Rogers writes both historical subjectivity and allegory, recognizing the importance of each for his revisionist version of the grand

---

28 Rogers writes near the beginning of his *Concise Account*, 'Certain I am, that no man besides has traveled over and seen so much of this part of the country as I have done ... I may say that the long and particular acquaintance I have had with several tribes and nations in both peace and war, has at least furnished me materials to treat the subject with propriety' (iv–v, vii).

29 Telling, for example, is that his comments on political geography in *Concise Account* frequently use language of possession rather than merely occupation. See, for example, pages 174–6 on the Five Nations and Great Lakes Mississaugas. He also explicitly rejects contemporary arguments against an Indigenous sense of private property in his description of the Nippisongs: 'there is such a thing as private property among them, which they transfer to one another, by way of bargain and exchange, and if taken out of the compass of fair dealing, the aggressor is stigmatized, and punished with disdain' (Rogers 157).

colonial narrative. As I will argue in the following pages, Ponteach is offered historical subjectivity; the Mohawk princess Monelia is his allegory. The play in some ways functions as a metadramatic embodiment of the pattern of ambivalent colonial mimicry that is so central to Rogers' depiction: it is a text about the conquest of the Ottawas by the colonists, and as such is, of course, a reflection of the great colonial mythologies of conversion and civilization. But making Pontiac the central consciousness in the depiction of that ostensibly universally recognized narrative leaves it *'almost the same, but not quite'* (Bhabha, 'Mimicry' 126; original emphasis) – a near perfect reflection of the privileged cultural narrative, but one that recognizes its inversion in a clear assertion of ambivalence. As Homi Bhabha explains, mimicry is 'the sign of a double articulation; a complex strategy of reform, regulation, and discipline, which "appropriates" the Other as it visualizes power. Mimicry is also the sign of the inappropriate, however, a difference or recalcitrance which coheres the dominant strategic function of colonial power, intensifies surveillance, and poses an immanent threat to both "normalized" knowledges and disciplinary powers' ('Mimicry,' 126).

Bhabha's concept of mimicry is typically applied to a situation in which Indigenous writers in a colonized culture mimic the colonizers' discourse, and it is not conventionally operated by writers from the colonizing culture. That said, Rogers' *Ponteach* is clearly written as a document of resistance, existing both within and outside of the dominant British culture. Rogers himself occupied an oddly marginal position in transatlantic British culture: born in North America, he is outside Britain, and yet is often on the fringe of (or even firmly rejected by) agencies of official authority in America. Rogers' perspective thus originates from shifting affiliative ground, his own voice hybridized by a lifetime spent in sites where no single discourse was entirely dominant, at the fringes of empire, but firmly surrounded by Indian cultures and modes of authority. Susan Castillo terms such figures 'Creole settlers' who move 'between identifications with the European colonizing power and the native, alternately invoking and suppressing the indigenous components of it symbolic economy' (198).

The 'double vision' of *Ponteach*'s Creole colonial mimicry, 'which in disclosing the ambivalence of colonial discourse also disrupts its authority' (Bhabha, 'Mimicry' 129), is articulated throughout the play, but in terms of Ponteach's characterization as historical subject, the play's first three acts make explicit that his actions are neither simple nor natural, but enforced upon him by the acts of dishonest traders, murderous hunters, and negligent, embezzling administrators. Rogers' play uses a language of metaphor (the same, but not) to assert categorically that Ponteach is not an example of the natural man or noble savage, but rather the product of a compulsory savagism imposed upon him by the negotiated fictions of a prescriptive culture that, in defining itself as superior, required that resistance be located in acts outside of its social and linguistic control, limiting others to marginal speech and acts of violence or other extremity.

This play, though, is very explicitly not just about Pontiac the man, but at several points directly articulates the connection between the private and public realms between which Ponteach/Pontiac moves in the play and in history. The traders', soldiers', and governors' serial gestures of disrespect in the first act demand a violent response because Rogers writes their actions to be emblematic of the larger political treatment of Indigenous North Americans. The play's depiction of racial conflicts that are relatively small and personal allow easier comprehension by a European audience trained on heroic drama and conventional tragedy: it is much more possible to identify with humiliation and betrayal on that scale than on the scale of the attempts at cultural eradication that Rogers witnessed in person and records in the play.[30] The fundamental implication of Rogers' staging of the motivations behind Pontiac's conspiracy is very much the early recognition that the personal is indeed political.

This twentieth-century truism is articulated in eighteenth-century terms at several points through the play, most significantly in the scene where several sachems meet in a war council.[31] Ponteach asserts that

'Tis better thus to die than be despis'd;
Better to die than be a Slave to Cowards,
Better to die than see my Friends abus'd;
The Aged scorn'd, the Young despis'd and spurn'd.
Better to die than see my Country ruin'd.

---

30 Whether Rogers knew of it or not, the most significant effort at eradication occurred during the siege of Fort Pitt, when Captain Simon Ecuyer and William Trent (in a tactic later approved by Amherst and Bouquet) presented to two Delaware leaders two blankets and two handkerchiefs that had been intentionally contaminated with smallpox. Smallpox subsequently broke out among the Delawares and Shawnees, though historians debate whether the blankets or another vector might be the cause. This contamination was a deliberate contradiction of the traditional European rules of war, which specifically precluded killing enemies by poison. For detailed discussion, see Dowd, 190 and 211, and Nester, 112–15.

31 Gordon Sayre analyses this scene and other major speeches in conjunction in his discussion of the historical Pontiac as part of his argument that 'scenes of dramatic encounter between Native American and Euro-American people – at frontier treaty councils, in theatres, or in open-air spectacles – supports a definition of cultural and racial identity as performative' (*Indian Chiefs* 16). He argues that 'Pontiac offers our best opportunity to examine how a Native American leader adopted the rhetoric and ideology of European and colonial politics. Pontiac was savvy enough to employ imperial ideology against itself' (133).

His adviser Tenesco reasserts the necessary equation between private acts of disrespect and larger acts of cultural violence as he notes the need to challenge 'Their Pride and Insults, Knavery and Frauds, / Their large Encroachments on our common Rights ...What calls on us more loudly for Revenge, / Is their Contempt and Breach of public Faith.' Tenesco ends his speech with, 'Wrongs like these are national and public, / Concern us all, and call for public Vengeance.' To which Ponteach's fictionalized son Phillip tellingly replies, 'Public or private Wrongs, no matter which' (III iii).

By politicizing so explicitly the personal experience of Ponteach, Rogers' play removes itself from the sphere of the constructed noble savage, allowing its protagonist to be bitterly angry at the English; treacherous in his plotting to 'reign alone' over all of the Indian tribes once the colonists have been driven off by the confederacy's collective might;[32] monstrous in his willingness to torture the innocent; and greedy in his decision to save them only for future ransoms. Rogers' Ponteach is not Rousseau's pure natural man,[33] but a complex human character driven to horrific acts by deceits and manipulations great and small that are the more debilitating because, as one of the better-known Indigenous leaders of his day, Pontiac's personal humiliations are witnessed and borne by all of his people. Had it been widely staged, Rogers' play might have been the first devastatingly human representation of the colonial agenda to audiences who, more or less accepting the myths of noble generosity or animalized savages needing civilization, did not fully fathom the human costs of their beaver hats and tobacco.

By the middle of the eighteenth century, ethnographic information on Indigenous cultures was fairly widely available in sources ranging in accuracy from the informed first-person accounts of *The Jesuit Relations* (1610–73),[34]

---

32 Rogers' *Concise Account* intimates this ambition as well: 'He often intimated to me, that he could be content to reign in his country in subordination to the King of Great Britain, and was willing to pay him such annual acknowledgement as he was able in furs, and to call him his uncle' (181, this volume). On the implication of that particular model of familial relationship, see pages 50–1.

33 Ponteach's atypical complexity of characterization is my point here, but Hayden White does argue that even the noble savage is not as straightforward in its implications as we might assume. White argues that the ideological effect of the term 'noble savage' is 'to draw a distinction between presumed types of humanity on manifestly qualitative grounds, rather than such superficial bases as skin color, physiognomy, or social status' (17). Ania Loomba presses this further, noting that the idea of the noble savage 'represents a rupture, a contradiction, a point at which the seamless connections between inferiority and the external characteristics are disturbed' (103).

34 *The Jesuit Relations* were reports from North America published annually in France from 1633 to 1673. Different accounts were collected, translated, or republished through the

for example, in French and Cadwallader Colden's *History of the Five Indian Nations* (1747) in English, to innumerable scurrilous knockoffs like Ned Ward's *A Trip to New England*, a detailed first-person travel and ethnographic account cobbled together from previously published accounts: Ward had never set foot on North American soil. As Benjamin Bissell's old, but still useful overview of English accounts of North American Indians puts it, 'Taken together, these works constitute a very large bulk of printed matter, a curious mixture of fact and fiction regarding the Indian's character, customs, and mode of life: sometimes correct observations exaggerated or misunderstood; sometimes novel theories, showing the writer's imagination or ingenious fancy' (12). Though accurate sources were available, more widely read outside of political circles were the necessarily short accounts in popular media like *The Spectator* and *The Gentleman's Magazine*,[35] and the generally highly fictionalized and often lurid and extremely violent accounts of captivity narratives from America.[36] In between fall contemporary novels such as Charles Jonstone's popular *Chrysal, or the Adventures of a Guinea* (1760), in which a section on Sir William Johnson offers both some reasonably accurate information and some egregious exaggeration of Indigenous sexual practice, and Tobias Smollett's later *Humphrey Clinker* (1771), with its interpolated captivity narrative. Several less financially successful novels also offered fictionalized accounts around the same time, including the pseudonymous Unca Eliza Winkfield's *The Female American* (1767) and Frances Brooke's *The History of Emily Montague* (1769).

As Linda Colley documents in her discussion of captivity narratives, 'Before 1756, most of what British newspapers and magazines printed about America had been brief, factual and overwhelmingly commercial, often little more than a record of incoming and outgoing transatlantic vessels at specific ports. But as the war advanced, far more attention was devoted in papers, pamphlets and books to the American interior, to issues other than trade, and to human interest

---

eighteenth century in England, though the fully collected texts were not available in English until Reuben Gold Thwaites' edition of 1902, which also includes allied documents from as early as 1610.

35 See, for example, *The Tatler* 50 (27 April 1711) for a fictionalized account of the opinions of London held by one of the famed 'Four Indian Kings' who visited London in 1710. For a later example, see *The Gentleman's Magazine* 35 (1765) on the visit of three Cherokee Chiefs to London.

36 The earliest and most famous being Mary Rowlandson's account of 1682, though hundreds of captivity narratives were published between 1682 and the mid-nineteenth century. For a useful overview of the genre and its cultural implications, see Kathryn Derounian-Stodola and James Levernier's *The Indian Captivity Narrative, 1550–1900*.

stories, understandably so, since individual Britons and different varieties of American were now encountering each other at a hitherto unknown rate and degree of intensity' (*Captives* 174). Variously accurate information was available to Londoners in the eighteenth century, then, though, given the demands of readership and the political requirements of the colonial mission, only intelligent and devoted readers could reasonably be expected to have substantive knowledge of North American Indian people and the specific political and military actions underlying the economies of trade and colonialism between North America and Britain. Rogers' *Journals*, the *Concise Account*, and even *Ponteach* benefited from and contributed to a surge of interest in the lives of various types of Americans around the time of the Seven Years' War, when troops from Britain (and often their families) were sent to North America in substantial numbers. Under these circumstances, in the late 1750s, 'this vast territory and all its complex dangers came to seem to Britons at home infinitely more real and absorbing' (Colley, *Captives* 161).

Even with the much clearer historical picture available to modern readers, part of the challenge of discussing *Ponteach* is this problem of reading Ponteach (and Pontiac). It is dangerously easy to allow the character to slip into archetypes of the noble savage. For Marilyn Anderson, for example, Ponteach speaks 'wisdom based on an intimate knowledge of nature' (236), and embodies 'all of the virtues of the noble savage, [and so] is set up as a model for white Americans to emulate ... [since] according to the criterion for heroic dramas, *someone* had to be representative of the very highest of virtue and honour' (226, 228; original emphasis). In contrast, Laura Tanner and James Krasner argue that the view of Ponteach as a hero, noble and tragic, is actually based only on the first act, and that in fact even other characters recognize him as petulant, self-absorbed, and dangerously misguided in his ambition. This seems to me a better, though still not fully nuanced sense of Ponteach's characterization. Tanner and Krasner, however, go on to use this insight to argue that the play is written only as an allegory: a warning on the nature of rebellion in the days preceding the American Revolution, with Rogers a 'political playwright, lampooning American revolutionary leaders as crafty, two-faced savages, trying to rob the king of his fairly gained land' (17). The problem of this reading of *Ponteach* is that in neither the play nor Rogers' historical publications is there any substantive evidence that he had the literary talent for a cultural critique so subtly inlaid that it was universally missed by contemporary readers and reviewers. And it seems hugely problematic to assume that a play engaging almost exclusively Native North American cultures, written by a man who knew Pontiac and had recorded concerns about his mistreatment, is significant merely as a volley between Whig and Tory in London.

Given the play's tone throughout, I can see no way to argue that the 'intensity of Rogers' condemnation of Ponteach demonstrates the fury with which Whig revolutionary rhetoric was attacked by Tories' (16). It is true, though, that the character of Ponteach becomes increasingly unattractive as the play goes on, driven by a series of small snubs to press his confederacy to great violence and what would be enormous losses, and condoning the on-stage torture of even the wife and babies of the villain Honnyman until he is reminded that they will bring a large ransom at the end of the conflict. Susan Castillo notes this change as well, though she too attributes it more to Rogers' political experience than to his sense of Pontiac, arguing that Rogers 'is ventriloquizing the character of Ponteach in order to enact some of the dilemmas of Creole subjectivity that he himself had encountered ... and the transformation of Ponteach from noble statesman to treacherous bloodthirsty savage mirrors Rogers's own shifting allegiances and his increasing inclination towards the British view of the American rebels as the embodiment of chaos and anarchy' (222–3).

While any play by a writer so consistently pulled in different cultural directions might be expected to reflect the sort of multiple cultures of reference that Castillo and Tanner and Krasner point out, *Ponteach*'s representation of a real, widely known and politically important Indigenous leader cannot be written off as significant primarily as English anxiety in disguise. Questions of constructions and performances of identity are, however, extremely important here. The Ponteach of Act I certainly is noble, and speaks with dismay at the distinction between word and act that he perceives in the 'false, deceitful, knavish' British (II ii). He has been unable to construct any consistent identity on which to base negotiation because, the play suggests, North Americans and Britons maintain incompatibly distinct understandings of the relationship between public and private identity. It is not just that national identities and languages are different, which of course, forms the most basic obstacle to communication and coexistence; it is that the very conception of identity is a product of nation. Rogers' representation of British identity in the conflict is a reinscription of Mandevilleanism, set up to commend honourable public appearance regardless of private virtue. Private vice has public benefit for Rogers' hunters, traders, and colonists, but that private vice is also one of the roots of violence in the Indigenous/colonial relationship. Perhaps by virtue of practical necessity for the sort of early colonists Rogers depicts here, that which is valued is nationally self-serving, regardless of conventional ideas of honesty or virtue; the latter qualities have become merely reassuring linguistic touchstones without further implication.

As Honnyman's Act I speech makes clear, Rogers draws the colonial British identity as one that manipulates private wrongs such that they disappear in the absence of their publicity: if no one knows, there is no crime. In response to Orsbourn's anxious query after they have shot and scalped two Indian hunters, 'd'ye think this is not Murder? / I vow I'm shock'd a little to see them scalp'd,' Honnyman replies, 'It's no more Murder than to crack a Louse, / That is, if you've the Wit to keep it private ... as they live like Beasts, like Beasts' they die.' This leaves Orsbourn 'content; my Scruples are remov'd. / And what I've done, my Conscience justifies' (I ii).[37] Honnyman advises Orsbourn to 'conceal yourself': both the man and the evidence of his actions. The word 'conceal' is repeated several times in this scene: Honnyman warns Orsbourn, 'conceal yourself, and mind your Eye'; after the murders they 'must conceal the tawny Dogs'; and after covering them with brush, 'There they will lie conceal'd and snug enough' (I ii). Honnyman and Orsbourn thus seem to affirm a convention of concealment and deceit among at least certain types of British settlers. This accepted disparity of appearances and actuality among the colonists leaves Ponteach's Ottawas vulnerable because they expect equation, at least until they become 'poisoned by the infection of our Foes' (III iii): 'Whose very Language is a downright Lie? / Who swear and call on Gods when they mean nothing? / Who call it complaisant, polite good Breeding, / To say Ten thousand things they don't intend, / And tell their nearest Friends the basest Falsehoods?' (III i). With the exception of Ponteach and Philip, both described as contaminated by English values, Rogers' representatives of the Great Lakes Nations are purported to speak honestly and directly and to expect the same of others, assuming that they are judged and valued upon their acts and the words that represent them: 'I call no Man bad, till such he's found, / Then I condemn him and cast him from my Sight; / And no more trust him as a Friend and Brother' (I iv). *Ponteach* depicts its Ottawa and Mohawk cultural identities as ones in which ideal self relies on a congruent relationship between public and private identification.

---

37 The traders Murphey and M'Dole are not so violent, but establish from the play's opening scene that for British characters, 'Our fundamental Maxim then is this, / That it's no Crime to cheat and gull an *Indian* ... A Thousand Opportunities present / To take Advantage of their Ignorance' (I i). The Governors Sharp, Gripe, and Catchum similarly exploit their belief that the Ottawas 'are ignorant of the Worth / Of single things, nor know they how to add / Or calculate, and cast the whole Amount.' Sharp adds, 'How thankful should we be that we have Schools, / And better taught and bred than these poor Heathen' (I iv). Susan Castillo suggests there is potentially further significance to this discussion of trade by characters with respectively Irish and Scottish names, noting that the names evoke 'two nations on the periphery of English empire, as were (Rogers may be implying) England's American Colonies' (216). The use of names typical of other British colonies may attempt to assert equality, rather than hierarchy, among those who were identified as not-English.

The play also individualizes the Ottawas' and Mohawks' struggle to engage the Europeans' contradictory construction of identity and its destabilizing effect on their own perception of identity and relationships with each other. Ponteach's second son Chekitan, for example, proclaims effusively his love for Monelia, but the Mohawk princess replies, 'Hoh! now your Talk is so much like a Christian's, / That I must be excus'd if I distrust you.' Chekitan is horrified that she would 'compare an Indian Prince to those / Whose Trade it is to cheat, deceive, and flatter' (III i), but his ability to communicate has been contaminated. This leads to his immediate willingness to accept the word of his duplicitous brother Philip because Chekitan is unwilling to see any 'Indian Prince' in these English terms. And this culturally infused lapse of communication is what leads to the destruction of the second generation of Ottawas and Mohawks in Rogers' imagining.

In this crucial exchange that we see the fatal implications of the partial naturalization of Europeanness in the second-generation Ottawa and Mohawk characters. Without thinking, Chekitan has come to embody colonial ambivalence: he despises the Europeans and their dishonesty, yet emulates their patterns of romantic speech and their inherent iteration of gendered identity. It is reminiscent of what Bhabha terms 'the White man's artifice inscribed on the Black man's body. It is in relation to this impossible object that emerges the liminal problem of colonial identity and its vicissitudes' ('Remembering' 117). Here, Chekitan's contamination of identity performs double duty. First, it radicalizes his relationships upon purely racial lines, rendering him vulnerable to his treacherous brother, and thus contributes to Ponteach's military defeat; and second, it prevents reproduction and regeneration, driving the lovers apart because they can no longer presume to speak the same figurative language.[38]

The foreboding sense of The Wolf that each generation has been weakened more than the last is confirmed:

We're poison'd with the Infection of our Foes,
Their very Looks and Actions are infectious,
And in deep Silence spread Destruction round them.
Bethink yourselves while any Strength remains;
Dare to be like your Fathers, brave and strong,
Nor further let the growing Poison Spread. (III iii)

---

38 Castillo argues, 'The sons of Ponteach also reflect some of the difficult choices faced by Rogers as a first-generation Creole; the pacific Chekitan is a loyal son and subject, while the warlike Philip is a vision of the darker, fratricidal side of the brewing American revolt' (223).

Not just for Ponteach, then (himself 'infected' with deceitful ambition), but for all of the allied sachems, the fear of loss of control of identity is definitive. The young need to emulate not just their literal fathers, but also myriad preceding generations, with ideas of self and nation established long before every inter-action required mediation by the 'version of themselves the other side invented' (White, 'Fictions' 64). Nation is no longer about territory, history, or family: even nations often traditionally in conflict are united for survival 'while any Strength remains.'

Ponteach's first appearance in the play follows the shocking scene of the hunters Honnyman and Orsbourn murdering and scalping two Indians to steal their load of furs, justifying the act with the argument that 'It's no more Murder than to crack a Louse' (I ii).[39] These scenes can be interpreted in different ways, of course, but though I find Julie Ellison's discussion of *Ponteach* often persuasive, I cannot agree in any way with her reading of the opening scenes 'exposing the crimes of French and English traders and settlers against the Indians' as 'low comic scenes' (90). It seems to me that *Ponteach*'s tragedy begins from its first moments, and to read it otherwise is to trivialize the most historically detailed and accurate (and angry) section of the play. The play calls for the events of Act I scene ii, as well as later murders, scalpings, and the torture of an innocent woman and her breastfeeding infant, to occur on stage rather than off. Staging these scenes of violence would render their physical quality as sickening as Honnyman's philosophy and its consequences, and there can be no surprise that the next scene establishes a direct and simple contrast between the cursing, overconfident English military leaders and the idealized Ponteach of the play's first act. Ponteach's response to Colonel Cockum's and Captain Fisk's insults (whose more horrific human and economic implications have been established in the first two scenes) is

So ho! Know you whose Country you are in?
Think you, because you have subdu'd the French,
That *Indians* too are now become your Slaves?
This Country's mine, and here I reign as King;
I value not your Threats, nor Forts, nor Guns;

---

39 Colley documents effectively several historical contexts analogous to this depiction of British brutality, noting that some Britons emerged from the experience of the Seven Years' War 'convinced that Native Americans were irredeemably bestial, cruel to captives and cruel in essence. But other Britons recognized – on the basis of what they read in letters or print – that their own regular troops in America (like French and colonial troops there) sometimes behaved not much differently' (*Captives* 186).

I have got Warriors, Courage, Strength, and Skill.
Colonel, take care; the Wound is very deep,
Consider well, for it is hard to cure. (I iii)

This assertion of dominion is only a lead-in, though, for the next increment in the play's movement from private encounters between private citizens, to semi-private military encounters, and finally to public political exchanges between Ponteach and the three governors of the colony: Sharp, Gripe, and Catchum. Rogers' allegiance in the latter scene is obvious in names alone, and his *Concise Account* accuses those promoted above him of exactly such ignorance. But the slights move beyond private morality as the governors embezzle the king's gifts to the sachems, and then the sachems' gifts to the king, until their own greed has left the chiefs insulted and vulnerable to Ponteach's calls for rebellion, and their nations at war. Ponteach comes to stand in both for the plight of the devalued individual in revisionist colonial systems of hierarchy and for the 'doomed Indian' stereotype that would be so widely referenced in the nineteenth century; the difference between Rogers' portrayal and those typical of the eighteenth century is that Ponteach is shown to be complicated, human, and respected by a fellow warrior even as that warrior depicts his end.[40]

Though both the play and eighteenth-century English culture in general tend to assume that women are to be excluded from political public discourse, it is not just Ponteach to whom Rogers gives a split significance. The Mohawk princess Monelia is certainly rendered a passive, typically feminized object that men desire and over which they do battle, but she is also significant in much more emblematic ways. Of course, the myths and metaphors surrounding colonist-colonized sexual relationships are myriad, from nations figured as naked women awaiting plunder by the colonial master to the dark-skinned rapist attacking white women who stand in for European or colonial culture. There is also a conventional narrative of European men preventing barbaric colonized men from mistreating women, which Gayatri Spivak summarizes as 'White men are saving brown women from brown men' (296), and finally the Pocahontas tradition of the Indian princess who falls in love with a European man, which Peter Hulme suggests uses romance narratives to assert 'the ideal

---

40 For an intriguing point of comparison on the depiction of an Indian human nature with more in common than different from that of Europeans, see Peter Williamson's *French and Indian Cruelty* (1757). Frequently revised and reprinted, and widely read over the next hundred years, Williamson's captivity narrative acknowledges from its title page Indian 'cruelties,' but frequently also criticizes both the English and French for their own brutality, notably in deceitful trade and the use of alcohol to manipulate Indian partners.

of a cultural harmony through romance' (141). Elements of *Ponteach* conflict with the larger cultural myths of colonialism in their articulation of a slightly distorted version of a narrative widely assumed natural and true. Much to the same effect, Rogers rewrites interracial sexuality in a way that allows Monelia in particular not only to stand in for America in the larger project of colonialism, but also to embody the selectivity of consent in the ostensibly collaborative systems of trade and exchange among colonists and Indians.

As Ania Loomba has observed, narratives of romantic consensuality frequently parallel trade: colonial trade 'is projected as a transaction desired by both parties, an enterprise mutually beneficial and entered into via the exercise of free will' (134). Loomba's examples come from colonial India, but a nicely parallel study is offered in Sylvia van Kirk's *Many Tender Ties*, which documents in a less metaphorical way the links among trade and romantic partnership in cases where sachems of various nations married their daughters to Hudson's Bay Company fur traders in order to cement trade benefits. Such cases suggest that mutually beneficial visions of colonialism may be fictionalized through narratives of romantic alliances, but that those fictions are also based on historical actualities. *Ponteach*, though, asserts a coercive nature in intercultural trade: in Act I, two Indian hunters are murdered and scalped because Honnyman and Orsbourn are unsuccessful hunters but still desire profit through trade; a second man is cheated when a European trader gives him alcohol, uses a weighted scale, and takes advantage of different systems of quantification; and Sharp, Gripe, and Catchum cheat the Ottawas as a group of both goods and good will by skimming both sides of exchanges of gifts of respect. In these scenes, Rogers does not appear to object to the idea of colonialism as a potentially mutually beneficial trade relationship, but he does seem to object to the ignorance and short-sightedness behind such greed. Rogers observed at first hand the effects of cheating traders and of corrupt officials who opted to ignore the fact that colonial trade (and the peace that it helped to maintain) depended upon mutualism: both sides must benefit from trade (though not necessarily equally), or there is no benefit to the Indians in allowing colonists access to their traditional resources. *Ponteach* does not suggest that trade inevitably leads to coercion and retaliatory violence – Rogers benefited too much himself from cross-cultural trade to make such a case – but his play makes clear the need for some sort of balanced reciprocity in line with both established Indigenous traditions and traditional trade among Europeans. Throughout the series of scenes in Act I in particular, Rogers legitimizes the case for rebellion as he depicts a complete disregard for expectations of reciprocity and informed consent. The relationships are neither mutually beneficial nor, because they are based on violence and deceit, consensual.

The same tactics are used in the scene between Monelia and the French Roman Catholic priest. He has earlier attempted to initiate a sexual transaction through the language of romance and seduction that Hulme identifies (and that parallels the exchanges of gifts and statements of friendship of the governors). When circumstances take away the time needed to claim Monelia by seduction, the Priest resorts to brute physical force, much like Honnyman does to claim the furs he desires. And when the attempted rape is interrupted, the Priest attempts to impose a blatantly falsified system of reason, naturalism, and balance in God's will (rather like the supposed exact rightness and balance of the traders' scales): 'I have a Dispensation from St. *Peter* / To quench the Fire of Love when it grows painful, / This makes it innocent like Marriage Vows; And all our holy Priests, and she herself, / Commits no Sin in this Relief of Nature: / For, being holy, there is no Pollution / Communicated from us as from others' (IV ii). Even under its conventional anti-French, anti-Catholic cover, this scene replicates symbolically the economic and political relationships that have been set up in Act I. Once again, the elements of the narrative are entirely typical – corrupt French priest, beautiful maiden, last-moment rescue – and yet it is not the same. This is first because Monelia is rescued by Chekitan, which gives the Native man the qualities of virtuous heroism that Britons conventionally imagined in themselves and in their staged representations. Locating heroic virtue in Chekitan emphasizes the absence of such qualities in the British colonists in the play, a point that is pressed even closer to home by the fact that the action of the French priest is aligned so explicitly to the earlier acts of the English that the scene becomes one of equation, rather than differentiation of the two European nations and their relative values.[41]

Rogers' play uses metaphors of rape and gender consistently (though not universally) to translate the threat of cultural violation into a form that English audiences might be expected to understand more easily. Such metaphors can be read as a two-step aid to identification: the articulation of Indigenous identity in the play depends at times upon the conventionalized vulnerability of the feminine, and the idea of an identity eradicable by force is rendered through metaphors of rape. This is, of course, not a new set of connections in colonial

---

41 Dowd offers a specific historical context. He notes that many Indigenous women were kept as mistresses or even prostitutes in colonial garrisons, and that 'sexuality emerged as a definite issue between Britons and Indians. When Miamis took Fort Miami in 1763, they deployed a ruse involving the Indian lover of the garrison commander. And in the first violence of the war, on the St Clair River far north of Detroit, Ojibwa women would use seductive gestures very effectively to entice willing British boatmen into the gun sights of hidden Ojibwa warriors. In these instances there are hints that Indians resented a British assumption of sexual access to Indian women' (88).

imagery, even in the eighteenth century. *Ponteach*'s metaphors of sexual vulnerability fall into alignment (both perfect and skewed) with long-standing
conventions of personifications of North America as a sexually vulnerable
Indigenous woman, most memorably in Theodore Galle's 1580 engraving
America (reprinted here, page 57).[42] The alignment is perfect in the assumed
powerlessness of the not-European, not-male, but skewed in that images like
America were not, at least initially, expected to suggest abuse and eradication, but rather potential for germination, in ideas of conversion, illumination, and economic expansion. Rogers' play implies that those naïve if noble
goals have led not to an expanded age of enlightenment, but to something
altogether less noble.

In *Ponteach*, the threat of subordination is quite consistently framed in gendered terms: those who are disinclined to be brought to battle in the name of
small, hugely emblematic acts of disrespect and betrayal or by arguments of
avenging the deaths of a few with the deaths of the many, are described by the
battle-ready men as 'womanish' and 'unmanned.' When Chekitan suggests
that reason must rule over passion in matters of war, Philip accuses him of being 'a very Woman in thy Heart.' Chekitan retorts, 'Is it all womanish to re-
consider / And weight the Consequences of our Action, Before we desperately
rush upon them? / Let me then be the Coward, a mere Woman / Mine be the
Praise of Coolness, yours of Rage' (II ii). Every character uses a language
of assumed weakness in femininity, and such language appears even in unexpected places: the lover Chekitan uses it to ironize Philip's view of war, and
later to communicate his fear of being 'unman'd' by love. Similarly, the monstrous villain Honnyman is allowed a sympathetic moment as he fears he will
have to witness the torture and murder of his children, but until he is 'unman'd'
by the thought that 'Dear *Tommy* too must die' his response is to prohibit his
good wife from prayer, concerned that his captors will 'say Religion makes us
all mere Women' (IV iv). In this similarity between Philip's speech and that of
the worst of colonists, it is, of course, possible that such echoes are simply the
effects of an inexperienced writer, failing to differentiate the speech patterns of
different characters. But given that Philip and Chekitan do explicitly discuss
the significance of this feminized language to their own identities, the potential
complexity signified by its use seems plausibly significant. We may see in
characters on both sides of the conflict the conundrum that Julie Ellison
points out in Anglo-American modes of masculine sensibility: many men

---

42 Galle's image is after a drawing by Jan Vander Straet. For detailed discussion of this particu-
    lar metaphor in American culture, see Annette Kolodny's *Lay of the Land*.

who mocked women for their emotional excesses 'wrote at times in the pathetic vein themselves, read and admired the literature of sensibility, and, all told, were able to justify their own emotionalism while rejecting the emotional displays of women. A man could have his sensibility, in other words, and despise it too' (20).

Citing Adam Smith's *Theory of Moral Sentiments*, Ellison sets forth a foundational premise that 'effects fundamental to the genres of sensibility are organized by gender and race' (7).[43] As Edward Said and others have similarly noted, there is a long-standing association of femininity and weakness with the racialized Other (figured as East in Said's analysis), and masculinity and strength with the West. In the speeches cited above, however, Rogers has both the colonist and colonized cultures make the same equation, demonstrating the absorption of the colonists' valuations of both gender and race by the Ottawa and Mohawk men. This in spite of the likelihood that both Rogers and the Indigenous men he knew would almost certainly have been familiar with nearby communities such as the Huron, who had a partially matriarchal political and familial system. As in so many representations of colonial transculturation, though, the mimicry is ambivalent: the very hostile Philip accepts the characterization despite his hatred of those who make it (using the language of power as it is used by those who devalue and disempower him), while Chekitan who, as we have seen, has absorbed other modes of European language, both accepts and rearticulates that formulation in an example of the slightly distorted way in which the colonized repeat the colonizers' discourse. His speech reflects a version of the gendering of racial identity that is '*almost but not quite*' European (Bhabha, 'Mimicry' 126; original emphasis) as he infuses reason and consciousness into that which is presumptively passionate and reactionary, creating space for the same possibility of rearticulation in the parallel construction of race in colonial discourse.

And though powerless in the broad movements of the play, women are at the centre of every action – they are, as Chekitan observes, 'the Tie, the Centre of the Whole' (V iv). Philip betrays his brother and murders the Mohawk prince and princess Monelia and Torax because his brother has sold as a slave a woman whom he would like to have kept once he 'saw her and instantly loved her.' Chekitan initially argues against Ponteach's plan to go to war without the

---

43 Ellison argues that particularly in eighteenth-century America, discourses of sensibility fostered an increased acceptance and even valuation of 'tenderhearted manhood' (12), but in making her argument, she also notes the long association of derogatory uses of language of femininity when describing men.

Mohawks because it will risk alienating him from his beloved Monelia; he then leaves Monelia alone in the forest so that he can lead a team in war (instead of his more qualified brother) because Philip tells him that this is the best way to protect Monelia. The French Priest betrays Ponteach's plan to the French in part because he is angry that Chekitan has thwarted his attempt to rape Monelia; and even Ponteach sees himself as constantly in service to the Fates, which are gendered female here.

Certainly, heroic drama, tragedy, and republican drama all tend to depend upon such roots to some degree, but here the central role of women – their vulnerability and the desire for revenge they can foster – is not just about establishing masculinity through the defence of femininity. What Rogers foresees as the broad outcome of the North American conflict is to some degree emblematized in the figure of Monelia and in her violent death in a struggle for the succession of power. Despite the historical problem of locating the metaphor for Indian vulnerability in a Mohawk woman,[44] Monelia's body does function in the play as a fairly straightforward metaphor of the body politic. As a character, Monelia owns no discursive strategies to counter her relegation to dehumanized object and geographical metaphor (whose presence forces others to act, even if only to claim possession), and her psychic and physiological resources are presumed available for consumption. Even in sympathetic European accounts like that of Rogers, indigeneity as identity is performed defensively, enforced by an increasingly dominant European presence.

History always diverges from its accounts, of course, and in fact the British were much more successful at negotiated settlements than in violent conflict with the Great Lakes Nations, but *Ponteach* is like so many contemporary representations of indigeneity (even the sympathetic ones) in its fostering of popular perceptions of the idea of the Indian. Had his play been produced, Rogers might reasonably have expected it to be influential in some degree. As Colley shows, though many North American colonists' direct experience might have led to a 'gut fear and dislike of Indians,' Britons' understandings of North American Indians were still being developed in the 1760s: 'On the British side of the Atlantic, things were different. Overwhelmingly preoccupied for

---

44 It is ironic that Rogers chooses a Mohawk woman in whom to locate his metaphor. Throughout the eighteenth century, the Mohawks were the most politically powerful Indigenous nation in North America, through a combination of their historical dominance among the Iroquois and neighbouring nations (noted by Rogers in his *Concise Account*) and their successful alliance with the British (noted in *Ponteach*). While Rogers may have been relatively accurate in the general outcomes his play expects – and renders in metaphor through Monelia – the Mohawks were among the least vulnerable Indigenous groups in 1766.

so long with European enemies, and substantially ignorant of Indians – as of much else about the land across the Atlantic – many Britons at home held understandably to a wider spectrum of attitudes' (*Captives* 161). Rogers' play strives to establish the humanity and human range of temperament and experience among the Ottawas, the Mohawks, and other nations, perhaps contributing to what Felicity Nussbaum calls the 'inconsistencies and confusion ... characteristic of racial discourse' (139) in the eighteenth century.[45] Even with his efforts at individuation, however, conventions of constructed identity are concurrently interrogated and entrenched by Rogers: even as he points out the errors of perceptions of identity and the tragic outcomes of a political strategy based on misconstruction, his play cannot help but contribute to the mythology of the doomed Indian, driven to presumed extinction by failures to communicate effectively through performative identity. As K. Anthony Appiah puts it for the modern context, 'Between the politics of recognition and the politics of compulsion, there is no bright line' (163).

The metaphor of Monelia suggests that Rogers is to some degree aware of devaluatory metaphors being imposed around him in the service of colonialism. The particular metaphors that Rogers invokes in his play most consistently are those that render Indigenous men weak through a language of feminization or ignorant through a language of savagery, confirming the presumptive universal positive of Christian European masculinity. Judith Butler has argued in the specific terms of gender and sexuality that the distinctions between public and private or personal and political are socially functional fictions, constructed to substantiate the status quo, such that even the most ostensibly private and personal acts are scripted to some degree by compulsory ideology and social convention.[46] She notes that 'as an intentionally organized materiality, the body is always an embodying *of* possibilities both conditional and circumscribed by historical convention. In other words, the body *is* a historical situation, as Beauvior has claimed, and is a manner of doing, dramatizing, and *reproducing* a historical situation' (521; original emphasis).

---

45 Nussbaum summarizes ideas of race in the eighteenth century thus: 'Concepts of race and its signifiers were sufficiently incoherent and inconsistent to make launching of a stable identity for English people versus the non-English fraught and complicated, though not impossible. In sum, inconsistencies and confusion are *characteristic* of racial discourse and related cultural practices in mid eighteenth-century England rather than the exception' (139). For a detailed historical overview of eighteenth-century ideas on race, see Nicholas Hudson's 'From "Nation" to "Race": The Origin of Racial Classification in Eighteenth-Century Thought.'

46 As Butler puts it, 'The personal is thus implicitly political inasmuch as it is conditioned by shared social structures, but the personal has also been immunized against political challenge to the extent that public/private distinctions endure' (523).

Rogers' metaphors of race and nation in both Ponteach and Monelia function in much this way.[47] To varying degrees among its representations of different characters, the play is one of perhaps only a few instances where the eastern North American Indigenous body of the eighteenth century can be understood as constituted by discourse and its performative embodiment: the audience of English readers and imagined viewers can be expected to have no first-hand knowledge of the identity represented on stage. Pontiac the man, of course, existed and struggled with social demand; Ponteach the character creates Pontiac as a linguistic construction. In Rogers' mediated representation of recent history, the raced construction is often articulated in the language of European ideas of marginal femininity, such that the naturalized or unmarked qualities of the feminine inform disempowered difference. The character of Monelia suggests this relationship most specifically, but the texts' links among the language of the feminine and the language of race are both articulated by and directly affect the other characters too, from Tenesco and The Wolf, to Ponteach, Philip, and Chekitan.

And as the near-rape and eventual murder of Monelia demonstrate, Ponteach is right to attempt to manage through both speech and action the metaphors of intercultural negotiation. Throughout the play, he attempts to force his conversations with the governors into metaphors of brotherhood, friendship, and even paternalism. Ponteach calls the English 'Brothers,' and pledges to treat them as 'Friends and Brothers' (I iv), but remembers with ironic fondness the French colonists who 'Call'd us their Friends, nay, what is more, their Children, / And seem'd like Fathers anxious for our Welfare.' And despite the mistreatment of his people, he is even willing to 'call their King my Friend, / Yea, and honour and obey him as my Father ... would he keep his own Sea, / And leave these distant Lakes and Streams to us' (II ii). This might seem straightforward, even uncharacteristically submissive for Ponteach, but as Richard White documents, the balances of power implied by these relationships are not as direct as modern readers might assume. In many of the surviving historical documents, 'the fictional identity of brothers was accepted by both sides, but the meaning of that identity, "the firmest bonds of Love and Friendship," was an American, not Algonquian construction ... For the Algonquians, fraternity

---

47 Butler herself applies her theory of compulsory performance of bodily difference to questions of race only sparingly; however, her sense that 'it's not so much a double consciousness – gender and race as the two axes, as if they're determined only in relation to one another, I think that's a mistake – but I think the unmarked character of the one very often becomes the condition of the articulation of the other' (quoted in Bell 168) seems exactly at the crux of Rogers' metaphors of race and power in Ponteach.

was a more neutral relation than paternity ... fraternal relations were relations of equality, but of all the kinship terms of Indian diplomacy, brother seems, except for cousin, the one least fraught with mutual obligation.' Still, these questions of brother, father, uncle, or cousin are crucial, as 'each side had to agree on its metaphorical identity, on the fictions that would govern negotiations. Once established, images became part of larger reality and certain images of the Other demanded certain responses regardless of what the Other actually said or what concessions the Other offered' ('Fictions' 68–71). White cites speeches by Wyandot chief Tarhe to suggest the Indigenous metaphor of fatherhood (for which Ponteach is willing to settle in defeat) is 'not a stern patriarch; a father was a generous friend' (83). Still, the father can demand respect and deference. Ponteach reaches this point, however, only after he attempts to construct the relationship in terms of other metaphors such as the more equal and at times violent fraternity. For example, White notes that 'the [next generation] Ottawa chief Aguishiway meant to elevate the Americans in standing when he told Anthony Wayne that he did not consider him a brother but rather a friend. Even as the Americans and confederated Indians killed each other, they addressed each other as brothers' (69).

The familial metaphors that Rogers cites thus again both illuminate and problematize the types of relationships that might be possible. Rogers' audience assumes that it knows what these metaphors imply, but the instability and unreliability of their presumptively universal knowledge of family ultimately affirms instead their cultural ignorance and the dangerous ramifications that assumed knowledge can have in culturally mediated conflict with those who are almost the same, but not quite. Much in the same way that White describes nineteenth-century diplomatic councils,

> the middle ground was a realm of constant invention that once agreed upon by both sides, became convention. The central and defining aspect of the middle ground was a willingness, born of necessity, for one set of people to justify their actions in terms of what they perceived to be their partners' cultural premises. In seeking to persuade others to act, they sought out congruences, either perceived or actual, between the two cultures. The congruences arrived at often seemed – and, indeed, were – results of misunderstandings or accidents. Indeed, the explanations offered by members of one society for the practices of another often were ludicrous. This, however, did not matter. Any congruence, no matter how tenuous, could be put to work and take on a life of its own as long as it was accepted by both sides. (66)

This ongoing process of definition and self/other identification is always in masculine terms, ever attempting to redress the creep of devaluatory metaphors of feminization, because outside of those relationships one of the only two other options is to be womanly – like Monelia, obedient, threatened, nearly ruined by representatives of European Christianity, and finally, violently dead. Or they can become enemies, which is, of course, where the relationship ends up, leaving both the Mohawk king and Ponteach holding only the dead and dying bodies of their children and the future they are written explicitly to warn against.[48]

Ironically, though, not one is dead at the hand of the English: Monelia and her brother Torax are stabbed by Philip in the name of revenging himself on Chekitan, who discovers the murders, killing Philip and then himself in a telling rage:

> There is no Kindred, Friendship, Faith, or Love
> Among Mankind – Monelia's dead – The World
> Is all unhing'd – There's universal War –
> She was the Tie, the Centre of the Whole;
> And she remov'd, all is one general Jar. (V iv)

After both fraternal and romantic affiliation have been destroyed, there is nothing left but a war that is pointless because it cannot serve kindred, friendship, faith, or love. The world as colonized by the English is so changed that the next generation of Ottawa and Mohawk leaders end in a cycle of self-destruction, overwhelmed by the example and control of the English into a dissipated identity.

As early as Act I, Ponteach eloquently summarizes the elements of the colonial relationship that will lead to the contamination of identity that constitutes the play's tragic end:

> *Indians* a'n't Fools, if White Men think us so;
> We see, we hear, we think as well as you;
> We know they're Lies, and Mischiefs in the World;
> We don't know whom to trust, nor when to fear. (I iv)

The actual killing does not have to be done by the English – the cultural chaos they have created is enough. Of course, Rogers himself likely killed dozens of Indigenous men on one side of the French and Indian War, and served in battle

---

48 That these children are all fictional makes the more clear their metaphorical function, as they all end the play threatened, contaminated, and eventually dead, much like Rogers expected their nations to be without changes in colonial management.

with hundreds more on the other side. *Ponteach* doesn't deny Rogers' own acts of brutal violence, but it does seem to suggest that he recognized more of their implications than did many soldiers. His play uses the universalized identifiability of the sexual, physical, and social vulnerability of femininity to allow European audiences a glimpse into the position of the Indigenous people of North America, to render on a human scale the enormous acts of cultural violence carried out around the French and Indian War and in the smaller-scale, but equally destructive conflicts among settlers and Indians. And by allowing Ponteach to be both brilliant and monstrous, both defeated and autonomous, Rogers demonstrates the fallacy of the mythologies that were being marketed in Europe to justify the privileging of settlers' interests over those of established Indigenous populations.

The play ends as Ponteach's forces are being defeated in battle and Tenesco tells him that he must retreat with them or face alone 'the Fury of a conquering Foe.' Ponteach's final speech begins with a tragic Lear-like cry,

Will they desert their King in such an Hour,
When Pity might induce them to protect him?
Kings like the Gods are valued and ador'd,
When Men expect their Bounties in Return,
Place them in Want, destroy the giving Power,
All Sacrifices and Regards will cease.

Neither the play nor Ponteach ends there, though, in the posture of tragic defeat and powerlessness demanded by most North American settlers and some Britons. Ponteach then calls to the fields and streams, fountains and trees,

I am no more your Owner and your King.
But witness for me to your new base Lords,
That my unconquer'd Mind defies them still;
And though I fly, 'tis on the Wings of Hope ...
Britons may boast, the Gods may have their Will,
Ponteach I am, and shall be *Ponteach* still. (V v)

Rogers' dramatization of Pontiac's life thus refuses to end with the submission that might have pleased British and American audiences, affirming the rightness of the colonization or extermination of those driven by revenge to act against what they have perhaps convinced even Ponteach himself is God's will. Instead, Ponteach lays claim to individual agency and begins his plans for 'more Sons, fresh Troops ... and other Schemes of future Greatness,' no longer willing to collaborate with either European power in the destruction of Indigenous autonomy, but planning to act against both.

In the end, of course, the historical Pontiac was only sporadically successful, but the rebellion that bears his name was one of the last major challenges to British colonialism in eastern North America. Rogers rejects both noble and savage ideological constructions of Indigenous identity and creates a dramatization of a fellow great military leader that is human and powerful. Rogers' Ponteach embodies the tragedy of his people in such a way that an inattentive reading can make it all seem personal and petty, with the deaths of hundreds of European and Indigenous people caused by wounded pride and ignorant ambition. But Rogers asks his audience to see Ponteach not as he was misread by fools like Cockum and Frisk, Sharp, and Gripe, but as the personal face of a political act, where acts of violence and degradation are all both 'public or private, it matters not.' As a survivor of the war himself, Rogers tries to show London audiences the human face of the North American pawns at the centre of the Seven Years' War between England and France. In *Ponteach*, Indianness is both granted historical specificity in the figure of Ponteach and a metaphor in Monelia. And when these two characters are grouped with Chekitan and his ambivalent relationship to colonial culture, it is possible to read their (written) Indianness as performance whose function is both to give specificity to those typically rendered merely symbolic, and in a similarly critical gesture, to expose colonial and European performance as itself savage, violent, and spiritually and economically corrupt, embodied by violent men deliberately reinterpreting both law and policy set by perhaps well-meaning but ignorant men abroad. It is perhaps no wonder that the play was not embraced in its day. It has much, however, to say to us.

Robert Rogers, engraved by Thomas Hart, 1776 (William L. Clements Library, The University of Michigan).

Pontiac, artist and year unknown (Ohio Historical Society).

Theodore Galle, *America*, ca. 1580 (Print Collection, Miriam and Ira D. Wallach Division of Art, Prints and Photographs, The New York Public Library, Astor, Lenox, and Tilden Foundations).

PONTEACH:

OR THE

Savages of America.

A

TRAGEDY.

LONDON:
Printed for the Author ; and Sold by J. MILLAN,
oppofite the *Admiralty, Whitehall.*

M.DCC.LXVI.
[Price 2 s. 6 d.]

Dramatis Personae.

PONTEACH,	Indian *Emperor on the great Lakes*.
PHILIP *and* CHEKITAN,	*Sons of* Ponteach.
TENESCO,	*His chief Counsellor and Generalissimo*.
ASTINACO, The BEAR, The WOLF,	Indian *Kings who join with* Ponteach.
TORAX *and* MONELIA	*Son and Daughter to* Hendrick, *Emperor of the* Mohawks.
Indian	*Conjuror.*
French	*Priest.*
SHARP, GRIPE, CATCHUM,	*Three* English *Governors.*
Colonel COCKUM, Captain FRISK,	*Commanders at a Garrison in* Ponteach*'s Country.*
M'DOLE *and* MURPHEY,	*Two* Indian *Traders.*
HONNYMAN *and* ORSBOURN,	*Two* English *Hunters.*
Mrs. HONNYMAN,	*Wife* to Honnyman *the Hunter.*

Warriors, Messengers, &c.

PONTEACH:

OR THE

Savages of America.

ACT I.

SCENE I.

An Indian *Trading House.*

Enter M'Dole *and* Murphey, *Two* Indian *Traders, and their Servants.*
M'Dole.
So, *Murphey*, you are come to try your Fortune
Among the Savages in this wild Desart?[1]

Murphey. Ay, any Thing to get an honest Living,
Which 'faith I find it hard enough to do;
Times are so dull, and Traders are so plenty,   5
That Gains are small, and Profits come but slow.

M'Dole. Are you experience'd in this kind of Trade?
Know you the Principles by which it prospers,
And how to make it lucrative and safe?
If not, you're like a Ship without a Rudder,   10
That drives at random, and must surely sink.

Murphey. I'm unacquainted with your *Indian* Commerce,
And gladly would I learn the Arts from you,
Who're old, and practis'd in them many Years.

M'Dole. That is the curst Misfortune of our Traders,   15
A thousand Fools attempt to live this Way,
Who might as well turn Ministers of State.
But, as you are a Friend, I will inform you

---

1 In the eighteenth century the term desert was not yet limited to an arid climate, but indicated
  uninhabited wilderness, including forest land.

Of all the secret Arts by which we thrive,
Which if all practis'd, we might all grow rich,   20
Nor circumvent each other in our Gains.
What have you got to part with to the *Indians?*

Murphey. I've Rum and Blankets, Wampum,[2] Powder,[3] Bells,
And such-like Trifles as they're wont to prize.

M'Dole. 'Tis very well: your Articles are good: 25
But now the Thing's to make a Profit from them,
Worth all your Toil and Pains of coming hither.
Our fundamental Maxim then is this,
That it's no Crime to cheat and gull an *Indian.*

Murphey. How! Not a Sin to cheat an *Indian,* say you?   30
Are they not Men? hav'nt they a Right to Justice
As well as we, though savage in their Manners?

M'Dole. Ah! If you boggle[4] here, I say no more;
This is the very Quintessence of Trade,
And ev'ry Hope of Gain depends upon it;   35
None who neglect it ever did grow rich,
Or ever will, or can by *Indian* Commerce.
By this old *Ogden*[5] built his stately House,

---

2 Cylindrical beads made from polished whelk shells. Wampum was generally threaded or
  woven into belts, often up to six feet in length. Wampum belts were widely used as currency
  between Europeans and eastern North American Indigenous groups, but because they were
  sturdy and travelled well, they were traditionally more significant as a mode of communication
  and as a memory aid in cultures of oral tradition. A wampum belt painted red, for example,
  could be sent as a summons to war. See Rogers' description in the excerpt from *A Concise
  Account of North America*, reprinted in this volume.
3 Gunpowder.
4 Hesitate or startle.
5 While no specific Ogden can be identified from this reference, it seems possible that it refers
  to the Ogden family of New Jersey. They were among the earliest settlers to the area, and
  might have been known to the playwright(s) in several ways. One of the soldiers closest to
  Rogers' in his famed efforts to save his men after the attack on St Francis was a Captain
  Ogden. Perhaps more likely is a link through Nathaniel Potter, who attended New Jersey
  College at a time when the Ogden family was prominent because of the legislator John Ogden,
  who was in turn the father of Aaron Ogden, later New Jersey's fifth governor, who graduated
  from New Jersey College in 1773. The two men would likely not have known one another, but
  the Ogden family was certainly affluent and well known, and the legislative connection would
  make a nice pun on 'stately house.'

Purchas'd Estates, and grew a little King.
He, like an honest Man, bought all by Weight,   40
And made the ign'rant Savages believe
That his Right Foot exactly weigh'd a Pound:[6]
By this for many Years he bought their Furs,
And died in Quiet like an honest Dealer.

Murphey. Well, I'll not stick at what is necessary;   45
But his Device is now grown old and stale,
Nor could I manage such a barefac'd Fraud.

M'Dole. A thousand Opportunities present
To take Advantage of their Ignorance;[7]
But the great Engine I employ is Rum,   50
More pow'rful made by certain strength'ning Drugs.[8]
This I distribute with a lib'ral Hand,
Urge them to drink till they grow mad and valiant;
Which makes them think me generous and just,
And gives full Scope to practise all my Art.   55
I then begin my Trade with water'd Rum,
The cooling Draught well suits their scorching Throats.
Their Fur and Peltry[9] come in quick Return:
My Scales are honest, but so well contriv'd,
That one small Slip will turn Three Pounds to One;   60
Which they, poor silly Souls! ignorant of Weights
And Rules of Balancing, do not perceive.
But here they come; you'll see how I proceed.
Jack, is the Rum prepar'd as I commanded?

---

6 This particular mode of dishonest trade is described in satirical detail in Washington Irving's
   1809 *A History of New-York from the Beginning of the World to the End of the Dutch Dynasty,*
   by Diedrich Knickerbocker

7 In 1761, Lord Egremont, one of George III's ministers, wrote to General Amherst to complain
   that 'The Indians are disgusted & their minds alienated from His Majesty's Government by the
   shamefull manner in which business is transacted between them and our traders, the latter
   making no scruple of using every low trick and artifice to overreach and cheat those unguarded
   ignorant people in their dealings with them, while the French by a different conduct, and worthy of our immitation, deservedly gain their confidence' (Nester 53).

8 G.M. Wrong and others report that some traders spiked rum with laudanum, as 'drugged rum
   was a great ally of trade' (89).

9 M'Dole distinguishes between the furs of larger animals, such as the beaver, and the pelts of
   smaller animals. In *Concise Account*, Rogers notes that 'the fur of [the skunk or pole-cat], with
   that of the Ermin, Otter, and Martin, make up what they call the small peltry' (189).

Jack. Yes, Sir, all's ready when you please to call.   65

M'Dole. Bring here the Scales and Weights immediately.
You see the Trick is easy and conceal'd.
                                        [*Shewing how to flip the Scales.*

Murphey. By *Jupiter*, it's artfully contriv'd;
And was I King, I swear I'd knight th' Inventor.
—*Tom*, mind the Part that you will have to act.   70

Tom. Ah, never fear, I'll do as well as Jack.
But then, you know, an honest Servant's Pains
Deserves Reward.[10]

Murphey.   O! I'll take care of that.
                        Enter a Number of Indians, with Packs of Fur.

1ˢᵗ Indian. So, what you trade with *Indians* here to-day?

M'Dole. Yes, if my Goods will suit, and we agree.   75

2ᵈ Indian. 'Tis Rum we want, we're tired, hot, and thirsty.

3ᵈ Indian. You, Mr. *Englishman*, have you got Rum?

M'Dole. Jack, bring a Bottle, pour them each a Gill.[11]
You know which Cask contains the Rum. The Rum?

1ˢᵗ Indian. It's good strong Rum, I feel it very soon.   80

M'Dole. Give me a Glass. Here's Honesty in Trade;
We *English* always drink before we deal.

2ᵈ Indian. Good Way enough; it makes one sharp and cunning.

---

10 Perhaps an allusion to the fact that a substantial number of servants in North America were
     'convict servants': persons convicted of a crime in England (usually theft) and then transport-
     ed to America.
11 Four ounces, or a quarter pint, a substantial amount of rum, even if not augmented with
     laudanum.

M'Dole. Hand round another Gill. You're very welcome.

3ᵈ Indian. Some say you *Englishmen* are sometimes Rogues;   85
You make poor *Indians* drunk, and then you cheat.

1ˢᵗ Indian. No, *English* good. The *Frenchmen* give no Rum.

2ᵈ Indian. I think it's best to trade with *Englishmen.*

M'Dole. What is your Price for Beaver Skins *per* Pound?[12]

1ˢᵗ Indian. How much you ask *per* Quart for this strong Rum?   90

M'Dole. Five Pounds of Beaver for One Quart of Rum.

1ˢᵗ Indian. Five Pounds? Too much. Which is't you call Five Pound?

M'Dole. This little Weight. I cannot give you more.

1ˢᵗ Indian. Well, take 'em; weigh 'em. Don't you cheat us now.

M'Dole. No : He that cheats an *Indian* should be hang'd.   95
                                        [*weighing the Packs.*
There's Thirty Pounds precisely of the Whole;
Five times Six is Thirty. Six Quarts of Rum.
Jack, measure it to them; you know the Cask.
This Rum is sold. You draw it off the best.
                                        [*Exeunt* Indians *to receive their Rum.*

Murphey. By *Jove*, you've gain'd more in a single Hour   100
Than ever I have done in Half a Year:
Curse on my Honesty! I might have been
A *little King*, and liv'd without Concern,
Had I but known the proper Arts to thrive.

M'Dole. Ay, there's the Way, my honest Friend, to live.   105
                                        [*clapping his Shoulder.*
There's Ninety Weight of Sterling Beaver for you,

---

12 Alexander Henry's *Travels and Adventures* reports that in 1765, a pound of beaver skins
   traded for 2s 6p or a half-pound of powder.

Worth all the Rum and Trinkets in my Store;
And, would my Conscience let me do the Thing,
I might enhance my Price, and lessen theirs,
And raise my Profits to an higher Pitch.   110

Murphey. I can't but thank you for your kind Instructions,
As from them I expect to reap Advantage.
But should the Dogs detect me in the Fraud,
They are malicious, and would have Revenge.

M'Dole. Can't you avoid them? Let their Vengeance light   115
On others Heads, no matter whose, if you
Are but secure, and have the Gain in Hand:
For they're indiff'rent where they take Revenge,[13]
Whether on him that cheated, or his Friend,
Or on a Stranger whom they never saw,   120
Perhaps an honest Peasant, who ne'er dreamt
Of Fraud or Villainy in all his Life;
Such let them murder, if they will a Score,
The Guilt is theirs, while we secure the Gain,
Nor shall we feel the bleeding Victims Pain.   [*Exeunt.*

SCENE II.

A Desart.

Enter Orsbourn *and* Honnyman, *Two* English *Hunters.*

Orsbourn.
Long have we toil'd, and rang'd the Woods in vain,
No Game, nor Track, nor Sign of any Kind
Is to be seen; I swear I am discourag'd
And weary'd out with this long fruitless Hunt.

---

13 See Rogers' *Concise Account* in this volume: 'if any quarrels happen, they never make use of
    oaths, or any indecent expressions, or call one another by hard names; but, at the same time, no
    duration can put a period to their revenge; it is often a legacy transferred from generation to
    generation, and left as a bequest from father to son, till an opportunity offers of taking ample
    satisfaction, perhaps in the third or fourth generation from those who first did the injury' (177).

No Life on Earth besides is half so hard,   5
So full of Disappointments, as a Hunter's:
Each Morn he wakes he views the destin'd Prey,
And counts the Profits of th'ensuing Day;
Each Ev'ning at his curs'd ill Fortune pines,
And till next Day his Hope of Gain resigns.   10
By *Jove*,[14] I'll from these Deserts hasten home,
And swear that never more I'll touch a Gun.

Honnyman. These hateful *Indians* kidnap all the Game.
Curse their black Heads! they fright the Deer and Bear,
And ev'ry Animal that haunts the Wood,   15
Or by their Witchcraft conjure them away.
No *Englishman* can get a single Shot,
While they go loaded home with Skins and Furs.
'Twere to be wish'd not one of them survived,
Thus to infest the World, and plague Mankind.   20
Curs'd Heathen Infidels! mere savage Beasts!
They don't deserve to breathe in Christian Air,
And should be hunted down like other Brutes.

Orsbourn. I only wish the Laws permitted us
To hunt the savage Herd where-e'er they're found;   25
I'd never leave the Trade of Hunting then,
While one remain'd to tread and range the Wood.

Honnyman. Curse on the Law, I say, that makes it Death[15]
To kill an *Indian*, more than to kill a Snake.
What if 'tis Peace? these Dogs deserve no Mercy;   30
Cursed revengeful, cruel, faithless Devils!
They kill'd my Father and my eldest Brother.

---

14 A mild curse, referring to Jove or Jupiter, the Roman sky god, head of the gods, and ironically – given the rest of this scene – disburser of justice.
15 Outside of times of war, in most states the formal laws at least declined to distinguish on the
basis of race in terms of murder and other crimes. North Carolina's laws of 1715 note, for example, that 'whatever white man shall defraud or take from any of the Indians his goods, or
shall beat, abuse, or injure his person … shall suffer such other punishment as he should
or ought to have done had the offense been committed to an Englishman,' and Georgia's
'Murder of Free Indians' Act of 1774 states, 'to murder any free Indian, in amity with this
province, is, but the law of the land, as penal, to all intents and purposes whatsoever, as to
murder any white person.'

Since which I hate their very Looks and Name.

Orsbourn. And I, since they betray'd and kill'd my Uncle;
Hell seize their cruel, unrelenting Souls!   35
Tho' these are not the same, 'twould ease my Heart
To cleave their painted Heads, and spill their Blood.[16]
I abhor, detest, and hate them all,
And now cou'd eat an *Indian*'s Heart with Pleasure.

Honnyman. I'd join you, and soop his savage Brains for Sauce;[17]   40
I lose all Patience when I think of them,
And, if you will, we'll quickly have Amends
For our long Travel and successless Hunt,
And the sweet Pleasure of Revenge to boot.

Orsbourn. What will you do? Present, and pop one down?   45

Honnyman. Yes, faith, the first we meet well fraught with Furs;
Or if there's Two, and we can make sure Work,
By *Jove*, we'll ease the Rascals of their Packs,
And send them empty home to their own Country.
But then observe, that what we do is secret,   50
Or the Hangman will come in for Snacks.[18]

Orsbourn. Trust me for that; I'll join with all my Heart;
Nor with a nicer Aim, or steadier Hand,
Would shoot a Tyger[19] than I would an *Indian*.
There is a Couple stalking now this Way   55

---

16 Orsbourn here repeats from his own point of view what M'Dole has said of the Indians in Ii
    (see note 13).
17 A reversal of conventional typifications of North American Indians as cannibals. Such de-
    scriptions were typically false, though the Ottawa did practise occasional ritual cannibalism.
    The 1766 text clearly reads 'soop' (possibly as in liquefy), rather than the perhaps more intui-
    tive 'scoop.'
18 'Come in for snacks' is a colloquialism meaning to claim a share or portion. The hunters
    could be hanged if their actions were discovered.
19 Though of course there were no tigers in North America, many accounts and government
    documents use the word, probably to refer to the mountain lion or other large cat. For
    example, Carolina's 1696 act requiring Indians to bring in skins as back payment for
    European clothing and other ostensible gifts of the past requires each adult Indian
    man to provide 'yearly, one wolf's skin, one tiger's skin, or one bear skin, or two cat
    skins.'

With lusty Packs; Heav'n favour our Design.

Honnyman.[20] Silence; conceal yourself, and mind your Eye.

Orsbourn. Are you well charg'd?[21]

Honnyman.   I am. Take you the nearest,
And mind to fire exactly when I do.

Orsbourn. A charming Chance!

Honnyman.   Hush, let them still come nearer.   60
                    [*They shoot, and run to rifle the* Indians.
They're down, old Boy, a Brace of noble Bucks!

Orsbourn. Well tallow'd, faith, and noble Hides upon 'em.
                                        [*Taking up a Pack.*
We might have hunted all the Season thro'
For Half this Game, and thought ourselves well paid.

Honnyman. By *Jove*, we might, and been at great Expence   65
For Lead and Powder, here's a single Shot.

Orsbourn. I swear I've got as much as I can carry.

Honnyman. And faith I'm not behind; this Pack is heavy.
But stop; we must conceal the tawny Dogs,
Or their blood-thirsty Countrymen will find them,   70
And then we're bit. There'll be the Devil to pay,
They'll murder us, and cheat the Hangman too.[22]

Orsbourn. Right. We'll prevent all Mischief of this Kind.
Where shall we hide their savage Carcases?

Honnyman. There they will lie conceal'd and snug enough—   75
                                        [*They cover them.*

---

20 Corrected from *Hon.*

21 Is your gun ready and charged with gunpowder?

22 If the hunters are killed by the countrymen of those they have murdered, they will not face
   English justice and the risk of death by hanging.

But stay—perhaps ere long there'll be a War,
And then their Scalps will sell for ready Cash,
Two Hundred Crowns at least, and that's worth saving.[23]

Orsbourn. Well! that is true, no sooner said than done—
                                                        [*Drawing his Knife.*
I'll strip the Fellow's painted greasy Skull.[24]   80
                                                        [*Strips off the Scalp.*[25]

Honnyman. A damn'd tough Hide, or my Knife's devilish dull—
                                                        [*Takes the other Scalp.*
Now let them sleep to Night without their Caps,
And pleasant Dreams attend their long Repose.[26]

Orsbourn. Their Guns and Hatchets now are lawful Prize,
For they'll not need them on their present Journey.[27]   85

Honnyman. The Devil hates Arms, and dreads the Smell of Powder;[28]

---

23 Amounts paid for the scalps (as evidence of the killing of an Indian) varied widely over time,
    geography, and circumstance, but Honnyman's estimate seems reasonably apt, given, for
    example, Pennsylvania's 1764 proclamation offering $134 'for every male above ten years,
    scalped, being killed.' Live captives were worth $150 (male) or $130 (female). During King
    George's War, Sir William Johnson offered substantial bounties for scalps, including half-
    bounties for the scalps of children. Johnson would later be instrumental in reaffirming the
    Covenant Chain, the alliance between the Iroquois nations and the English.
24 Many Indigenous nations, including the Five Nations and Great Lakes Nations, used body
    and face paint, often made from bear's grease, to signify status and to mark important events,
    including battle.
25 Though there was a brief scholarly vogue in the 1970s for arguments that scalping was intro-
    duced to North America by Europeans, James Axtell argues convincingly that such arguments
    are misplaced, and that there is substantial evidence that North American Indians had tradi-
    tions of scalping that predate European contact. Axtell, however, does make clear that both
    Indians and Europeans used the practice in North America, including the 1688 example of
    the French governor of Canada offering ten beaver skins for every enemy scalp – Indian or
    Christian; in 1696 the Council of New York offered six pounds for every Indian or French
    scalp (Axtell and Sturtevant 470).
26 Corrected from Repo se.
27 As Rogers himself notes in *Concise Account*, most Algonquian nations shared the custom of
    burying people with valuable items such as pipes, tobacco, bows, and arrows 'that they might
    not be in want of any thing when he comes to the other country.' See page 171, this volume.
    Orsbourne's comment thus affirms either his ignorance or his disrespect of such customs.
28 John Milton's *Paradise Lost* famously identifies Satan as the inventor of gunpowder, but he is
    driven from heaven after losing the war with the angels.

He'll not allow such Instruments about him,
They're free from training[29] now, they're in his Clutches.

Orsbourn. But, *Honnyman*, d'ye think this is not Murder?
I vow I'm shock'd a little to see them scalp'd,   90
And fear their Ghosts will haunt us in the Dark.

Honnyman. It's no more Murder than to crack a Louse,
That is, if you've the Wit to keep it private.
And as to Haunting, *Indians* have no Ghosts,
But as they live like Beasts, like Beasts they die.   95
I've kill'd a Dozen in this self-same Way,
And never yet was troubled with their Spirits.

Orsourn. Then I'm content; my Scruples[30] are remov'd.
And what I've done, my Conscience justifies.
But we must have these Guns and Hatchets alter'd,   100
Or they'll detect th'Affair, and hang us both.

Honnyman. That's quickly done—Let us with Speed return,
And think no more of being hang'd or haunted;
But turn our Fur to Gold, our Gold to Wine,
Thus gaily spend what we've so slily won,   105
And bless the first Inventor of a Gun.

[*Exuent.*

SCENE III.

An English *Fort.*

Enter Colonel Cockum *and Captain* Frisk.

Cockum.
What shall we do with these damn'd bawling *Indians?*

---

29 In this context, either dragging meat on the ground to attract animals to the hunt, or spreading
    gunpowder on the ground to ignite a fire.
30 Corrected from myScruples.

They're swarming every Day with their Complaints
Of Wrongs and Injuries, and God knows what—
I wish the Devil would take them to himself.

Frisk. Your Honour's right to wish the Devil his Due.   5
I'd send the noisy Helhounds packing hence,
Nor spend a Moment in debating with them.
The more you give Attention to their Murmurs,
The more they'll plague and haunt you every Day,
Besides, their old King *Ponteach* grows damn'd saucy,   10
Talks of his Power, and threatens what he'll do.
Perdition to their faithless sooty Souls,
I'd let 'em know at once to keep their Distance.

Cockum. Captain, You're right; their Insolence is such
As beats my Patience; cursed Miscreants!   15
They are encroaching; fain would be familiar:[31]
I'll send their painted Heads to Hell with Thunder!
I swear I'll blow 'em hence with Cannon Ball,
And give the Devil a Hundred for his Supper.

Frisk. They're coming here; you see they scent your Track,   20
And while you'll listen, they will ne'er be silent,
But every Day improve in Insolence.

Cockum. I'll soon dispatch and storm them from my Presence.

Enter Ponteach, *and other* Indian *Chiefs.*

Ponteach. Well, Mr. Colonel *Cockum*, what d' they call you?
You give no Answer yet to my Complaint;   25
Your Men give my Men always too much Rum,
Then trade and cheat 'em.[32] What! d' ye think this right?

---

31 Cockum's phrasing alludes to the language of class: 'insolence' suggests misbehaviour by an
   inferior; 'encroaching' suggests moving into inappropriate space owned by another; and to be
   'familiar' is to be intimate, but with the negative implication of unwelcome intimacy or intru-
   sion in this case. In the eighteenth century 'miscreant' conveyed not merely bad behaviour,
   but also often the religious implication of disbelief or paganism.

32 This was a common complaint about the treatment of Indigenous nations in the colonial
   period. In 1762, Colonel Henry Bouquet had ordered that because the 'use of rum and all

Cockum. Tush! Silence! hold your noisy cursed Nonsense;
I've heard enough of it; what is it to me?

Ponteach. What! you a Colonel, and not command your Men?   30
Let ev'ry one be a Rogue that has a Mind to't.

Cockum. Why, curse your Men, I suppose they wanted Rum;
They'll rarely be content, I know, without it.

Ponteach.[33] What then? If *Indians* are such Fools, I think
White Men like you should stop and teach them better.   35

Cockum. I'm not a Pedagogue to your curs'd *Indians.*   [*aside.*

Ponteach. Colonel, I hope that you'll consider this.

Frisk. Why don't you see the Colonel will not hear you?
You'd better go and watch your Men yourself,
Nor plague us with your cursed endless Noise;   40
We've something else to do of more Importance.

Ponteach. Hah! Captain *Frisk,* what! you a great man too?
My[34] Bus'ness here is only with your Colonel;
And I'll be heard, or know the Reason why.

1ˢᵗ Chief. I thought the *English* had been better Men.   45

2ᵈ Chief. Frenchmen would always hear an *Indian* speak,
And answer fair, and make good Promises.

Cockum. You may be d—d, and all your *Frenchmen* too.

Ponteach. Be d—d! what's that? I do not understand.

---

strong liquors is destructive to the Indians and attended with the most pernicious consequences, all Indian traders and others are expressly forbid' to sell liquor to Indians. Pontiac's
spiritual leader, the Delaware Prophet Neolin, claimed that in his vision the Master of Life
had specifically ordered his followers to cease drinking to excess and also to end trade with
the English.

33 Corrected from *Ponteack.*
34 Corrected from By.

Cockum. The Devil teach you; he'll do it without a Fee.   50

Ponteach. The Devil teach! I think you one great Fool.
Did your King[35] tell you thus to treat the *Indians?*
Had he been such a Dunce he ne'er had conquer'd,
And made the running *French* for Quarter cry.
I always mind that such proud Fools are Cowards,   55
And never do aught that is great or good.

Cockum. Forbear your Impudence, you curs'd old Thief;
This Moment leave my fort, and to your Country.
Let me hear no more of your hellish Clamour,
Or to D—n I will blow you all,   60
And feast the Devil with one hearty Meal.

Ponteach. So ho! Know you whose Country you are in?
Think you, because you have subdu'd the *French*,
That *Indians* too are now become your Slaves?
This Country's mine, and here I reign as King;[36]   65
I value not your Threats, nor Forts, nor Guns;
I have got Warriors, Courage, Strength, and Skill.
Colonel, take care; the Wound is very deep,
Consider well, for it is hard to cure.   *[Exeunt* Indians.

Frisk. Vile Infidels! observe their Insolence;   70
Old *Ponteach* puts on a mighty Air.

Cockum. They'll always be a Torment till destroy'd
And sent all headlong to the Devil's Kitchen.
This curs'd old Thief, no doubt, will give us Trouble,
Provok'd and madded at his cool Reception.   75

---

35 King George III had become king in 1760. He and his ministers were disturbed by stories of
    mistreatment of North American Indians. Nester's account of Pontiac's Rebellion documents
    several correspondences asserting that 'His Majesty's interests may be promoted by treating
    the Indians upon the same principles of humanity and proper indulgence' as settlers (53).

36 For Rogers' account of Ponteach's sense of his own status, see *Concise Account* in this vol-
    ume: 'his whole conversation sufficiently indicated that he was far from considering himself
    as a conquered Prince, and that he expected to be treated with the respect and honour due a
    King or Emperor by all who came into his country or treated with him' (181).

Frisk. Oh! Colonel, they are never worth our minding,
What can they do against our Bombs and Cannon?
True, they may skulk, and kill and scalp a few,
But, Heav'n be thank'd, we're safe within these Walls:[37]
Besides, I think the Governors are coming,   80
To make them Presents, and establish Peace.

Cockum. That may perhaps appease their bloody Minds,
And keep them quiet for some little Term.
God send the Day that puts them all to sleep,
Come, will you crack a Bottle at my Tent?   85

Frisk. With all my Heart, and drink D—n to them.

Cockum. I can in nothing more sincerely join.   [*Exeunt.*

SCENE IV.

An Apartment in the Fort.

Enter Governors Sharp, Gripe, *and* Catchum.[38]

Sharp.

Here are we met to represent our King,
And by his royal Bounties to conciliate
These *Indians* Minds to Friendship, Peace, and Love.
But he that would an honest Living get

---

37 Of course, this confidence turns out to be misplaced. Almost simultaneously in the late spring
    and early summer of 1763, several forts were attacked and breached in the beginning of
    Pontiac's Rebellion. On 4 June 1763, for example, a group of Ojibwe (also called Cherokee)
    men played lacrosse outside Fort Michillimackinac; when soldiers came to watch the game,
    warriors entered the fort and killed almost all of its occupants. See Act IV scene iii for refer-
    ence to a similar event.
38 The names are obviously indicative of values. Sharp likely alludes to his being a sharper or
    cheat, as in 'card sharp' (which later evolved to 'shark'). Historians such as Gregory Evans
    Dowd have read the character of Sharp as a specific attack on Major Henry Gladwin, a fellow
    officer under whom Rogers served in 1763. The Navarre *Journal of Pontiac's Conspiracy* also
    lays blame for the attack on Detroit on insult Pontiac believed he had had from Gladwin (17).

In Times so hard and difficult as these,   5
Must mind that good old Rule, Take care of One.

Gripe. Ay, Christian Charity begins at home;
I think it's in the Bible, I know I've read it.[39]

Catchum. I join with *Paul*, that he's an Infidel
Who does not for himself and Friends provide.[40]   10

Sharp. Yes, *Paul* in fact was no bad Politician;
And understood himself as well as most.
All good and wise Men certainly take care
To help themselves and Families the first;
Thus dictates Nature, Instinct, and Religion,   15
Whose easy Precepts ought to be obey'd.

Gripe. But how does this affect our present Purpose?
We've heard the Doctrine; what's the Application?

Sharp. We are intrusted with these *Indian* Presents.
A Thousand Pound was granted by the King,   20
To satisfy them of his Royal Goodness,
His constant Disposition to their Welfare,
And reconcile their savage Minds to Peace.
Five hundred's gone; you know our late Division,
Our great Expence, *Et cetera*, no matter: 25
The other Half was laid out for these Goods,
To be distributed as we think proper;
And whether Half (I only put the Question)
Of these said Goods won't answer every End,

---

39 This quotation actually appears to originate in Terence's classical Roman play *Andria* from
    the second century B.C.E., and was known in the eighteenth century from sources like Francis
    Beaumont and John Fletcher's *Wit without Malice* (in which it is used ironically: 'Charity and
    beating begins at home' (V ii). Sir Thomas Browne also used the exact phrase in the 1642
    Religio Medici: 'Charity begins at home, is the voice of the world: yet is every man his greatest
    enemy.' Gripe's biblical sourcing could simply be incorrect, or may allude to Paul's advice to
    widows with children in 1 Timothy 5:4: 'Let them learn first to show piety at home.'
40 Catchum misrepresents the intention of Paul's advice in 1 Timothy 5:8: 'But if any provide
    not for his own, and specially for those of his own house, he hath denied the faith, and is
    worse than an infidel.'

And bring about as long a lasting Peace   30
As tho' the Whole were lavishly bestow'd?

Catchum. I'm clear upon't they will, if we affirm
That Half's the Whole was sent them by the King.

Gripe. There is no doubt but that One Third wou'd answer,
For they, poor Souls! are ign'rant of the Worth   35
Of single Things, nor know they how to add
Or calculate, and cast the whole Amount.

Sharp. Ay, Want of Learning is a great Misfortune.
How thankful should we be that we have Schools,
And better taught and bred than these poor Heathen.   40

Catchum. Yes, only these Two simple easy Rules,
Addition and Subtraction, are great Helps,
And much contribute to our Happiness.

Sharp. 'Tis these I mean to put in Practice now;
Subtraction from these Royal Presents makes   45
Addition to our Gains without a Fraction.
But let us overhawl and take the best,
Things may be given that won't do to sell.

                            [*They overhawl the Goods,* &c.

Catchum. Lay these aside; they'll fetch a noble Price.

Gripe. And these are very saleable, I think.   50

Sharp. The *Indians* will be very fond of these.
Is there the Half, think you?

Gripe.   It's thereabouts.

Catchum. This Bag of Wampum may be added yet.

Sharp. Here, Lads, convey these Goods to our Apartment.

Servant. The *Indians,* Sir, are waiting at the Gate.   55

Gripe. Conduct them in when you've disposed of these.

Catchum. This should have been new-drawn before they enter'd.
                    [*pulling out an Inventory of the whole Goods.*

Gripe. What matters that? They cannot read, you know,
And you can read to them in gen'ral Terms.

        Enter Ponteach, *with several of his Chieftains.*

Sharp. Welcome, my Brothers, we are glad to meet you,   60
And hope that you will not repent our coming.

Ponteach. We're glad to see our Brothers here the *English.*
If honourable Peace be your Desire,
We'd always have the Hatchet buried deep,
While Sun and Moon, Rivers and Lakes endure,   65
And Trees and Herbs within our Country grow.
But then you must not cheat and wrong the *Indians,*
Or treat us with Reproach, Contempt, and Scorn;
Else we will raise the Hatchet to the Sky,
And let it never touch the Earth again,   70
Sharpen its Edge, and keep it bright as Silver,
Or stain it red with Murder and with Blood.
Mind what I say, I do not tell you Lies.

Sharp. We hope you have no Reason to complain
That *Englishmen* conduct to you amiss;   75
We're griev'd if they have given you Offence,
And fain would heal the Wound while it is fresh,
Lest it should spread, grow painful, and severe.

Ponteach. Your Men make *Indians* drunk, and then they cheat 'em.
Your Officers, your Colonels, and your Captains   80
Are proud, morose, ill-natur'd, churlish[41] Men,
Treat us with Disrespect, Contempt, and Scorn.
I tell you plainly this will never do,
We never thus were treated by the *French,*

---

41 Vulgar or rude.

Them we thought bad enough, but think you worse. 85

Sharp. There's good and bad, you know, in every Nation;
There's some good *Indians*, some are the reverse,
Whom you can't govern, and restrain from ill;
So there's some *Englishmen* that will be bad.
You must not mind the Conduct of a few, 90
Nor judge the rest by what you see of them.

Ponteach. If you've some good, why don't you send them here?
These every one are Rogues, and Knaves, and Fools,
And think no more of *Indians* than of Dogs.
Your King had better send his good Men hither, 95
And keep his bad ones in some other Country;
Then you would find that *Indians* would do well,
Be peaceable, and honest in their Trade;
We'd love you, treat you, as our Friends and Brothers,
And Raise the Hatchet[42] only in your Cause[43] 100

Sharp. Our King is very anxious for your Welfare,
And greatly wishes for your Love and Friendship;
He would not have the Hatchet ever raised,
But buried deep, stamp'd down and cover'd o'er,
As with a Mountain that can never move: 105
For this he sent us to your distant Country,
Bid us deliver you these friendly Belts,

[*holding out Belts of Wampum.*

All cover'd over with his Love and Kindness.
He like a Father loves you as his Children;
And like a Brother wishes you all Good;[44] 110
We'll let him know the Wounds that you complain of,
And he'll be speedy to apply the Cure,
And clear the Path to Friendship, Peace, and Trade.

---

42 To take up arms. This is the opposite of 'bury the hatchet' (below) meaning to end hostilities
and lay down arms.

43 There is no period here in the 1766 printing, perhaps indicating interruption.

44 Throughout these scenes relationships are described in familial terms that carried quite different significance for Europeans and the Ottawa. See Introduction, pages 50–1 for detailed
discussion.

Ponteach. Your King, I hear's a good and upright Man,
True to his word, and friendly in his Heart;   115
Not proud and insolent, morose and sour,
Like these his petty Officers and Servants:
I want to see your King, and let him know
What must be done to keep the Hatchet dull,[45]
And how the Path of Friendship, Peace, and Trade   120
May be kept clean and solid as a Rock.

Sharp. Our King is distant over the great Lake,
But we can quckly send him your Requests;
To which he'll listen with attentive Ear,
And act as tho' you told him with your Tongue.   125

Ponteach. Let him know then his People here are Rogues,
And cheat and wrong and use the *Indians* ill.
Tell him to send good Officers, and call
These proud ill natur'd Fellows from my Country,
And keep his Hunters from my hunting Ground.   130
He must do this, and do it quickly too,
Or he will find the Path between us bloody.

Sharp. Of this we will acquaint our gracious King,
And hope you and your Chiefs will now confirm
A solid Peace as if our King was present;   135
We're his Ambassadors, and represent him,
And bring these Tokens of his Royal Friendship
To you, your Captains, Chiefs, and valiant Men.
Read Mr. *Catchum*, you've the Inventory.

Catchum. The *British* King, of his great Bounty, sends   140
To *Ponteach*, King upon the Lakes, and his Chiefs,
Two hundred, No [*aside*] a Number of fine Blankets,
Six hundred [*aside*] Yes, and several Dozen Hatchets,
Twenty thousand [*aside*] and a Bag of Wampum,
A Parcel too of Pans, and Knives, and Kettles.   145

Sharp. This rich and royal Bounty you'll accept,

---

45 Rather than sharpened, in preparation for violence.

And as you please distribute to your Chiefs,
And let them know they come from *England*'s King,
As Tokens to them of his Love and Favour.
We've taken this long Journey at great Charge,   150
To see and hold with you this friendly Talk;
We hope your Minds are all disposed to Peace,
And that you like our Sovereign Bounty well.

1ˢᵗ Chief. We think it very small, we heard of more.
Most of our Chiefs and Warriors are not here,   155
They all expect to share a Part with us.

2ᵈ Chief. These won't reach round to more than half our Tribes,
Few of our Chiefs will have a single Token
Of your King's Bounty, that you speak so much of.

3ᵈ Chief. And those who have'nt will be dissatisfied,   160
Think themselves slighted, think your King is stingy,
Or else that you his Governors are Rogues,
And keep your Master's Bounty for yourselves.

4ᵗʰ Chief. We hear such Tricks are sometimes play'd with *Indians*,
King *Astenaco*,[46] the great Southern Chief,   165
Who's been in *England*, and has seen your King,
Told me that he was generous, kind, and true,
But that his Officers were Rogues and Knaves,
And cheated *Indians* out of what he gave.

Gripe. The Devil's in't, I fear that we're detected   [*aside.* 170

Ponteach. Indians a'n't Fools, if White Men think us so;
We see, we hear, we think as well as you;
We know there're Lies, and Mischiefs in the World;

---

46 Commonly recorded as Ostenaco or Outacity, one of three Cherokee men who travelled to
   England in the summer of 1762, escorted by Henry Timberlake. The names of the other
   two men are less consistently reported, but the anglicizations of their names are The Pouting
   Pigeon (Tohanohawighton) and The Stalking Turkey (Kanagagota). Though the three were
   not particularly pleased with their reception, they did eventually meet King George III. For
   highlights of the visit, see *The Gentleman's Magazine* 'Historical Chronicle' for June, July,
   and August 1762.

We don't know whom to trust, nor when to fear;
Men are uncertain, changing as the Wind,   175
Inconstant as the Waters of the Lakes,
Some smooth and fair, and pleasant as the Sun,
Some rough and boist'rous, like the Winter Storm;
Some are Insidious as the subtle Snake,
Some innocent, and harmless as the Dove;   180
Some like the Tyger raging, cruel, fierce,
Some like the Lamb, humble, submissive, mild,
And scarcely one is every Day the same;
But I call no Man bad, till such he's found,
Then I condemn him and cast him from my Sight;   185
And no more trust him as a Friend and Brother.
I hope to find you honest Men and true.

Sharp. Indeed you may depend upon our Honours,
We're faithful Servants of the best of Kings;
We scorn an imposition on your ignorance,   190
Abhor the Arts of Falshood and Deceit.
These are the Presents our great Monarch sent,
He's of a bounteous, noble, princely Mind
And had he known the Numbers of your Chiefs,
Each would have largely shar'd his Royal Goodness;   195
But these are rich and worthy your Acceptance,
Few Kings on Earth can such as these bestow,
For Goodness, Beauty, Excellence, and Worth.

Ponteach. These Presents from your Sovereign I accept,
His friendly Belts to us shall be preserved,   200
And in Return convey you those to him.   [*Belts and Furs.*
Which let him know our Mind, and what we wish,
That we dislike his crusty Officers,
And wish the Path of Peace was made more plain,
The Calumet[47] I do not chuse to smoak,   205
Till I see further, and my other Chiefs

---

47 A type of pipe with a long, ornamented stem and a bowl made of clay or stone. It is used as a
   signifier of agreement among many North American Indian nations. To smoke the pipe signi-
   fies peace or friendship; to refuse to smoke communicates disagreement or a rejection of
   offered terms. See *Concise Account* 173–4, this volume.

Have been consulted. Tell your King from me,
That first or last a Rogue will be detected,
That I have Warriors, am myself a King,
And will be honour'd and obey'd as such;   210
Tell him my Subjects shall not be oppress'd,
But I will seek Redress and take Revenge;
Tell your King this; I have no more to say.

Sharp. To our great King your Gifts we will convey,
And let him know the Talk we've had with you;   215
We're griev'd we cannot smoak the Pipe of Peace,
And part with stronger Proofs of Love and Friendship;
Mean time we hope you'll so consider Matters,
As still to keep the Hatchet dull and buried,
And open wide the shining Path of Peace,   220
That you and we may walk without a Blunder.   [*Exeunt Indians.*

Gripe. Th' appear not fully satisfied, I think.

Catchum. I do not like old *Ponteach's* Talk and Air,
He seems suspicious, and inclin'd to war.

Sharp. They're always jealous, bloody, and revengeful,   225
You see that they distrust our Word and Honour;
No wonder then if they suspect the Traders,
And often charge them with downright Injustice.

Gripe. True, when even we that come to make them Presents,
Cannot escape their Fears and Jealousies.   230

Catchum. Well, we have this, at least, to comfort us;
Their good Opinion is no Commendation,
Nor their foul Slanders any Stain to Honour.
I think we've done whatever Men could do
To reconcile their savage Minds to Peace.   235
If they're displeas'd, our Honour is acquitted,
And we have not been wanting in our Duty
To them, our King, our Country, and our Friends.

Gripe. But what Returns are these they've left behind?

These Belts are valuable, and neatly wrought.[48]   240

Catchum. This Pack of Furs is very weighty too;
The Skins are pick'd, and of the choicest Kind.

Sharp. By *Jove*, they're worth more Money than their Presents.

Gripe. Indeed they are; the King will be no Loser.

Sharp. The King! who ever sent such Trumpery to him?   245

Catchum. What would the King of *England* do with Wampum?
Or Beaver Skins, d'ye think? He's not a Hatter![49]

Gripe. Then it's a Perquisite belongs to us?[50]

Sharp. Yes, they're become our lawful Goods and Chattels,
By all the Rules and Laws of *Indian* Treaties.   250
The King would scorn to take a Gift from *Indians*,
And think us Madmen should we send them to him.[51]

Catchum. I understand we make a fair Division,
And have no Words nor Fraud among ourselves.

Sharp. We throw the whole into one common Stock,   255
And go Copartners in the Loss and Gain.
Thus most who handle Money for the Crown
Find means to make the better Half their own;
And, to your better Judgments with Submission,
The self Neglecter's a poor Politician.   260
These Gifts, you see, will all Expences pay;

---

48 Wampum belts. See note 2.
49 A maker of hats. Beaver skin was a luxury material used in fashionable hats in England in the
    eighteenth century.
50 A bonus in addition to the regular pay of a position. In modern terms, a 'perk' of the job.
51 Sharp misrepresents English policy; in fact such valuable goods as furs were the property of
    the Crown, though not necessarily the king personally. Many artefacts from this period
    are held by royal descendants and beneficiaries, however, so some goods did clearly reach
    the king directly. No period ends this sentence in the 1766 printing.

Heav'n send an *Indian* Treaty every Day;
We dearly love to serve our King this Way.

The End of the First ACT.

ACT II.

SCENE I.

An Indian *House.*

Enter Philip[52] *and* Chekitan,[53] *from hunting, loaded with Venison.*[54]

Philip.
The Day's Toil's ended, and the Ev'ning smiles
With all the Joy and Pleasantness of Plenty.
Our good Success and Fortune in the Chace
Will make us Mirth and Pastime for the Night.
How will the old King and his Hunters smile   5
To see us loaded with the fatt'ning Prey,
And joyously relate their own Adventures?
Not the brave Victor's Shout, or Spoils of War,
Would give such Pleasure to their gladden'd Hearts.

Chekitan. These, *Philip,* are the unstain'd Fruits of Peace,   10
Effected by the conqu'ring *British* Troops.
Now may we hunt the Wilds secure from Foes,[55]

---

52 Philip's name may allude to Wampanoag sachem Metacomet, called King Philip by
   Europeans, and the leader of several nations in what became known as King Philip's War
   (1675–6).
53 The two fictional sons of Ponteach. There is no record that the historical Pontiac had sons
   who were involved in his rebellion. See Introduction note 6.
54 The flesh of an animal killed in hunting and used as food; in the eighteenth century the term
   encompassed all game animals, including deer, boar, hare, and rabbit.
55 King George III's Royal Proclamation of 1763 included provision that 'the several Nations
   or Tribes of Indians with whom We are connected, and who live under our Protection,

And seek our Food and Cloathing by the Chace,
While Ease and Plenty thro' our Country reign.

Philip. Happy Effects indeed! long may they last!   15
But I suspect the Term will be but short,
Ere this our happy Realm is curs'd afresh
With all the Noise and Miseries of War,
And Blood and Murder stain our Land again.

Chekitan. What hast thou heard that seems to threaten this,   20
Or is it idle Fancy and Conjectures?

Philip. Our Father's late Behaviour and Discourse
Unite to raise Suspicions in my Mind
Of his Designs? Hast thou not yet observ'd,
That tho' at first he favour'd *England*'s Troops,   25
When they late landed on our fertile Shore,
Proclaim'd his Approbation of their March,
Convoy'd their Stores, protected them from Harm,
Nay, put them in Possession of *Detroit*;[56]
And join'd to fill the Air with loud Huzza's   30
When *England*'s Flag was planted on its Walls?
Yet, since, he seems displeas'd at their Success,
Thinks himself injured, treated with Neglect
By their Commanders, as of no Account,[57]
As one, whose Right to Empire now is lost,   35

---

should not be molested or disturbed in the Possession of such Parts of Our Dominions and
Territories as, not having been ceded to or purchased by Us, are reserved to them, or any of
them, as their Hunting Grounds.'
56 Rogers' *Concise Account* reports that in 1760 while on their way to secure Fort Detroit, he
and his Rangers encountered Pontiac, who granted them safe passage through his territory to
Detroit (see pages 180–2 in this volume). Though Rogers may embellish the individual role
of Pontiac in the meeting, the Ottawa did negotiate free passage for the British through the
exchange of gifts and smoking of the calumet.
57 As William Nester documents, Jeffrey Amherst, commander of the king's forces in North
America in 1759, instituted a policy that reduced gifts and munitions to the Indians in an
effort to reduce administrative costs, weaken Indian military capacity, and force them to
return to hunting by traditional means. Gifts were seen by most Indian nations as payment
for access to their lands, while Amherst considered them unnecessary and undeserved
presents.

And he became a Vassal[58] of their Power,
Instead of an Ally. At this he's mov'd,
And in his Royal Bosom glows Revenge,
Which I suspect will sudden burst and spread
Like Lightning from the Summer's burning Cloud,[59]   40
That instant sets whole Forests in a Blaze.

Chekitan. Something like this I have indeed perceiv'd;
And this explains what I but now beheld,
Returning from the Chace, myself concealed,
Our Royal Father basking in the Shade,   45
His Looks severe, Revenge was in his Eyes,
All his great Soul seem'd mounted in his Face,
And bent on something hazardous and great.
With pensive Air he view'd the Forest round;
Smote on his Breast as if oppress'd with Wrongs,   50
With Indignation stamp'd upon the Ground;
Extended then and shook his mighty Arm,
As in Defiance of a coming Foe;
Then like the hunted Elk he forward sprung,
As tho' to trample his Assailants down.   55
The broken Accents murmur'd from his Tongue,
As rumbling Thunder from a distant Cloud,
Distinct I heard, 'Tis fix'd, I'll be reveng'd;
'I will make War; I'll drown this Land in Blood.'
He disappear'd like the fresh-started Doe   60
Pursu'd by Hounds o'er rocky Hills and Dales,
That instant leaves the anxious Hunter's Eye;
Such was his Speed towards the other Chiefs.

Philip. He's gone to sound their Minds to Peace and War,
And learn who'll join the Hazards in his Cause.   65
The Fox, the Bear, the Eagle, Otter, Wolf,[60]

---

58 A subordinate or servant. The more specific definition, from feudal England, is also relevant: a person permitted by a superior to hold lands, but only on the condition of homage and allegiance.

59 Sheet lightning, wherein a wide surface is illuminated at once, often appearing to be the whole sky or a large cloud.

60 Animal names widely represent clans within tribes. Bear, Eagle, and Wolf are common clan names, used by several nations, including the Hurons, whose clans included Bear, Wolf,

And other valiant Princes of the Empire,
Have late resorted hither for some End
Of common Import. Time will soon reveal
Their secret Counsels and their fix'd Decrees.   70
Peace has its Charms for those who love their Ease,
But active Souls like mine delight in Blood.

Chekitan. Should War be wag'd, what Discords may we fear
Among ourselves? The powerful *Mohawk* King
Will ne'er consent to fight against the *English*,[61]   75
Nay more, will join them as a firm Ally,
And influence other Chiefs by his Example,[62]
To muster all their Strength against our Father.
Fathers perhaps will fight against their Sons,
And nearest Friends pursue each other's Lives;   80
Blood, Murder, Death, and Horror will be rife,
Where Peace and Love, and Friendship triumph now.

Philip. Such stale Conjectures smell of Cowardice.
Our Father's Temper shews us the reverse:
All Danger he defies, and, once resolv'd,   85
No Arguments will move him to relent,
No Motives change his Purpose of Revenge,
No Prayers prevail upon him to delay
The Execution of his fix'd Design:
Like the starv'd Tyger in Pursuit of Prey,   90
No Opposition will retard his Course;
Like the wing'd Eagle that looks down on Clouds,

Hawk, and Heron. Pontiac himself used the otter symbol, and Fox is a clan name that came
to represent a nation (the Fox, part of the Algonquian language group, are now part of the
Sac and Fox Nation). Rogers' *Concise Account* asserts that the Five Nations of the Iroquois
Confederacy were identified with the bear, otter, wolf, tortoise, and eagle, but given the historical hostility between the Great Lakes and Iroquois Nations, the implication of Huron
clans seems more likely.

61 The Mohawk and the larger Iroquois Confederacy had a long-standing alliance with the Eng-
    lish, known as the Covenant Chain. The Mohawks declared the Chain broken in 1753, but the
    agreement was re-established in 1755, and held through Pontiac's Rebellion.
62 Rogers' *Concise Account* asserts that the Mohawk were the most successful, powerful, and
    feared nation in eastern America, commanding emulation by neighbouring nations. See
    Concise Account in this volume, pages 166–7.

All Hindrances are little in his Eye,
And his great Mind knows not the Pain of Fear.

Chekitan. Such Hurricanes of Courage often lead   95
To Shame and Disappointment in the End,
And tumble blindfold on their own Disgrace.
True Valour's flow, deliberate, and cool,
Considers well the End, the Way, the Means,
And weighs each Circumstance attending them.   100
Imaginary Dangers it detects,
And guards itself against all real Evils.
But here *Tenesco* comes with Speed important;
His Looks and Face presage us something new.

Tenesco. Hail, noble Youth! the News of your Return   105
And great Success has reach'd your Father's Ears.
Great is his Joy; but something more important
Seems to rest heavy on his anxious Mind,
And he commands your Presence at his Cabbin.

Philip. We will attend his Call with utmost Speed,   110
Nor wait Refreshment after our Day's Toil   [*Exeunt.*

SCENE II.

Ponteach's *Cabbin.*

Ponteach, Philip, Chekitan, *and* Tenesco.

Ponteach.
My Sons, and trusty Counsellor *Tenesco,*
As the sweet smelling Rose, when yet a Bud,
Lies close conceal'd, till Time and the Sun's Warmth
Hath swell'd, matur'd, and brought it forth to View,
So these my Purposes I now reveal   5
Are to be kept with You, on pain of Death,
Till Time hath ripen'd my aspiring Plan,
And Fortune's Sunshine shall disclose the Whole;

Or should we fail, and Fortune prove perverse,
Let it be never known how far we fail'd,   10
Lest Fools shou'd triumph, or our Foes rejoice.

Tenesco. The Life of great Designs is Secrecy,
And in Affairs of State 'tis Honour's Guard;
For Wisdom cannot form a Scheme so well,
But Fools will laugh if it should prove abortive;   15
And our Designs once known, our Honour's made
Dependent on the Fickleness of Fortune.

Philip. What may your great and secret Purpose be,
That thus requires Concealment in its Birth?

Ponteach. To raise the Hatchet from its short Repose,   20
Brighten its Edge, and stain it deep with Blood;
To scourge my proud, insulting, haughty Foes,
To enlarge my Empire; which will soon be yours:
Your Interest, Glory, Grandeur, I consult,
And therefore hope with Vigour you'll pursue   25
And execute whatever I command.

Chekitan. When we refuse Obedience to your Will,
We are not worthy to be call'd your Sons.

Tenesco. Spoke like yourselves, the Sons of *Ponteach*;
Strength, Courage, and Obedience form the Soldier,   30
And the firm Base of all true Greatness lay.

Ponteach. Our Empire now is large, our Forces strong,
Our Chiefs are wise, our Warriors valiant Men;
We all are furnish'd with the best of Arms,
And all things requisite to curb a Foe;   35
And now's our Time, if ever, to secure
Our Country, Kindred, Empire, all that's dear,
From these Invaders of our Rights, the *English*,
And set their Bounds towards the rising Sun.
Long have I seen with a suspicious Eye   40
The Strength and growing Numbers of the *French*;
Their Forts and Settlements I've view'd as Snakes

Of mortal Bite, bound by the Winter Frost,
Which in some future warm reviving Day
Would stir and hiss, and spit their Poison forth,   45
And spread Destruction through our happy Land.
Where are we now? The *French* are all subdued,[63]
But who are in their Stead become our Lords?
A proud, imperious, churlish, haughty Band.
The *French* familiarized themselves with us,   50
Studied our Tongue, and Manners, wore our Dress,
Married our Daughters, and our Sons their Maids,
Dealt honestly, and well supplied our Wants,
Used no One ill, and treated with Respect
Our Kings, our Captains, and our aged Men;   55
Call'd us their Friends, nay, what is more, their Children,
And seem'd like Fathers anxious for our Welfare.
Whom see we now? their haughty Conquerors
Possess'd of every Fort, and Lake, and Pass,
Big with their Victories so often gain'd;   60
On us they look with deep Contempt and Scorn,
Are false, deceitful, knavish, insolent;
Nay think us conquered, and our Country theirs,
Without a Purchase, or ev'n asking for it.[64]
With Pleasure I wou'd call their King my Friend,   65
Yea, honour and obey him as my Father;
I'd be content, would he keep his own Sea,
And leave these distant Lakes and Streams to us;
Nay I would pay him Homage, if requested,
And furnish Warriors to support his Cause.   70
But thus to lose my Country and my Empire,
To be a Vassal to his low Commanders,
Treated with Disrespect and public Scorn
By Knaves, by Miscreants, Creatures of his Power;

---

63 The governor of New France had agreed to the Capitulation of Montreal on 8 September
   1760, surrendering North American territories to Britain; the Peace of Paris was signed in
   February 1763 to formalize the end of the Seven Years' War.
64 This was a common complaint, voiced also, for example, by Shawnee diplomat Nimwha
   during peace negotiations with George Croghan at Fort Pitt in 1768: 'You think yourselves
   Masters of this Country, because you have taken it from the French, who, you know, had no
   Right to it, as it is the Property of us Indians.'

Can this become a King like *Ponteach*,   75
Whose Empire's measured only by the Sun?
No, I'll assert my Right, the Hatchet raise,
And drive these *Britons* hence like frighted Deer,
Destroy their Forts, and make them rue the Day
That to our fertile Land they found the Way.   80

Tenesco. No Contradiction to your great Design;
But will not such Proceeding injure us?
Where is our Trade and Commerce to be carry'd?
For they're possess'd of all the Country round,
Or whence Supplies of Implements for War?   85

Ponteach. Whence? Take them from our conquered running Foes.
Their Fortresses are Magazines[65] of Death,
Which we can quickly turn against themselves;
And when they're driven to their destin'd Bounds,
Their Love of Gain will soon renew their Trade.   90
The heartless *French*,[66] whene'er they see us conquer,
Will join their little Force to help us on.[67]
Nay many of their own brave trusty Soldiers,
In Hope of Gain, will give us their Assistance;
For Gain's their great Commander, and will lead them   95
Where their brave Generals cannot force their March:
Some have engag'd, when they see hope of Plunder,
In sly Disguise to kill their Countrymen.

Chekitan. These Things indeed are promising and fair,
And seem a Prelude to our full Success.   100
But will not many *Indian* Chiefs refuse
To join the Lists,[68] and hold themselves oblig'd
T'assist the Foe when hardly press'd[69] by us?

---

65 A room designated for the storage of weapons and ammunition.
66 Not cruel, but rather lacking the spirit to win in battle.
67 Ponteach expects that the defeated French will return to battle once they see a possibility of
    victory against the English. The 1763 Peace of Paris agreement that ended the Seven Years'
    War would preclude this, however, a circumstance that contributed to the eventual failure of
    Pontiac's Rebellion.
68 A catalogue of soldiers.
69 Vigorously encouraged.

Ponteach. I've sounded all their Minds; there's but a few
That are not warm and hearty in our Cause, 105
And those faint Hearts we'll punish at our Leisure:
For hither tends my Purpose; to subdue
The Tribes who now their annual Homage pay
To the imperious haughty *Mohawk* Chief,
Whose Pride and Insolence 'tis Time to curb. 110
He ever boasts the Greatness of his Empire,
The Swiftness, Skill and Valour of his Warriors,
His former Conquests, and his fresh Exploits,
The Terror of his Arms in distant Lands,
And on a Footing puts himself with me, 115
For Wisdom to contrive, and Power to do.
Such a proud Rival must not breath the Air;
I'll die in fighting, or I'll reign alone
O'er every *Indian* Nation, Tribe, and Chief.
But this in solemn Silence we conceal, 120
Till they're drawn in to fight the common Foe,
Then from my Fact, the sly Disguise I'll cast,
And shew them *Ponteach* to their Surprize.

Tenesco. Thy Plan is wise, and may Success attend it;
May all the warlike numerous Tribes unite, 125
Nor cease to conquer while thou hast a Foe!
Then may they join and own thee for their Sovereign,
Pay full Submission to thy scepter'd Arm,
And universal Empire be thy own!

Chekitan. Would you the *Mohawk* Emperor displease, 130
And wage a bloody War, by which you made
Him and his num'rous Tribes your certain Foes?

Ponteach.[70] Most of his Tribes will welcome the Proposal;
For long their galled Necks have felt the Yoke,[71]
Long wish'd for Freedom from his partial Sway, 135
In favour of the proud incroaching *Britons.*

---

70 Corrected from *Ponteack.*
71 Figurative language communicating a sense of oppression or humiliation, derived from the
   device used to couple together beasts of burden such as oxen.

Nay, they have oft, in spite of his Displeasure,
Rush'd forth like Wolves upon their naked Borders,
And now, like Tygers broken from their Chains,
They'll glut themselves, and revel in their Blood.   140

Philip. Myself will undertake to make even *Hendrick*[72]
Our zealous Friend against the common Foe;
His strong Attachment to them I'll dissolve,
And make them rage, and thirst for Vengeance on them.

Ponteach. This would be doing Honour to thyself,   145
And make thee worthy of thy Father's Crown.
The secret Means I will not now inquire,
Nor doubt but thus engag'd you will perform.
The Chiefs in part are knowing to my Purpose,
And think of nought but War, and Blood, and Plunder,   150
Till in full Council we declare our Pleasure.
But first my last Night's Dream I will relate,
Which much disturb'd my weary anxious Mind,
And must portend some signal grand Event
Of Good or Evil both to me or mine.[73]   155
On yonder Plain I saw the lordly Elk[74]
Snuffing the empty Air in seeming Sport,
Tossing his Head aloft, as if in Pride
Of his great Bulk and nervous active Limbs,

---

72 The Mohawk leader Theyanoguin was known as Hendrick. Though he had been killed in
    battle in 1755 in the Seven Years' War, before the events of Rogers' play, the name is prob-
    ably used here because the Mohawk 'King Hendrick' could be expected to be remembered in
    England as one of the 'Four Indian Kings' whose visit created a sensation in London in 1711.
    In fact, however, as Barbara Sivertsen has shown, there were actually two different Mohawk
    sachems called Hendrick Peters by Europeans. The two have been conflated by generations
    of historians, but as Dean Snow has recently documented, the sachem known to the Mohawks
    as Tejonihokarawa was a member of the Wolf Clan born around 1660, while the Hendrick
    Peters also known as Theyanoguin was a member of the Bear Clan born in 1692.
73 Rogers' *Concise Account* reports, 'The Indians depend much upon their dreams, and really
    believe that they dream the whole history of their future life … for which reason they make
    dreaming a kind of religious ceremony when they come to sufficient years' (170).
74 See the excerpt from Rogers' *Concise Account* in this volume: 'The Indians have a great ven-
    eration for this animal, and imagine that to dream of it portends good fortune and long life …
    It is dangerous to approach very near this animal when he is hunted, as he sometimes springs
    furiously on his pursuers, and tramples them to pieces' (188).

And Scorn of every Beast that haunts the Wood.   160
With mighty Stride he travelled to and fro,
And as he mov'd his Size was still increas'd,
Till his wide Branches reached above the Trees,
And his extended Trunk across the Plain.
The other Beasts beheld with wild Amaze,   165
Stood trembling round, nor dare they to approach
Till the fierce Tyger yell'd the loud Alarm,
When Bears, Cats, Wolves, Panthers, and Porcupines,[75]
And other Beasts of Prey, with Force united
And savage Rage, attack'd the common Foe.   170
But as the busking Bull, when Summer Flies,
With keenest Sting disturb the grazing Herd,
Stands careless in some shady cool Retreat,
And from his Sides sweeps the invenom'd Mites,
Or shakes them with a Stamp into the Dust;   175
So he unmov'd amidst their Clamours stood,
Trampled and sprun'd them with his Hoofs and Horns,
Till all dispers'd in wild Disorder fled,
And left him Master of th'extended Plain.

Tenesco. This Dream no doubt is full of some great Meaning,   180
And in it bears the Fate of your Design,
But whether good or ill, to me's a Secret.

Philip. It ne'er was counted ill to dream of Elks,
But always thought portentous of Success,
Of happy Life, and Victories in War,   185
Or Fortune good when we attempt the Chace.

Chekitan. Such is the common Say; but here the Size
And all the Circumstances are uncommon,
And therefore can contain no common Meaning:
I fear these Things portend no Good to us,   190
That Mischiefs lurk like Serpents in the Grass,
Whose pois'nous deadly Bite precedes all Warning.
That this Design will end in mighty Ruin

---

75 Each of these animals is described in detail in Rogers' *Concise Account*. See pages 185–90 in
this volume.

To us and ours, Discord among our Friends,
And Triumph to our Foes.

Philip. A valiant Hero!   195
Thou always wast a Coward, and hated War,
And lov'st to loll on the soft Lap of Peace.
Thou art a very Woman in thy Heart,
And talk'st of Snakes and Bugbears in the Dark,
Till all is Horror and Amaze about thee,   200
And even thy own Shadow makes thee tremble.

Chekitan. Is there no Courage in delib'rate Wisdom?
Is all rank Cowardice but Fire and Fury?
Is it all womanish to re-consider
And weigh the Consequences of our Actions,   205
Before we desperately rush upon them?
Let me then be the Coward, a mere Woman,
Mine be the Praise of Coolness, yours of Rage.

Ponteach. Peace, Peace, my Sons, nor let this casual Strife
Divide your Hearts; both mean the common Good;   210
Go Hand in Hand to conquer and promote it.
I'll to our worthy Doctor and the Priest,
Who for our Souls Salvation come from *France*;[76]
They sure can solve the Mysteries of Fate,
And all the Secrets of a Dream explain;   215
Mean while, *Tenesco*, warn the other Chiefs
That they attend my Call within an Hour.
                                   [*Exeunt* Pont. & Tenesco.

Philip. My Warmth perhaps has carried me too far,
But it's not in me to be cool and backward
To act or speak when Kingdoms are the Prize.   220

---

76 The Roman Catholic Church dispatched large numbers of priests to North America on conversion missions. There were two priests at Detroit during the time covered by the play, and
one, Father Potier, Jesuit missionary to the Hurons, was closely associated with habitant
Pierre Meloche, who was a friend and adviser to Pontiac. There is no historical evidence,
however, of Potier's having any sort of personal advisory relationship with Pontiac, and certainly no record of any conduct like that depicted later in the play. Father Potier's accounts
are included in *The Jesuit Relations*.

My Blood runs high at the sweet Sound of Empire,
Such as our Father's Plan ensures to us,
And I'm impatient of the least Delay.

Chekitan. Thy Fire thou hast a Right to stile a Virtue;
Heat is our Friend when kept within due bounds,   225
But if unbridled and allowed to rage,
It burns and blisters, torments, and consumes.
And, Torrent-like, sweeps every Comfort by.
Think if our Father's Plan should prove abortive,
Our Troops repuls'd, or in th' Encounter slain,   230
Where are our conquer'd Kingdoms then to share,
Where are our Vict'ries, Trophies, Triumphs, Crowns,
That dazzle in thy Eye, and swell thy Heart;
That nerve thy Arm, and wing thy Feet to War
With this impetuous Violence and Speed?   235
Crest-fallen then, our native Empire lost,
In captive Chains we drag a wretched Life,
Or fly inglorious from the conquering Foe
To barren Mountains from this fertile Land,
There to repent our Folly when too late,   240
In Anguish mourn, and curse our wretched Fate.

Philip. But why so much of Mischiefs that may happen?
These are mere Possibilities at most;
Creatures of Thought, which ne'er can be Objections,
In valiant Minds, to any great Attempt;   245
They're empty Echoes of a tim'rous Soul,
Like Bubbles driv'n by the tempestuous Storm,
The Breath of Resolution sweeps them off.
Nor dost thou judge them solid from thy Heart,
I know the secret Motive in thy Breast,   250
Thus to oppose our Father's great Design,
And from an Undertaking to dissuade,
In which thoul't share the Profit and the Glory.
Hendrick, the King of *Mohawks*, hath a Daughter,
With whom I saw you dallying in the Shade,   255
And thought you then a Captive to her Charms.
The bright *Monelia* hangs upon thy Heart,
And softens all the Passions of thy Soul;

Her thou think'st lost should we proclaim a War,
In which the King her Father will not join.   260

Chekitan. What if I have a Value for *Monelia*,
Is it a Crime? Does she not merit Love
From all who see her move, or hear her speak?

Philip. True, she is engaging, has a charming Air;
And if thy Love is fix'd, I will assist it,   265
And put thee in Possession of the Joy
That thou desirest more than Crowns and Empire.

Chekitan. As how, dear *Philip?* Should we wage a War
Which *Hendrick* disapproves, the Prize is lost.
Not Empires then could make *Monelia* mine;   270
All Hopes are dash'd upon that fatal Rock;
Nor Gold, nor Prayers, nor Tears, nor Promises,
Nor all the Engin'ry of Love at Work,
Could save a single Moment of my Joy.

Philip. Yes, I will save it all, and make her thine,   275
Act but thy Part, and do as I prescribe,
In Peace or War thou shalt possess the Prize.

Chekitan. Thy Words revive my half-despairing Heart.
What must I act? or which Way must I turn?
I'll brave all Dangers, every Ill defy,   280
Risque Life itself, to call *Monelia* mine.
Help me, my *Philip*, and I'll be thy Slave,
Resign my Share of Empire to thy Hand,
And lay a Claim to nothing but *Monelia*.

Philip. Rewards I do not ask; I am thy Brother,   285
And hold my Kindness to thee as a Debt.
Thou know'st I have engag'd to bring king *Hendrick*
To join the Lists, and fight against our Foes,
To rouse him to Revenge, and Rage, and War,
And make him zealous in the common Cause.   290
Nay, with uncommon Fury he shall rave,
And urge his Warriors on to Blood and Murder.

When this is done, *Monelia* may be thine,
Hendrick will court Alliance to our Tribe,
And joy to call great *Ponteach*'s Son his own. 295

Chekitan. But should you fail in these Attempts, and he
Prove obstinately fix'd against the War,
Where's then *Monelia?* where is *Chekitan?*
My Hopes are blasted, all my Joys are fled,
Like the vain Phantoms of a Midnight Dream,[77] 300
Are scattered like the Dust before a Whirlwind,
And all my Soul is left a Void for Pain,
Vexation, Madness, Phrensy, and Despair,
And all the Pains of disappointed Love.
Better I ne'er had flattered my fond Heart, 305
Nor sooth'd my Mind with Prospects of my Joy,
Than thus to perish on the Point of Hope.

Philip. Leave all to me; I so concerted Matters,
That I defy ev'n Fate.to disappoint me.
Exert thyself, and to *Monelia* go, 310
Before th' assembled Chiefs in Council meet;
Urge it to her, and to her Brother *Torax*,
That should their Father prove refractory,
Withdraw himself, and order his Domesticks
To hasten home at News of our Design; 315
Urge it, I say, to them; *Torax* loves War;
To linger here in Hopes of his Return,
Which tell them I'll effect ere twice the Sun
Has run the Circuit of his daily Race.[78]
Here they may loiter careless, range the Woods, 320
As tho' the Noise of War had not been heard.
This will give full Success to both our Wishes:
Thoul't gain the Prize of Love, and I of Wrath,
In favour to our Family and State.

---

77 Given the play's epic mode of the heroic, this may refer specifically to Alexander Pope's
1725–6 translation of Homer's *Odyssey*, in which a 'phantom' speaks to Penelope: 'O why,
Penelope, this causeless fear, / To render sleep's soft blessing insincere? / Alike devote to
sorrow's dire extreme / The day-reflection and the midnight-dream!' (IV 1063).
78 Two days.

Thoul't[79] tame the Turtle, I shall rouse the Tyger;[80]   325
The one will soothe thy Soul to soft Repose,
The other prove a Terror to our Foes.

Chekitan. I see the subtle Argument thou'lt use,
And how thou'lt work upon the old King's Weakness.
Thoul't set his strong Affection for his Children   330
At War against his Kindness for our Foes,
By urging their Attachment to our Cause,
That they'll endure ev'n Banishment and Death,
Rather than cease to be our stedfast Friends.

Philip. All this I'll urge, nay more, I will convince him,   335
These Foes to us can be no Friends to him;
I'll thunder in his Ears their growing Power,
Their Villainies and Cheats upon his Subjects:
That their fair Shew of Love is foul Disguise;
That in their Hearts they hate the Name of *Indians*,   340
And court his Friendship only for their Profit;
That when no longer he subserves their Ends,
He may go whistle up some other Friends.

Chekitan. This must alarm and bring him to our Mind.
I'll hasten to my Charge with utmost Speed,   345
Strain every Nerve, and every Power exert;
Plead, promise, swear like any Christian Trader;
But I'll detain them till our Ends are answer'd,
And you have won their Father to our Purpose.   [*Exit.*

Philip, solus.
Oh! what a wretched Thing is a Man in Love!   350
All Fear—all Hope—all Diffidence—all Faith—
Distrusts the greatest Strength, depends on Straws—
Soften'd, unprovident, disarm'd, unman'd,

---

79 Throughout this section, the contraction for 'thou shalt' is inconsistent.
80 Though turtles are highly symbolic in the Great Lakes Indigenous cultures, this line seems
    rather to allude to European tradition, in which the turtle alludes to the turtledove, an emblem
    of romantic love. Turtle is also one of the traditional Mohawk clans, but the historical Hendrick
    (Theyanoguin, long dead by the events of the play) was a member of the Bear Clan.

Led blindfold; every Power denies its Aid,
And every Passion's but a Slave to this;   355
Honour, Revenge, Ambition, Interest, all
Upon its Altar bleed—Kingdoms and Crowns
Are slighted and contemn'd and all the ties
Of Nature are dissolv'd by this poor Passion:
Once I have felt its Poison in my Heart,   360
When this same *Chekitan* a Captive led
The fair *Donata* from the *Illinois*;[81]
I saw, admir'd, and lov'd the charming Maid,
And as a Favour ask'd her from his Hands,
But he refus'd and sold her for a Slave.[82]   365
My Love is dead, but my Resentment lives,
And now's my Time to let the Flame break forth,
For while I pay this antient Debt of Vengeance,
I'll serve my Country, and advance myself.
He loves *Monelia*—*Hendrick* must be won—   370
Monelia and her Brother both must bleed—
This is my Vengeance on her Lover's Head—
Then I'll affirm, 'twas done by *Englishmen*—
And to gain Credit both with my Friends and Foes,
I'll wound myself, and say that I receiv'd it   375
By striving to assist them in the Combat.
This will rouse *Hendrick*'s Wrath, and arm his Troops
To Blood and Vengeance on the common Foe.
And further still my Profit may extend;
My Brother's Rage will lead him into Danger,   380
And, he cut off, the Empire's all my own.
Thus am I fix'd; my Scheme of Goodness laid,
And I'll effect it, tho' thro' Blood I wade,

---

81 A collective term for the confederacy of Algonquian tribes, formerly occupying south
   Wisconsin, northern Illinois, and sections of Iowa and Missouri, comprising the Cahokia,
   Kaskaskia, Michigamea, Moingwena, Peoria, and Tamaroa. Ironically, the historical Pontiac
   would be murdered in 1769 by a Kaskaskia man, provoking the vengeance of the Lake tribes
   on the Illinois, and contributing to a highly destructive war.
82 Among the Ottawas, as among most nations, captives faced several possible fates. They
   could be killed, adopted into a family, ransomed, kept as a slave, sold as a slave to another
   community, or some combination of these. As the captor, Chekitan would normally have
   chosen how the captive would be disposed of, unless a woman in the community claimed
   the captive for adoption.

To desperate Wounds apply a desperate Cure,
And to tall Structures lay Foundations sure;   385
To Fame and Empire hence my Course I bend,
And every Step I take shall thither tend.

End of the Second ACT.

ACT III.

SCENE I.

A Forest.

Chekitan *seeing* Torax *and* Monelia *coming towards them.*[83]

As the young Hunter, anxious in the Chace,
With beating Heart and quivering Hand espies
The Wish'd for Game, and trembles for th' Event,
So I behold the bright *Monelia*'s Steps,
Whom anxiously I've[84] sought, approach this way—   5
What shall I say? or how shall I accost her?
It is a fatal Minute to mistake in.
The Joy or Grief of Life depends upon't;
It is the important Crisis of my Fate.
I've thought a thousand things to say and do,   10
But know not which to say or do the first.
Shall I begin with my old Tale of Love?
Or shall I shock her with the News of War?
Must I put on the Face of Joy or Grief?
Seem unconcern'd or full of Doubts and Fears?   15
How unprepar'd I am for the Encounter?
I'd rather stand against an Host of Foes—
But she draws near, and Fate must guide me now,

---

83 It seems likely that this stage direction should change 'them' to 'him' but it has been left un-
     corrected to recognize the ambiguity of movement implied by the comma missing from either
     after Chekitan or after Monelia.
84 Corrected from Iv'e.

Enter Torax *and* Monelia

Where tend your Steps with such an Air of Joy?

Torax. To view the Beauties of th' extended Lake,   20
And on its mossy Bank recline at Ease,
While we behold the Sports of Fish and Fowl,
Which in this Calm no doubt will be diverting.
And these are new Amusements to *Monelia,*
She never saw the Sea or Lakes before.[85]   25

Chekitan. I'm glad our Country's aught to give such Pleasure
To one deservedly so welcome in it.

Monelia. That I am welcome you have oft assur'd me,
That I deserve it you may be mistaken.
The outside Shew, the Form, the Dress, the Air,   30
That please at first Acquaintance, oft deceive us,
And prove more Mimickers of true Desert,
Which always brightens by a further Trial,
Appears more lovely as we know it better,
At least can never suffer by Acquaintance.   35
Perhaps then you To-morrow will despise
What you esteem to Day, and call deserving.

Chekitan. My Love to you, *Monelia,* cannot change.
Your Beauty, like the Sun, for ever pleases,
And like the Earth, my Love can never move.   40

Monelia. The Earth itself is sometimes known to shake,[86]
And the bright Sun by Clouds is oft conceal'd.
And gloomy Night succeeds the Smiles of Day;
So Beauty oft by foulest Faults is veil'd,

---

85 Traditional Mohawk territory was east of the Great Lakes, with its eastern boundary approxi-
    mately parallel to Lake Champlain and southern boundary proximate to the Mohawk River.
    The territory spread over what is now divided between New York and Quebec.
86 Earthquakes were recorded in the eastern Great Lakes and St Lawrence Valley in 1638, 1661,
    1663, 1727, and 1732, with the strongest on 18 December 1737, which was also felt in
    Boston, Philadelphia, and Delaware.

And after one short Blaze admir'd no more,   45
Loses its Lustre, drops its sparkling Charms,
The Lover sickens, and his Passion dies.
Nay worse, he hates what he so doted on.
Time only proves the Truth of Worth and Love,
This one may be a Cheat, the other change,   50
And Fears, and Jealousies, and mortal Hate,
Succeed the Sunshine of the warmest Passion.

Chekitan. Have I not vow'd my Love to you, *Monelia*,
And open'd all the Weakness of my Heart?
You cannot think me false and insincere,   55
When I repeat my Vows to love you still;
Each time I see you move, or hear you speak,
It adds fresh Fuel to the growing Flame.
You're like the rising Sun, whose Beams increase
As he advances upward to our View;   60
We gaze with growing Wonder till we're blind,
And every Beauty fades and dies but his.
Thus shall I always view your growing Charm,
And every Day and Hour with fresh Delight.
Witness thou Sun and Moon, and Stars above,   65
Witness ye purling Streams and quivering Lakes,
Witness ye Shades, and the cool Fountain, where
I first espied the Image of her Charms,
And starting saw her on th' adjacent Bank,
If I to my *Monelia* prove untrue,   70

Monelia. Hoh! now your Talk is so much like a Christian's,
That I must be excus'd if I distrust you,
And think your fair Pretences all designing.
I once was courted by a spruce young Blade,[87]
A lac'd Coat Captain,[88] warlike, active, gay,   75
Cockaded Hat[89] and Medal on his Breast,

---

87 A gallant young man. Samuel Johnson's 1755 *Dictionary* provides a contemporary definition
     as 'a brisk man, either fierce or gay, called so in contempt.'
88 Eighteenth-century military uniforms were often extremely ornate, with brightly coloured
     wool, gilded trim, knots, and lace, colour coded to indicate regiment.
89 Decorated with a knot of ribbons or rosette, often as a marker of office.

And every thing was clever but his Tongue;
He swore he lov'd, O! how he swore he lov'd,
Call'd on his God and Stars to witness for him,
Wish'd he might die, be blown to Hell and damn'd,   80
If ever he lov'd Woman so before:
Call'd me his Princess, Charmer, Angel, Goddess,
Swore nothing else was ever half so pretty,
So dear, so sweet, so much to please his Taste,
He kiss'd, he squeez'd, and press'd me to his Bosom,   85
Vow'd nothing could abate his ardent Passion,
Swore he should die, should drown, or hang himself,
Could not exist if I denied his Suit,
And said a thousand Things I cannot Name:
My simple Heart, made soft by so much Heat,   90
Half gave Consent, meaning to be his Bride.
The Moment thus unguarded, he embrac'd,
And impudently ask'd to stain my Virtue.[90]
With just Disdain I push'd him from my Arms,
And let him know he'd kindled by Resentment;   95
The Scene was chang'd from Sunshine to a Storm,
O! then he curs'd, and swore, and damn'd, and sunk,
Call'd me proud Bitch, pray'd Heav'n to blast my Soul,
Wish'd Furies, Hell, and Devils had my Body,
To say no more; bid me begone in Haste   100
Without the smallest Mark of his Affection.
This was an *Englishman*, a Christian Lover.

Chekitan. Would you compare an *Indian* Prince to those
Whose Trade it is to cheat, deceive and flatter?
Who rarely speak the Meaning of their Hearts?   105
Whose Tongues are full of Promises and Vows?
Whose very Language is a downright Lie?
Who swear and call on Gods when they mean nothing?

---

90 There were many fewer restrictions on premarital sexuality in Iroquois and Great Lakes cultures than in European ones. In most communities, a young woman's body was her own until
   marriage, and sexual activity was not prohibited. Monelia's language of virtue is obviously as
   explicitly 'Christian' as Chekitan's language of love, despite her objections.

Who call it complaisant,[91] polite good Breeding,[92]
To say Ten thousand things they don't intend,   110
And tell their nearest Friends the basest Falsehoods?
I know you cannot think me so perverse,
Such Baseness dwells not in an *Indian's* Heart,
And I'll convince you that I am no Christian.

Monelia. Then do not swear, nor vow, nor promise much,   115
An honest Heart needs none of this Parade;
Its Sense steals softly to the listning Ear,
And Love, like a rich Jewel we most value,
When we ourselves by Chance espy its Blaze
And none proclaims where we may find the Prize.   120
Mistake me not, I don't impeach your Honour,
Nor think you undeserving my Esteem;
When our Hands join you may repeat your Love,
But save these Repetitions from the Tongue.

Chekitan. Forgive me, if my Fondness is too pressing,   125
'Tis Fear, 'tis anxious Fear, that makes it so.

Monelia. What do you fear? have I not said enough?
Or would you have me swear some Christian Oath?

Chekitan. No, but I fear our Love will be oppos'd,
Your Father will forbid our Hands to join.   130

Monelia. I cannot think it; you are *Ponteach*'s Son,
Heir to an Empire large and rich as his.

Chekitan. True; but your Father is a Friend to *Britons*,[93]
And mine a Foe, and now is fix'd on War,
Immediate War: This Day the Chiefs assemble,
To raise the Hatchet, and to arm the Troops.   135

Monelia. Then I must leave your Realm, and bid Adieu,

---

91 Agreeable and courteous.
92 Bearing and manners resulting from an appropriate upper-class education.
93 See note 72. The historical Hendrick was personally involved in the restoration of the
     Covenant Chain with Sir William Johnson.

In spite of your fond Passion, or my own;
For I can never disoblige my Father,
Though by it I were sure to gain an Empire.   140

Chekitan. Then *Chekitan's* undone, undone for ever,
Unless your Father by kind Fate is mov'd
To be our Friend, and join the Lists with mine.[94]

Torax. Nothing would please me better; I love War,
And think it time to curb the *English* Pride,   145
And give a check to their increasing Power.
The Land is ravag'd by their numberous Bands,
And every Day they're growing more our Lords,[95]

Chekitan. Are you sincere, or do you feign this Speech?

Torax. Indeed my Tongue does not bely my Heart;   150
And but my Father's wrong-turn'd Policy
Forbids, I'd instant join in War with you,
And help to set new Limits to their Power.

Chekitan. 'Tis plain, if they proceed, nor you nor I
Shall rule an Empire, or possess a Crown,   155
Our Countries all will soon become a Prey
To Strangers; we perhaps shall be their Slaves.
But will your Father be convinc'd of this?

Torax. I doubt[96] he'll not. The good old Man esteems
And dotes upon them as most worthy Friends;   160
I've told him often that he cherish'd Serpents
To bite his Children, and destroy his Friends.
But this he calls the Folly of my Youth,
Bids me be silent, shew Respect to Age,
Nor sow Sedition in my Father's Empire.   165

Chekitan. Stiff as he is, he may yet be subdued;

---

94 Join the war on the same side.
95 Torax's speech ends with a comma in the 1766 printing, perhaps indicating interruption rather
   than a full stop.
96 Suspect.

And I've a Power prepar'd that will attack him.
Should he refuse his Aid to our Design,
Retire himself, and bid his Troops to follow,
Yet *Philip* stands engag'd for his Return,   170
Ere twice the Sun hath ris'n and blest the Earth.
Philip is eloquent, and so prepar'd,
He cannot fail to bend him to our Purpose.
You and *Monelia* have a Part to act;
To linger here, should he in Haste retreat   175
Till *Philip* follows and employs his force.
Your Stay will add new Life to the Design,
And be of mighty Weight to gain Success.

Monelia. How shall we tarry midst the Noise of War,
In Danger of our Lives from Friends and Foes;   180
This will be deem'd a Madness by our Father,
And will deserve his most severe Rebuke.

Chekitan. Myself will be a Sponsor for your Safety;
And should your Father baffle our Attempts,
Conduct you home from all the Noise of War,   185
Where you may long in Peace and Plenty smile,
While I return to mourn my hapless Fate.
But should Success attend on *Philip*'s Purpose,
Your Father will not discommend your Stay,
But smiling give new Vigour to the War;   190
Which being ended, and our Foes subdu'd.
The happy Fruits of Peace succeed to all,
But we shall taste the greater Sweets of Love.

Torax. The Purport of our Stay is hid from me,
But *Philip*'s subtle, crafty as the Fox,[97]   195
We'll give full Scope to his inticing Art,
And help him what we can to take the Prey.

Monelia. In your Protection then I trust myself,
Nor will delay beyond th' appointed Term,
Lest anxious Fears possess our Father's Heart,   200

---

97 The fox is a trickster figure in Iroquois legend, so this reference is appropriate for the Mohawk
   Torax.

Or Mischiefs happen that incur his Anger.

Torax. It is agreed; we now pursue our Walk;
Mean time consult what else may be of Use,
You're pain'd with Love, and I'm in Pain for War.   [*Exeunt.*

Chekitan solus. The Game is sure—Her Brother's on my Side—   205
Her Brother and my own—My Force is strong—
But could her Father now be rous'd to War,
How should I triumph and defy even Fate?
But Fortune favours all advent'rous Souls:[98]
I'll now to *Philip;* tell him my Success,   210
And rouse up every Spark of Vigour in him:
He will conceive fresh Hopes, and be more zealous.

SCENE II.

Ponteach*'s* Cabbin.

Ponteach, *an* Indian *Conjurer, and* French *Priest.*

Ponteach.
Well! have you found the Secret of my Dream,
By all your Cries, and Howls, and Sweats, and Prayers?
Or is the Meaning still conceal'd from Man,
And only known to Genii and the Gods?

Conjurer. Two Hours I've lain within the sultry Stove,[99]   5

---

98 Perhaps a reference to Virgil's 'Fortune favors the brave' (*Aeneid* 10.284).

99 On what Rogers terms conjurers or jugglers, see the excerpts from *Concise Account* in this
volume: 'Among the Chickesaws, Creeks, Cherokees, and others to the southward, you will
find a conjuror in almost every village, who pretends to great things, both in politicks and
physick ... The conjuror, to prepare himself for these exploits, takes a sound sweat in a stove,
and directly after it plunges into a river or lake, be it ever so cold' (183). For the majority of
First Nations, including the Iroquois Nations, the sweat is a sacred ceremony that purifies or
cleanses the participant, in some cases to facilitate contact with the spiritual world. Hot
stones are placed in the centre of a small structure sometimes known as a sweat lodge, and
water is poured on them at regular intervals to produce steam. A sweat can last between several hours and several days, and usually also involves fasting and sexual abstinence.

While Floods of Sweat run trickling from my Skin;
With Howls and Cries and all the Force of Sound
Have I invok'd your Genius and my own,
Smote on my Breast, and beat against my Head,
To move an Answer, and the Secret learn.   10
But all in vain, no Answer can I have,
Till I first learn what secret Purposes
And great Designs are brooding in your Mind.

Priest. At our pure Virgin's Shrine I've bow'd my Knees,
And there in fervent Prayer pour'd out my Soul;   15
Call'd on Saint *Peter*, call'd on all the Saints
That know the Secrets both of Heaven and Earth,
And can reveal what Gods themselves can do:
I've us'd the Arts of our most holy Mother,
Which I receiv'd when I forsook the World,   20
And gave myself to Holiness and Heaven;
But can't obtain the Secret of your Dream,
Till first I know the Secrets of your Heart,
Or what you hope or wish to be effected.
'Tis on these Terms we learn the Will of God,   25
What Good or Ill awaits on Kings or Kingdoms;
And without this, St. *Peter's* Self can't tell,
But at a Dream like yours would be confounded.

Ponteach. You're well agreed—Our Gods are much alike—[100]
And I suspect both Rogues—What! wont[101] they tell!   30
Should they betray my Scheme, the whole is blown.
And yet I fain would know. I charge them first.   [*aside.*
Look here; if I disclose a Secret to you,
Tell it none but silent honest Gods;

---

100 Rogers makes this point on parallels among types of religious fraud more explicitly: 'Religious
     impostures are not less frequent among the Indians of America, than among the Christians of
     Europe; and some of them are very successful in persuading the multitude that they are filled
     with a divine enthusiasm, and a kind of inspiration, few knowing better how to act their part in
     this sacred juggle than they. ... They not only prescribe laws and rules, and persuade the popu-
     lace to believe them; but undertake to unfold the mysteries of religion and a future state, to
     solve and interpret all their dreams and visions, &c.' (*Concise Account*, this volume 170–1).
101 Apparently a misprint for 'won't.'

Death to you both, if you reveal to Men,   35

Both. We will, we will, the Gods alone shall know.

Ponteach. Know then that I have fix'd on speedy War,
To Drive these new Encroachers from my Country.
For this I meant t'engage our several Tribes,
And when our Foes are driven to their Bounds,   40
That we may stand and hold our Rights secure,
Unite our Strength under one common Head,
Whom all these Petty Kings must own their Lord,
Not even *Hendrick*'s self shall be excused.
This is my Purpose. Learn if it shall prosper,   45
Or will it end in Infamy and Shame?

*Conjurer. Smiting on his Breast, groaning, and muttering in
          his Cloak or Blanket, falls down upon the Ground,
          beats his Head against it, and pretends to listen; then
          rises, and says with a rumbling hideous Voice,*
Success and Victory shall attend your Arms;
You are the mighty Elk that none can conquer,
And all the Tribes shall own you for their King.
Thus, say the Genii, does your Dream intend.   50

*Priest. (looking up to Heaven in a praying Posture for a small
          Space, says)*
Had I but known you was resolv'd on War,
And War against those Hereticks the *English*,
I need not have ask'd a God or Saint
To signify the Import of your Dream.
Your great Design shall have a prosperous End,   55
'Tis by the Gods approv'd, and must succeed.
Angels and Saints are dancing now in Heaven:
Your Enemies are theirs, are hated by them,
And they'll protect and help you as their Champion,
That fights their Battles, and defends their Cause.   60
Our great St *Peter* is himself a Warrior;
He drew his Sword against such Infidels,
And now, like him, you'll gain immortal Honour,
And Gods in Heaven and Saints on Earth will praise you.

Ponteach. The Gods and Genii do as you have said.   65
I'll to the Chiefs, and hasten them to Arms.

                                      [*Exeunt* Pont. & Conj.

                          Priest, solus.
This, by St. *Peter*, goes as I would have it.
The Conjurer agreed with me to pump him,
Or else deny to solve his dubious Vision:
But, that we've so agreed in our Responses,   70
Is all mere Providence, and rul'd by Heaven,
To give us further Credit with this *Indian.*
Now he is fix'd—will wage immediate War—
This will be joyful News in *France* and *Rome,*[102]
That *Ponteach* is in Arms, and won't allow .   75
The *English* to possess their new-gain'd Empire:
That he has slain their Troops, destroy'd their Forts,
Expell'd them to the Lakes to their old Limits:
That he prefers the *French*, and will assist
To repossess them of this fertile Land.   80
By all the Saints, of this I'll make a Merit,
Declare myself to be the wise Projector;
This may advance me towards St. *Peter*'s Chair,[103]
And these blind Infidels by Accident
May have a Hand in making me a Pope—   85
But stop—Won't this defeat my other Purpose,
To gain the *Mohawk* Princess to my Wishes?
No—by the holy Virgin, I'll surprise her,[104]
And have one hearty Revel in her Charms.
By now I'll hasten to this *Indian* Council.   90
I May do something there that's à-propos.   [*Exit.*

---

102 The French and Indian War had ended with the Treaty of Paris in February of 1763, by
    which the French lost nearly all of their territory in North America to the English. The
    Roman Catholic Church had thus also lost much of its influence over the continent, as the
    English were of predominantly Protestant denominations. Both would be expected to be
    pleased by news of Ponteach's Rebellion against England.
103 The *Cathedra Petri* or Chair of Saint Peter is a particular chair preserved in St Peter's
    Basilica, Rome. It was once used by the popes and was often thought to have been used by
    Saint Peter himself, though it actually dates from 875. The Chair of Saint Peter has come to
    signify the episcopal office of the Pope, to which *Ponteach*'s Priest aspires.
104 The Priest swears his plan for Monelia's rape on Mary, the virgin mother of Jesus Christ.

SCENE III.

An Indian *Senate-house.*

Ponteach, Tenesco, Philip, Astinaco, Bear, Wolf, *and* French *Priest.*

Ponteach.
Are all the Chiefs and Warriors here assembled,[105]
That we expect to honour this Day's Council?

Tenesco. All are conven'd except the *Mohawk* King,
Who, as we are inform'd, denies his Presence.

Philip. I've half succeeded with the stubborn Chief.   5
He will not join in Council, but hath promised,
Till further Notice, not to be our Foe:
He'll see how we unite, and what Success
Attends our Arms; in short, he gives strong Hints
That he will soon befriend the common Cause.   10

Ponteach. Do what he will, 'tis this explains my Meaning;
                                        [*taking up the Hatchet.*
You are all well appris'd of my Design,
Which every passing Moment but confirms:
Nay, my Heart's pain'd while I with-hold my Hand
From Blood and Vengeance on our hated Foes.   15
Tho' I should stand alone, I'll try my Power
To punish their Encroachments, Frauds, and Pride;
Yet tho' I die, it is my Country's Cause,
'Tis better thus to die than be despis'd;
Better to die than be a Slave to Cowards,   20
Better to die than see my Friends abus'd;
The Aged scorn'd, the Young despis'd and spurn'd.

---

105 The *Journal of Pontiac's Conspiracy* records that the 27 April war council was attended by
   representatives from the Ottawas, Potawatomis, and the Huron Nations led by Takay
   (though not those led by Teata, who initially rejected the war belt). During the siege of
   Detroit, the *Journal* asserts that by June, 'there were two hundred fifty Ottawas under
   Pontiac; one hundred fifty Pottawattamies under Ninivois; fifty Hurons governed by Takay;
   two hundred fifty Chippewas under Wasson; one hundred seventy of the Chippewas under
   Sekahos' (160).

Better to die than see my Country ruin'd,
Myself, my Sons, my Friends reduc'd to Famine,
Expell'd from hence to barren Rocks and Mountains,[106]   25
To curse our wretched Fate and pine in Want;
Our pleasant Lakes and fertile Lands usurp'd
By Strangers, Ravagers, rapacious Christians.
Who is it don't prefer a Death in War
To this impending Wretchedness and Shame?   30
Who is it loves his Country, Friends, or Self,
And does not feel Resentment in his Soul?
Who is it sees their growing Strength and Power,
And how we waste and fail by swift Degrees,
That does not think it Time to rouse and arm,   35
And kill the Serpent ere we feel it sting,
And fall the Victims of its painful Poison?
Oh! could our Fathers from their Country see
Their antient Rights encroach'd upon and ravag'd,
And we their Children slow, supine, and careless   40
To keep the Liberty and Land they left us,
And tamely fall a Sacrifice to Knaves!
How would their Bosoms glow with patriot Shame,
To see their Offspring so unlike themselves?
They dared all Dangers to defend their Rights,   45
Nor tamely bore an Insult from a Foe.
Their plain rough Souls were brave and full of Fire,
Lovers of War, nor knew the Pain of Fear.
Rouse, then, ye Sons of antient Heroes, rouse,
Put on your Arms, and let us act a Part   50
Worthy the Sons of such renowned Chiefs.
Nor urge I you to Dangers that I shun,
Or mean to act my Part by Words alone;
This Hand shall wield the Hatchet in the Cause,
These Feet pursue the frighted running Foe,   55
This Body rush into the hottest Battle;
There should I fall, I shall secure my Honour,
And, dying, urge my Countrymen to Vengeance

---

106 Though the Great Lakes Nations had not been greatly affected by large influxes of British col-
    onists, their eastern allies the Shawnees and Delawares had experienced displacement like that
    described here, as the Thirteen Colonies pressed towards their territories in Ohio Country.

With more Success than all the Force of Words.
Should I survive, I'll shed the foremost Tear   60
O'er my brave Countrymen that chance to fall;
I'll be the foremost to revenge their Blood,
And, while I live, honour both them and theirs.
I add no more, but wait to hear your Minds.

Tenesco. Tho' I'm a Warrior, and delight in Arms,   65
Have oft with Pleasure heard the Sound of Battle,
And oft return'd with Victory and Triumph;
Yet I'm not fond to fight without just Cause,
Or shed the Blood of Men for my Diversion:
But I have seen, with my own Eyes I've seen,   70
High Provocations from our present Foes,
Their Pride and Insults, Knavery and Frauds,
Their large Encroachments on our common Rights,[107]
Which every Day increase, are seen by all,
And grown so common, they are disregarded.   75
What calls on us more loudly for Revenge,
Is their Contempt and Breach of public Faith.
When we complain, they sometimes promise fair;
When we grow restless, Treaties are propos'd,
And Promises are gilded then with Presents.   80
What is the End? Still the old Trade goes on;
Their Colonels, Governors, and mighty Men,
Cheat, lye, and break their solemn Promises,
And take no care to have our Wrongs redress'd.
Their King is distant, would he hear our Prayers: 85
Still we've no other Way to come to Justice,
But by our Arms to punish Wrongs like these,
And Wrongs like these are national and public,

---

107 Tenesco uses the language of English common law on property access to describe parallel
circumstances in North America. Common land included pasture, forests, rivers, and the
like, and signified land to which members of a specific community shared access and rights.
'Common rights' included gleaning the field stubble for animal feed after harvest, grazing
livestock on common land, collecting firewood, access to water, and even fishing rights. In
England, the land's actual owner held hunting rights, though this is not necessarily separate
in Tenesco's speech. Differences between European and Indigenous North American ideas
of property use and ownership are one source of the contentious colonial misperception that
much of America's land was available for claims of ownership.

Concern us all, and call for public Vengeance.
And Wrongs like these are recent in our Minds.   90

Philip. Public or private Wrongs, no matter which.
I think our Hunters ought to be reveng'd;
Their Bodies are found torn by rav'nous Beasts,
But who doubts they were kill'd by *Englishmen?*
Their Heads are scalp'd, their Arms and Jewels gone,   95
And Beasts of Prey can have no Use for these.
No, they were murdered, slily, basely shot,
And who that has Heart does not resent it?
O how I long to tear their mangled Limbs!
Yes, I could eat their Hearts, and drink their Blood,[108]   100
And revel in their Torments, Pains, and Tortures;
And, though I go alone, I'll seek Revenge.

Astinaco. This is the Fire and Madness of your Youth,
And must be curb'd to do your Country Service.
Facts are not always what they seem to be,   105
And this perhaps may be the Fault of One
Whom their Laws punish if you once detect him.
Shall we then, to revenge your Countrymen,
To recompence a Wrong by one committed,
Rouse all to Arms, and make a general Slaughter?   110
'Tis higher Motives move my Mind to War,
And make me zealous in the common Cause.
But hear me—'Tis no Trifle we're upon—
If we have Wisdom, it must now be used;
If we have Numbers, they must be united;   115
If we have Strength, it must be all exerted;
If we have Courage, it must be inflamed,
And every Art and Stratagem must be practis'd:
We've more to do than fright a Pigeon Roost,

---

108 An echo of Pontiac's speech to the French at Detroit 25 May 1763 as reported in the *Journal
     of Pontiac's Conspiracy*: 'When Mackinaw, the great chief of all these nations, said in his
     council that he would carry the head of your commander to his village, and devour his heart,
     and drink his blood, did I not take up your cause, and go to his village, and tell him that
     if he wanted to kill the French he would have to begin first with me and my men?' See
     Appendix B.

Or start a timorous Flock of running Deer;   120
Yes, we've a strong, a warlike stubborn Foe,
Unus'd to be repuls'd and quit the Field,
Nay, flush'd with Victories and long Success,
Their Numbers, Strength, and Courage all renown'd,
'Tis little of them that you see or know.   125
I've seen their Capital, their Troops and Stores,
And, what is more, I've seen their potent King,[109]
Who like a God sits over all the World,
And thunders forth his Vengeance thro' the Earth.
When he is pleas'd, Smiles fit upon his Face,   130
And Goodness flows in Rivers at his Feet;
When he's provok'd, 'tis like a fiery Tempest,
All's Terror and Amazement in his Presence,
And frighted Heroes trembling flee his Wrath.
And what then is to be done? what may we hope?   135
At most, by secret, sly, and subtle Means
To curb these vagrant Outcasts of his Subjects,
Secure our Countries from their further Ravage,
And make ourselves of more Importance to them,
Perhaps procure a Peace to our Advantage.   140
In this I'll join and head my valiant Troops,
Who will not fail to act a valiant Part.

The Bear.[110] What is the Greatness of their King to us?
What of his Strength or Wisdom? Shall we fear
A Lion chain'd, or in another World?[111]   145
Or what avails his flowing Goodness to us?
Does not the ravenous Tyger feed her Young?
And the fierce Panther fawn upon his Mate?
Do not the Wolves defend and help their Fellows
The poisonous Serpent feed her hissing Brood,   150
And open wide her Mouth for their Protection?

---

109 See note 46.
110 'The Bear' suggests a representative from the Huron Bear Clan.
111 The Bear's use of the Lion to emblematize England's king offers the tantalizing possibility
    that Rogers (or his editors) implies the levelling recognition that his own culture makes use
    of animal imagery in totemic ways nearly identical to those practised by many Indigenous
    cultures.

So this good King shews Kindness to his own,
And favours them, to make a Prey of others;
But at his Hands we may expect no Favour.
Look back, my Friends, to our Forefathers Time,   155
Where is their Country? where their pleasant Haunts?
The running Streams and shady Forests where?
They chas'd the flying Game, and liv'd in Plenty.
Lo, these proud Strangers now possess the Whole;
Their Cities, Towns, and Villages arise,   160
Forests are spoil'd, the Haunts of Game destroy'd,
And all the Sea Coasts made one general Waste:
Between the Rivers Torrent-like they sweep,
And drive our Tribes towards the setting Sun.
They who once liv'd on yon delightful Plains   165
Are now no more, their very Name is lost.[112]
The Sons of potent Kings, subdu'd and murder'd,
Are Vagrants, and unknown among their Neighbours.
Where will the Ravage stop? the Ruin where?
Does not the Torrent rush with growing Speed,   170
And hurry us to the same wretched End?
Let us grow wise then by our Fathers Folly,
Unite our Strength, too long it's been divided,
And mutual Fears and Jealousies obtain'd:
This has encourag'd our encroaching Foes,   175
But we'll convince them, once, we dare oppose them.

The Wolf.[113] Yet we have Strength by which we may oppose,
But every Day this Strength declines and fails.
Our great Forefathers, ere these Strangers came,

---

112 The very nature of a reference to a forgotten tribe of course makes this obscure, but The
     Bear may refer here to the Susquehannock Indians, depopulated by a smallpox outbreak in
     1661 and subsequent wars with the Delawares, the Maryland, and the Iroquois League as
     land pressures grew. The tribe was not exterminated, but survivors merged with other na-
     tions and tribal identity was lost.

113 Given the content of this speech, the most likely identification of The Wolf is Neolin, the
     Delaware Prophet, who was a member the Delaware Wolf Clan (see Introduction pages 10–
     13). However, Burton's annotations to the *Journal of Pontiac's Conspiracy* assert that 'Ma-
     higam, the Wolf' was one of the warriors involved in the attacks, citing *Lanman's History of
     Michigan*, so the Neolin identification cannot be absolute. 'The Wolf' could also refer more
     generally to a representative of the Huron or Delaware Wolf clans.

Liv'd by the Chace, with Nature's Gifts content,   180
The cooling Fountain quench'd their raging Thirst.
Doctors, and Drugs, and Med'cines were unknown,
Even Age itself was free from Pain and Sickness.
Swift as the Wind, o'er Rocks and Hills they chas'd
The flying Game, the bounding Stag outwinded,   185
And tir'd the savage Bear, and tam'd the Tyger;
At Evening feasted on the past Day's Toil,
Nor then fatigu'd; the merry Dance and Song
Succeeded; still with every rising Sun
The Sport renew'd; or if some daring Foe   190
Provok'd their Wrath, they bent the hostile Bow,
Nor waited his Approach, but rush'd with Speed,
Fearless of Hunger, Thirst, Fatigue, or Death.
But we their soften'd Sons, a puny Race,
Are weak in Youth, fear Dangers where they're not;   195
Are weary'd with what was to them a Sport,
Panting and breathless in One short Hour's Chace;
And every Effort of our Strength is feeble.
We're poison'd with the Infection of our Foes,
Their very Looks and Actions are infectious,   200
And in deep Silence spread Destruction round them.
Bethink yourselves while any Strength remains;
Dare to be like your Fathers, brave and strong,
Nor further let the growing Poison spread.
And would you stop it, you must resolve to conquer,   205
Destroy their Forts and Bulwarks, burn their Towns,
And keep them at a greater Distance from us.
O 'tis a Day I long have wish'd to see,
And, aged as I am, my Youth returns
To act with Vigour in so good a Cause.   210
Yes, you shall see the old Wolf will not fail
To head his Troops, and urge them on to Battle.

Ponteach. Your Minds are all for War, we'll not delay;
Nor doubt but others gladly will comply,
When they behold our Union and Success.   215

Tenesco. This Holy Priest has something to propose
That may excite us all to greater Zeal.

Ponteach. Let him be heard: 'Tis something from his Gods,
And may import the common Interest much.

Priest. (Coming from one Side, where he hath stood listening)
'Tis not to shew my Eloquence of Speech,   220
Or drown your Senses with unmeaning Sound,
That I desire Admittance to your Council;
It is an Impulse from the Gods that moves me,
That what I say will be to your Advantage.
Oh! With what secret Pleasure I behold   225
So many wise and valiant Kings unite,
And in a Cause by Gods and Saints espous'd.
Heaven smiles on your Design, and it shall prosper.
You're going to fight the Enemies of God;
Rebels and Traitors to the King of Kings;   230
Nay those who once betray'd and kill'd his Son,
Who came to save you *Indians* from Damnation—
He was an *Indian*, therefore they destroy'd him;[114]
He rose again and took his flight to Heaven;
But when his Foes are slain he'll quick return,   235
And be your kind Protector, Friend, and King.
Be therefore brave and fight his Battles for him;
Spare not his Enemies, where-e'r you find 'em:
The more you murder them, the more you please him;   240
Kill all you captivate, both old and young,
Mothers and Children, let them feel your Tortures;
He that shall kill a *Briton*, merits Heaven.
And should you chance to fall, you'll be convey'd
By flying Angels to your King that's there   245
Where these your hated Foes can never come.
Doubt you the Truth of this my Declaration?

---

114 Nevins reports that 'Doubtful authority has it that a part of the far-western Jesuit catechism
of the seventeenth century ran: 'Q. Who killed Jesus Christ? A. The bloody English' (225n).
Typical of the character, the Priest's account here serves his needs in the moment by literalizing
and overstating the parallel cultural metaphors sometimes used by the Jesuits to explain
Christianity. Such metaphors may have echoed for some time: the nineteenth-century English-
Sioux activist Charles Eastman (as contradictory as his actions often were), records a discussion
on religion with a Sioux elder in which the elder explains, 'I have come to the conclusion that
this Jesus was an Indian. He was opposed to material acquirement and to great possessions. He
was inclined to peace. He was as unpractical as any Indian and set no price upon his labor of
love. These are not the principles upon which the white man has founded his civilization' (143).

I have a Witness here that cannot lye

      [pulling out a burning Glass.[115]

This Glass was touch'd by your great Saviour's Hand,

And after left in holy *Peter*'s Care;   250

When I command, it brings down Fire from Heaven,

To witness for me that I tell no Lye

     [The Indians *gather round and gaze.*

Behold—Great God, send Fire, convince these *Indian* Kings

That I'm thy Servant, and report the Truth,

    [in a very Praying posture and solemn canting Tone.[116]

Am sent to teach them what they ought to do,   255

To kill and scalp, to torture and torment

Thy murderous treacherous Foes the hateful *English.*

     [it takes Fire, the Indians *are amaz'd, and retreat from it.]*

Ponteach. Who now can doubt the Justice of our Cause,

Or this Man's Mission from the King above,

And that we ought to follow his Commands?   260

Astinaco. 'Tis wonderful indeed—It must be so—

Tenesco. This cannot be a Cheat—It is from Heaven—

All. We are convinc'd and ready to obey;

We are impatient to revenge our King.

Ponteach. (Takes up the bloody Hatchet and flourishes it round)

Thus do I raise the Hatchet from the Ground,   265

Sharpen'd and bright may it be stain'd with Blood,

And never dull'd nor rusted till we've conquer'd,

And taught proud *Englishmen* to dread its Edge.

All. (Flourishing their Hatchets, and striking them upon a Block.)

Thus will we hew and carve their mangled Bodies,

And give them to the Beasts and Birds for Food.   270

Ponteach. And thus our Names and Honours will maintain

---

115 A lens that can be used to start fires by concentrating the sun's light.

116 Canting here refers to the formal or affected use of religious language, with the concurrent
  implication of a sing-song tone, both of which can imply hypocrisy.

While Sun and Moon, Rivers and Trees remain;
Our unborn Children shall rejoice to hear
How we their Fathers made the *English* fear.

The W A R   S O N G.

To the Tune of Over the Hills and far away,[117] *sung by*
Tenesco *the Head Warrior. They all join in the*
Chorus, and dance while that is singing in a Circle
round him; and during the Chorus the Musick plays.

Where-e'er the Sun displays his Light,   275
Or Moon is seen to shine by Night,
Where-e'er the noisy Rivers flow
Or Trees and Grass and Herbage grow.
                    Chorus.

Be't known that we this War begin
With Proud insulting *Englishmen*;   280
The Hatchet we have lifted high,
                    [*holding up their Hatchets.*]
And them we'll conquer or we'll die.
                    Chorus.

The Edge is keen, the Blade is bright,
Nothing saves them but their Flight;
And then like Heroes we'll pursue,   285
Over the Hills and Valleys through.
                    Chorus.

They'll like frighted Women quake,
When they behold a hissing Snake;
Or like timorous Deer away,

---

117 An English traditional song, first published in 1706 by Thomas D'Urfey with traditional
   courtship lyrics, and used in George Farquhar's *The Recruiting Officer* in the same year,
   with lyrics celebrating the freedom of the soldier from domestic responsibility as he goes
   off to battle in Portugal and Spain. It is also used in John Gay's *The Beggar's Opera* in
   1728, again with lyrics of courtship.

And leave both Goods and Arms a Prey.   290
                    Chorus.

Pain'd with Hunger, Cold, or Heat,
In Haste they'll from our Land retreat;
While we'll employ our scalping Knives—
                    [*drawing and flourishing their scalping Knives.*
Take off their Sculls, and spare their Lives.
                    Chorus.

Or in their Country they'll complain,   .   295
Nor ever dare return again;
Or if they should they'll rue the Day,
And curse the Guide that shew'd the Way.
                    Chorus.

If Fortune smiles, we'll not be long
Ere we return with Dance and Song,   300
But ah! if we should chance to die,
Dear Wives and Children do not cry.
                    Chorus.

Our Friends will ease your Grief and Woe,
By double Vengeance on the Foe;
Will kill, and scalp, and shed their Blood,   305
Where-e'er they find them thro' the Wood.
                    Chorus.

No pointing Foe shall ever say
'Twas there the vanquish'd *Indian* lay;
Or boasting to his Friends relate
The Tale of our unhappy Fate.   310
                    Chorus.

Let us with Courage then away
To hunt and seize the frighted Prey;
Nor think of Children, Friend, or Wife,
While there's an *Englishman* alive.
                    Chorus.

In Heat and Cold, thro' Wet and Dry,   315

Will we pursue, and they shall fly
To Seas which they a Refuge think,
In there in wretched Crouds they'll sink.

Chorus. Exeunt omnes singing.

The End of the Third ACT.

ACT IV.

SCENE I.

The Border of a Grove.

Enter Tenesco *to* Philip and Chekitan.

Tenesco.
The Troops are all assembled, some have march'd,
Perhaps are now engag'd, and warm in Battle;
The rest have Orders where to bend their Course.
Each Tribe is headed by a valiant Chief,
Except the *Bulls* which fall to one of you;[118]   5
The other stays to serve the State at home,
Or back us, should our Forces prove too weak.

Philip. The *Bulls* are brave, had they a brave Commander,
They'd push the Battle home with sure Success.
I'd chuse of all the Troops to be their Leader;   10
For tho' I'd neither Courage, Skill, nor Strength,
Honour attends the Man who heads the Brave;
Many are dubb'd for Heroes in these Times,
Who owe their Fame to those whom they commanded.

Tenesco. But we shall ne'er suspect your Title false;   15

---

118 Rogers' *Concise Account* describes a nation based north of Lake Superior calld the Bulls.
   Rogers asserts that they 'can raise about four thousand fighting men. They are originally of
   the Souties or Attawawas nation, as appears by the affinity between the two languages' (158).

Already you've confirm'd your Fame and Courage,
And prov'd your Skill and Strength as Commander.

Philip. Still, I'll endeavour to deserve your Praise,
Nor long delay the Honour you propose.

Chekitan. But this will interfere with your Design,   20
And oversets the Scheme of winning *Hendrick.*

Philip. Ah true—and kills your Hopes—This Man's in Love.
                                                    [*to* Tenesco.

Tenesco. Indeed! In Love with whom? King *Hendrick*'s Daughter?

Philip. The same; and I've engag'd to win her Father.

Tenesco. This may induce him to espouse our Cause,   25
Which likewise you engag'd should be effected.

Philip. But then I can't command as was propos'd
I must resign that Honour to this Lover,
While I conduct and form this double Treaty.

Tenesco. I am content if you but please yourselves   30
By Means and Ways not hurtful to the Public.

Chekitan. Was not the Public serv'd no private Ends
Would tempt me to detain him from the Field,
Or in his stead propose myself a Leader;
But every Power I have shall be exerted: 35
And if in Strength or Wisdom I should fail,
I dare presume you'll ever find me faithful.

Tenesco. I doubt it not—You'll not delay your Charge;
The Troops are all impatient for the Battle.
                                        [*Exeunt* Tenesco *and* Philip.

Chekitan, solus.
This is not to my Mind—But I must to it—   40
If *Philip* heads the Troops, my Hopes are blown—
I must prepare, and leave the Event to Fate

And him—'Tis fix'd—There is no other Choice;
Monelia I must leave, and think of Battles—
She will be safe—But Oh the Chance of War—   45
Perhaps I fall—and never see her more—
This shocks my Soul in spite of Resolution—
The bare Perhaps is more than Daggers to me—
To part for ever! I'd rather stand against
Embattled Troops than meet this single Thought;   50
A Thought in Poison dipp'd and pointed round;
O how it pains my doubting trembling Heart!
I must not harbour it—My Word is gone—
My Honour calls—and, what is more, my Love.
                    [*Noise of* Monelia *striving behind the Scene.*
What Sound is that?—Is it *Monelia*'s Voice;   55
And in Distress—What Monster gives her Pain?
                    [*Going towards the Sound, the Scene opens and discovers
                              the Priest with her*]

SCENE II.

Monelia and *Priest.*
What do I see? The holy Priest is with her.

*Monelia. (struggling with the Priest, and trying to disengage
    herself)*
No, I would sooner die than be dishonour'd—
Cut my own Throat, or drown me in the Lake.

Priest. Do you love *Indians* better than us white Men?

Monelia. Nay, should an *Indian* make the foul Attempt,   5
I'd murder him, or kill my wretched Self.[119]

---

119 There are very few reports in eighteenth-century accounts of rapes of Indigenous women by
    Indigenous men. George Croghan claimed that an Indian man would 'be putt to Death for
    Committing Rapes, which is a Crime they Despise.' As Sharon Block notes, however, a
    knowable public sentiment seems to affirm that 'rape was not unknown in Native American
    communities' (225–6).

Priest. I must, I can, and will enjoy you now.

Monelia. You must! You shan't, you cruel barbarous Christian.

Chekitan. Hold, thou mad Tyger—What Attempt is this?

[*Seizing him.*

Are you a Christian Priest? What do you here?   10

[*pushes him.*

What was his Will, *Monelia?* He is dumb.

Monelia. May he be dumb and blind, and senseless quite,
That has such brutal Baseness in his Mind.

Chekitan. Base, false Deceiver, what could you intend?

[*making towards him.*

Monelia. Oh I am faint—You have preserv'd my Honour,   15
Which he, foul Christian, thirsted to destroy.

[*Priest attempts to go.*

Chekitan. Stay; leave your Life to expiate your Crime:
Your heated Blood shall pay for your Presumption.

[*offering to strike him with a Hatchet.*

Priest. Good Prince, forbear your pious Hand from Blood;
I did not know you was this Maiden's Lover,   20
I took her for a Stranger, half your Foe.

Chekitan. Did you not know she was King *Hendrick*'s Daughter?
Did you not know that she was not your Wife?
Have you not told us, holy Men like you
Are by the Gods forbid all fleshly Converse?   25
Have you not told us, Death, and Fire, and Hell
Awaited those who are incontinent,[120]
Or dare to violate the Rites of Wedlock?[121]
That you God's Mother liv'd and died a Virgin,
And thereby set Example to her Sex?   30

---

120 Lacking in sexual self-restraint.
121 Premarital chastity and marital monogamy were two of the major moral emphases of religious missionaries of all denominations.

What means all of this? Say you such Things to us,
That you alone may revel in these Pleasures?

Priest. I have a Dispensation[122] from St. *Peter*
To quench the Fire of Love when it grows painful.
This makes it innocent like Marriage Vows;   35
And all our holy Priests, and she herself,
Commits no Sin in this Relief of Nature:
For, being holy, there is no Pollution
Communicated from us as from others;
Nay, Maids are holy after we've enjoy'd them,   40
And, should the Seed take Root, the Fruit is pure.

Chekitan. Oh, vain Pretence! Falshood, and foul Deception!
None but a Christian could devise such Lies!
Did I not fear it might provoke your Gods,
Your Tongue should never frame Deceit again.   45
If there are Gods, and such as you have told us,
They must abhor all Baseness and Deceit,
And will not fail to punish Crimes like yours.
To them I leave you—But avoid my Presence,
Nor let me ever see your hated Head,   50
Or hear your lying Tongue within this Country.

Priest. Now by St. *Peter*[123] I must go—He's raging.   [*aside.*

Chekitan. That Day I do, by your great dreadful God,
This Hand shall cleave your Head, and spill your Blood,
Not all your Prayers, and Lyes, and Saints shall save you.   55

Priest. I've got his Father's Secret, and will use it.

---

122 An exemption from a law or requirement, granted under special circumstances. In the
    Church, a dispensation can be granted by the Pope, an archbishop, or a bishop to do some-
    thing otherwise forbidden by ecclesiastical law. *Ponteach*'s Priest goes one step beyond this
    by claiming direct dispensation from Saint Peter, who, like most church figures before the
    fourth century, was married and a father. There is no historical evidence of anything resem-
    bling the permission the Priest claims.
123 There is no obvious reason that the Priest references and swears to Saint Peter so consistently.
    Peter did undertake missionary journeys, but it is more likely an indication of pride and
    ambition to the papacy.

Such disappointment ought to be reveng'd.

[aside.

Chekitan. Don't mutter here, and conjure up your Saints,
I value not their Curses, or your Prayers.

[stepping towards the Priest to hurry him.

Priest. By all the Saints, young Man, thou shalt repent it.   60

Monelia. Base, false Dissembler—Tyger, Snake, a Christian!
I hate the Sight; I fear the very Name.
O Prince, what has not your kind Presence sav'd me!

Chekitan. It sav'd to me more than my Father's Empire;
Far more than Crowns and Worlds—It sav'd *Monelia,*   65
The Hope of whom is more than the Creation.
In this I feel the Triumphs of an Hero,
And glory more than if I'd conquer'd Kingdoms.

Monelia. O I am thine, I'm more than ever thine;
I am your Captive now, your lawful Prize: 70
You've taken me in War, a dreadful War!
And snatch'd me from the hungry Tyger's Jaw.
More than my Life and Service is your Due,
And had I more I would devote it to you.

Chekitan. O my *Monelia!* rich is my Reward,   75
Had I lost Life itself in the Encounter;
But still I fear that Fate will snatch you from me,
Where is your Brother? Why was you alone?

Enter Torax, *from listening to their Discourse.*

Torax. Here am I: What would you of me?

Monelia.   Torax!
I've been assaulted by a barbarous Man,   80
And by mere Accident escap'd my Ruin.

Torax. What Foe is here? The *English* are not come?

Monelia. No: But a Christian lurk'd within the Grove,
And every Christian is a Foe to Virtue;
Insidious, subtle, cruel, base, and false!   85
Like Snakes, their very Eyes are full of Poison;[124]
And where they are not, Innocence is safe.

Torax. The holy Priest! Is he so vile a Man?
I heard him mutter Threat'nings as I past him.

Chekitan. I spar'd his guilty Life, but drove him hence,   90
On Pain of Death and Tortures, never more
To tread the Earth, or breathe the Air with me.
Be warn'd by this to better tend your Charge.
You see how Mischiefs lye conceal'd about us,
We tread on Serpents ere we hear them hiss,   95
And Tygers lurk to seize the incautious Prey.
I must this Hour lead forth my Troops to Battle,
They're now in Arms, and waiting my Command.

Monelia. What Safety shall I have when you are gone?
I must not, cannot, will not longer tarry,   100
Lest other Christians, or some other Foe,
Attempt my Ruin.

Chekitan. Torax will be your Guard.
My Honour suffers, should I now decline;
It is my Country's Cause; I've pawn'd my Word,   105
Prevented *Philip*, to make sure of you.
He stays. 'Tis all in favour to our Love:
We must at present please ourselves with Hopes.

Monelia. Oh! my fond Heart no more conceals its Flame;
I fear, my Prince, I fear our Fates are cruel: 110
There's something whispers in my anxious Breast,
That if you go, I ne'er shall see you more.

Chekitan. Oh! how her Words unman and melt my Soul!

---

124 In the eighteenth century, snakes were widely believed to hypnotize their prey with their
    eyes before attacking.

As if her Fears were Prophecies of Fate.   [*aside.*
I will not go and leave you thus in Fears;   115
I'll frame Excuses—*Philip* shall command—
I'll find some other Means to turn the King;
I'll venture Honour, Fortune, Life, and Love,
Rather than trust you from my Sight again.
For what avails all that the World can give?   120
If you're with-held, all other Gifts are Curses,
And Fame and Fortune serve to make me wretched.

Monelia. Now you grow wild—You must not think of staying;
Our only Hope, you know, depends on *Philip.*
I will not fear, but hope for his Success,   125
And your Return with Victory and Triumph,
That Love and Honour both may crown our Joy.

Chekitan. Now this is kind; I am myself again.
You had unman'd and soften'd all my Soul,
Disarm'd my Hand, and cowardiz'd my Heart: 130
But now in every Vein I feel an Hero,
Defy the thickest Tempest of the War:
Yes, like a Lion conscious of his Strength,
Fearless of Death I'll rush into the Battle;
I'll fight, I'll conquer, triumph and return;   135
Laurels[125] I'll gain, and lay them at your Feet.

Monelia. May the Success attend you that you wish!
May our whole Scheme of Happiness Succeed!
May our next Meeting put an End to Fear,
And Fortune shine upon us in full Blaze!   140

Chekitan. May Fate preserve you as her Darling Charge!
May all the Gods and Goddesses, and Saints,
If conscious of our Love, turn your Protectors!
And the great thundering God with Lightning burn
Him that but means to interrupt your Peace.   [*Exeunt.*   145

---

125 In ancient Rome, wreaths of laurel leaves were worn as markers of martial power or military
   victory.

SCENE III.

Indian *Senate-House.*

Ponteach *and* Philip.

Ponteach.
Say you that *Torax* then is fond of War?

Philip. He is, and waits impatient my Return.

Ponteach. 'Tis friendly in you thus to help your Brother;
But I suspect his Courage in the Field;
A love-sick Boy makes but a cow'rdly Captain.   5

Philip. His Love my spur him on with greater Courage;
He thinks he's fighting for a double Prize;
And but for this, and Hopes of greater Service
In forwarding the Treaty with the *Mohawk,*
I now had been in Arms and warm in Battle.   10

Ponteach. I much commend the Wisdom of your Stay.
Prepare yourself, and hasten to his Quarters;
You cannot make th'Attempt with too much Speed.
Urge ev'ry Argument with Force upon him,
Urge my strong Friendship, urge your Brother's Love,   15
His Daughter's Happiness, the common Good;
The general Sense of all the *Indian* Chiefs,
The Baseness of our Foes, our Hope of Conquest;
The Richness of the Plunder if we speed;
That we'll divide and share it as he pleases;   20
That our Success is certain if he joins us.
Urge these, and what besides to you occurs;
All cannot fail, I think, to change his Purpose.

Philip. You'd think so more if you knew all my Plan.   [*aside.*
I'm all prepar'd now I've receiv'd your Orders,   25
But first must speak t' his Children ere I part,
I am to meet them in the further Grove.

Ponteach. Hark! there's a Shout—We've News of some Success;
It is the Noise of Victory and Triumph.[126]

Enter a Messenger.

Huzza! for our brave Warriors are return'd   30
Loaded with Plunder and the Scalps of Christians.

Enter Warrior.

Ponteach. What have you done? Why all this Noise and Shouting?

1st Warrior. Three Forts are taken, all consum'd and plunder'd;[127]
The *English* in them all destroy'd by Fire,
Except some few escap'd to die with Hunger.   35

2d Warrior. We've smoak'd the Bear in spite of all his Craft,
Burnt up their Den, and made them take the Field:[128]
The mighty Colonel *Cockum* and his Captain
Have dull'd our Tomhocks; here are both their Scalps:
[*holding out the Two Scalps.*
Their Heads are split, our Dogs have eat their Brains.   40

Philip. If that be all they've eat, the Hounds will starve.

3d Warrior. These are the Scalps of those two famous Cheats
Who bought our Furs for Rum, and sold us Water.[129]
[*holding out the Scalps, which* Ponteach *takes.*
Our Men are loaded with their Furs again,

---

126 Rogers describes these shouts of battle victory in *Concise Account*, see page 177 in this
     volume.
127 Though Pontiac's Seige of Detroit began on 9 May, the first three forts to fall in Pontiac's
     Rebellion were Fort Sandusky, burned 16 May 1763 by the Wyandots; Fort St Joseph,
     captured 25 May by the Potawatomis; and Fort Miami, taken 27 May by the Miamis. As is
     typical in heroic tragedy, the play's timeline is highly condensed. According to the contem-
     porary *Journal of Pontiac's Conspiracy* word of the fall of Sandusky did not reach Detroit
     until 28 May, and word of Miami arrived 19 June.
128 One way to hunt bear is to track the animal to its den and light a fire at the entrance, filling
     the den with smoke and forcing the bear to emerge with little chance of escape.
129 M'Dole and Murphey, from Act I i.

And other Plunder from the Villains Stores.   45

Ponteach. All this is brave!   [*tossing up the Scalps, which others*
                                            catch, and toss and throw them about.
    This Way we'll serve them all.

Philip. We'll cover all our Cabbins with their Scalps.

Warriors. We'll fat our Dogs upon their Brains and Blood.

Ponteach. Ere long we'll have their Governors in Play.

Philip. And knock their grey-wig'd Scalps about this Way.   50

Ponteach. The Game is started; Warriors, hunt away,
Nor let them find a Place to shun your Hatchets.

All Warriors. We will: We will soon shew you other Scalps.

Philip. Bring some alive; I long to see them dance
In Fire and Flames, it us'd to make them caper.[130]   55

Warriors. Such Sport enough you'll have before we've done.

Ponteach. This still will help to move the *Mohawk* King.
Spare not to make the most of our Success.

Philip. Trust me for that—Hark; there's another Shout;
                                                      [*shouting without.*
A Shout for Prisoners—Now I have my Sport.   60

Ponteach. It is indeed; and there's a Number too.

                          Enter Warriors.
We've broke the Barrier, burnt their Magazines,

---

130 To dance and skip. Rogers describes types of torture of prisoners, including burning, in his
     Concise Account, page 178 this volume.

Slew Hundreds of them,[131] and pursu'd the rest
Quite to their Settlements.[132]

2ᵈ Warrior.   There we took
Their famous Hunters *Honnyman* and *Orsbourn*;   65
The last is slain, this is his bloody Scalp.

                                              [*tossing it up.*

With him we found the Guns of our lost Hunters,
And other Proofs that they're the Murderers;
Nay *Honnyman* confesses the base Deed,
And, boasting, says, he'd kill'd a Score of *Indians*.   70

3ᵈ Warrior. This is the bloody Hunter: This his Wife;
                  [*leading them forward, pinioned and tied together.*
With Two young Brats that will be like their Father.
We took them in their Nest, and spoil'd their Dreams.

Philip. Oh I could eat their Hearts, and drink their Blood,
Were they not Poison, and unfit for Dogs.   75
Here, you Blood-hunter, have you lost your Feeling?
You Tygress Bitch! You Breeder up of Serpents!
                  [*slapping* Honnyman *in the Face, and kicking his Wife.*

Ponteach. Stop—We must first consult which Way to torture,
And whether all shall die—We will retire.[133]

Philip, going.

---

131 While exact numbers of settlers and soldiers killed in the conflict are not possible, Dowd
     suggests that about 100 traders were killed in the early days of the war, and a majority
     of the soldiers in most of the forts that were taken were killed either in the initial attacks
     or later.
132 As word spread of Pontiac's siege and the fall of the first three forts (see note 127), other
     forts were taken. Fort Ouiatenon was taken by the Weas, Kickapoos, and Mascoutens on
     1 June 1763, with no English soldiers killed in the attack. Fort Michilimackinac was taken
     on 2 June by the Ojibwas; Fort Venango on 16 June and Fort Le Boeuf on 18 June by the
     Senecas; Fort Presque Isle was taken on 19 June by a large group of Ottawas, Ojibwas,
     Wyandots, and Senecas. Fort Pitt was held under siege from 22 June 22 to 20 August
     before being relieved by English troops under Colonel Henry Bouquet. Word of the fall of
     Fort Le Boeuf and Presque Isle arrived at Pontiac's camp on 20 June.
133 Rogers describes the process of allocating prisoners to adoption, slavery, or death in
     Concise Account, pages 177–8 this volume.

Take care they don't escape.

Warrior.   They're bound secure.   80

                              [*Exeunt* Indians; *manent Prisoners.*

SCENE IV.

Mrs. Honnyman.
O *Honnyman*, how desperate is our Case!
There's not a single Hope of Mercy left:
How savage, cruel, bloody did they look!
Rage and Revenge appear'd in every Face.

Honnyman. You may depend upon't, we all must die.   5
I've made such Havock, they'll have no Compassion;
They only wait to study our new Torments:
All that can be inflicted or endur'd,
We may expect from their relentless Hands.
Their brutal Eyes ne'er shed a pitying Tear;   10
Their savage Hearts ne'er had a Thought of Mercy;
Their Bosoms swell with Rancour and Revenge,
And, Devil-like, delight in others Plagues,
Love Torments, Torture, Anguish, Fire, and Pain,
The deep-fetch'd Groan, the melancholy Sigh,   15
And all the Terrors and Distress of Death,
These are their Musick, and enhance their Joy.
In Silence then submit yourself to Fate:
Make no Complaint, nor ask for their Compassion;
This will confound and half destroy their Mirth;   20
Nay, this may put a Stop to many Tortures,
To which our Prayers and Tears and Plaints would move them.[134]

Mrs. Hon. O dreadful Scene! Support me, mighty God,

---

134 According to Algonquian tradition, when faced with the prospect of capture and death by
ritual torture, many Algonquian captives distinguished themselves by bravely singing death
songs in the face of their enemies. This mark of bravery and nobility was reportedly at times
rewarded with release and adoption into the captor's community.

To pass the Terrors of this dismal Hour,
All dark with Horrors, Torments, Pains, and Death! 25
O let me not despair of thy kind Help;
Give Courage to my wretched groaning Heart!

Honnyman. Tush, Silence! You'll be overheard.

Mrs. Hon. O my dear Husband! 'Tis an Hour for Prayer,
An Infidel would pray in our Distress: 30
An Atheist would believe there was some God
To pity Pains and Miseries so great.

Honnyman. If there's a God, he knows our secret Wishes;
This Noise can be no Sacrifice to him;
It opens all the Springs of our weak Passions. 35
Besides, it will be Mirth to our Tormentors;
They'll laugh, and call this Cowardice in Christians,
And say Religion makes us all mere Women.

Mrs. Hon. I will suppress my Grief in Silence then,
And secretly implore the Aid of Heaven. 40
Forbid to pray! O dreadful Hour indeed! [*pausing.*
Think you they will not spare our dear sweet Babes?
Must these dear Innocents be put to Tortures,
Or dash'd[135] to Death, and share our wretched Fate?
Must this dear Babe that hangs upon my Breast 45
[*looking upon her Infant.*
Be snatch'd by savage Hands and torn in Pieces!
O how it rends my Heart! It is too much!
Tygers would kindly soothe a Grief like mine;
Unconscious Rocks would melt, and flow in Tears
At this last Anguish of a Mother's Soul. 50
[*pauses, and views her Child again.*
Sweet Innocent! It smiles at this Distress,
And fondly draws this final Comfort from me:

---

135 Smashed to pieces. Eighteenth-century captivity narratives in particular are replete with descriptions of captured infants being killed by having their heads dashed against trees or objects. While this almost certainly did happen at times, infants also had a strong likelihood of being adopted into a tribe upon capture.

Dear Baby, no more: Dear *Tommy* too must die,

                                    [looking at her other Child.

O my sweet First-born! Oh I'm overpower'd.   *[pausing.*

Honnyman. I had determin'd not to shed a Tear;   *[weeping.*   55
But you have all unman'd my Resolution;
You've call'd up all the Father in my Soul;
Why have you nam'd my Children? O my Son!

                                      [looking upon him.

My only Son—My Image—Other Self!
How have I doted on the charming Boy,   60
And fondly plann'd his Happiness in Life!
Now his Life ends: Oh the Soul-bursting Thought!
He falls a Victim for his Father's Folly.
Had I not kill'd their Friends, they might have spar'd
My Wife, my Children, and perhaps myself,   65
And this sad dreadful Scene had never happen'd.
But 'tis too late that I perceive my Folly;
If Heaven forgive, 'tis all I dare to hope for.

Mrs. Hon. What! have you been a Murderer indeed!
And kill'd the *Indians* for Revenge and Plunder?   70
I thought you rash to tempt their brutal Rage,
But did not dream you guilty as you said.

Honnyman. I am indeed. I murder'd many of them,
And thought it not amiss, but now I fear.

Mrs. Hon. O shocking Thought! Why have you let me know   75
Yourself thus guilty in the Eye of Heaven?
That I and my dear Babes were by you brought
To this Extreme of Wretchedness and Woe?
Why have you let me know the solemn Weight
Of horrid Guilt that lies upon us all?   80
To have died innocent, and seen these Babes
By savage Hands dash'd to immortal Rest,
This had been light, for this implies no Crime:
But now we die as guilty Murderers,
Not savage *Indians*, but just Heaven's Vengeance   85

Pursues our Lives with all these Pains and Tortures.
This is a Thought that points the keenest Sorrow,
And leaves no Room for Anguish to be heighten'd.

Honnyman. Upbraid me not, nor lay my Guilt to Heart;
You and the Fruits of our past Morning Love   90
Are Innocent. I feel the Smart and Anguish,
The Stings of Conscience, and my Soul on Fire.
There's not a Hell more painful than my Bosom,
Nor Torments for the Damn'd more keenly pointed.
How could I think to murder was not Sin?   95
Oh my lost Neighbour! I seduc'd him too.
Now Death with all its Terrors disappears,
And all I fear's a dreadful Something-after;
My Mind forebodes a horrid woful Scene,
Where Guilt is chain'd and tortur'd with Despair.   100

Mrs. Hon. The Mind oppress'd with Guilt may find Relief.

Honnyman. Oh could I reach the pitying Ear of Heaven,
And all my Soul evaporate in Sound,
'Twould ask Forgiveness! but I fear too late;
And next I'd ask that you and these dear Babes   105
Might bear no part in my just Punishment.
Who knows but by pathetic Prayers and Tears
Their savage Bosoms may relent towards you,
And fix their Vengeance where just Heaven points it?
I still will hope, and every Motive urge.   110
Should I succeed, and melt their rocky Hearts,
I'll take it as a Presage of my Pardon,
And die with Comfort when I see you live.

                              [*Death Halloo is heard without.*

Mrs. Hon. Hark! they are coming—Hear that dreadful Halloo.

Honnyman. It is Death's solemn Sentence to us all;   115
They are resolv'd, and all Intreaty's vain.
O horrid Scene! how shall I act my Part?
Was it but simple Death to me alone!
But all your Deaths are mine, and mine the Guilt.

Enter Indians, *with Stakes, Hatchets, and Firebrands.*

O horrid Preparation, more than Death!   120

Ponteach. Plant down the Stakes, and let them be confin'd:
                              [*they loose them from each other.*
First kill the Tygers, then destroy their Whelps.

Philip. This Brat is in our Way, I will dispatch it.
                              [*offering to snatch the sucking Infant.*

Mrs. Hon. No, my dear Babe shall in my Bosom die;
There is its Nourishment, and there its End.   125

Philip. Die both together then, 'twill mend the Sport;
Tie the other to his Father, make a Pair;
Then each will have a Consort in their Pains;
Their sweet Brats with them, to increase the Dance.
                    [*they are tied down facing each other upon their Knees,
                              and their Backs to the Stakes.*
Warrior. All now is ready; they are bound secure.   130

Philip. Whene'er you please, their jovial Dance begins.
                              [*to* Ponteach.

Mrs. Hon. O my dear Husband! What a Sight is this!
Could ever fabling Poet draw Distress
To such Perfection! Sad Catastrophe!
There are not colours for such deep-dyed Woe,   135
Nor Words expressive of such heighten'd Anguish.
Ourselves, our Babes, O cruel, cruel Fate!
This, this is Death indeed with all its Terrors.

Honnyman. Is there no secret Pity in your Minds?
Can you not feel some tender Passion move,   140
When you behold the Innocent distress'd?
True, I am guilty, and will bear your Tortures:
Take your Revenge by all the Arts of Torment;
Invent new Torments, lengthen out my Woe,
And let me feel the keenest Edge of Pain: 145

But spare this innocent afflicted Woman,
Those smiling Babes who never yet thought Ill,
They never did nor ever will offend you.

Philip. It cannot be: They are akin to you,
Well learnt to hunt and murder, kill and rob.   150

Ponteach. Who ever spar'd a Serpent in the Egg?
Or left young Tygers quiet in their Den?

Warrior. Or cherishes young Vipers in his Bosom?

Philip. Begin, begin; I'll lead the merry Dance.
                    [*offering at the Woman with a Firebrand.*[136]

Ponteach. Stop: Are we not unwise to kill this Woman?   155
Or sacrifice her Children to our Vengeance?
They have not wrong'd us; can't do present Mischief.
I know her Friends; they're rich and powerful,
And in their Turn will take severe Revenge:
But if we spare, they'll hold themselves oblig'd,   160
And purchase their Redemption with rich Presents.[137]
Is not this better than an Hour's Diversion,
To hear their Groans, and Plaints, and piteous Cries?

Warriors. Your Counsel's wise, and much deserves our Praise;
They shall be spar'd.

Ponteach.   Untie, and take them hence;   165
                    [*they untie the Woman and the oldest Child from
                    Honnyman, and retire a little to consult his Death.*
When the War ends her Friends shall pay us for it.

---

136 A burning piece of wood. Rare even in the eighteenth century was the intriguingly related
    definition of a person who deserves to burn in hell.
137 In times of peace, captives could often be 'redeemed' with cash payment or exchange of
    goods, allowing them to return home. Important figures in a community would be more
    expensive to redeem, and many communities took up collections or even held reserve funds
    for captive redemptions.

Philip. I'd rather have the Sport than all the Pay.

Honnyman. O now, kind Heaven, thou has heard my Prayer,
And what's to follow I can meet with Patience.

Mrs. Hon. O my dear Husband, could you too be freed!   [*weeping.*   170
Yet must I stay and suffer Torments with you.
This seeming Mercy is but Cruelty!
I cannot leave you in this Scene of Woe,
'Tis easier far to stay and die together!

Honnyman. Ah! but regard our Childrens Preservation;   175
Conduct their Youth, and form their Minds to Virtue;
Nor let them know their Father's wretched End,
Lest lawless Vengeance should betray them too.

Mrs. Hon. If I must live, I must retire from hence,
Nor see your fearful Agonies in Death;   180
This would be more than all the Train of Torments.
The horrid Sight would sink me to the Dust;
These helpless Infants would become a Prey
To worse than Beasts, to savage, bloody Men.

Honnyman. Leave me—They are prepar'd, and coming on—   185
Heav'n save you all! O 'tis the last dear Sight!

Mrs. Hon. Oh may we meet where Fear and Grief are banish'd!
Dearest of Men, adieu—Adieu till then.
                              [*Exit, weeping with her Children.*

Philip. Bring Fire and Knives, and Clubs, and Hatchets all;
Let the old Hunter feel the Smart of Pain.   190
                    [*they fall upon* Honnyman *with various
                              Instruments of Torture.*

Honnyman. Oh! this is exquisite![138]
                              [*groaning and struggling.*

1ˢᵗ Warrior. Hah! Does this make you dance?

---

138 Excruciatingly painful.

2ᵈ Warrior. This is fine fat Game!

Philip. Make him caper.

                          [*striking him with a Club, kicking,* &c.

Honnyman. O ye eternal Powers, that rule on high,
If in your Minds be Sense of human Woe,
Hear my Complaints, and pity my distress!   195

Philip. Ah call upon your Gods, you faint-heart Coward!

Honnyman. O dreadful Racks! When will this Torment end?
Oh for a Respite from all Sense of Pain!
'Tis come—I go—You can no more torment.   [*dies.*

Philip. He's dead; he'll hunt no more; h' as done with Game.   200
               [*striking the dead Body, and spitting in the Face.*

Ponteach. Drive hence his wretched Spirit, lest it plague us;
Let him go hunt the Woods; he's now disarm'd.
               [*They run round brushing the Walls,* &c. *to
                       dislodge the Spirit.*[139]

All. Out, Hunters, out, your Business here is done.
Out to the Wilds, but do not take your Gun.

Ponteach, (to the Spirit)
Go, tell our Countrymen, whose Blood you shed,   205
That the great Hunter *Honnyman* is dead:
That we're alive, we'll make the *English* know,
Whene'er they dare to serve us *Indians* so:
This will be joyful News to Friends from *France*,
We'll join the Chorus then, and have a Dance.   210
          [*Exeunt omnes, dancing, and singing the Two last Lines.*

               The End of the Fourth ACT.

---

139 This ritual is described in *Concise Account*, page 178 this volume.

ACT V.

SCENE I.

The Border of a Grove, in which Monelia *and* Torax *are asleep.*

Enter Philip, *speaking to himself.*
As a dark Tempest brewing in the Air,
For many Days hides Sun and Moon, and Stars,
At length grown ripe, burst forth and forms a Flood
That frights both Men and Beasts, and drowns the Land;
So my dark Purpose now must have its Birth,   5
Long nourish'd in my Bosom, 'tis matur'd,
And ready to astonish and embroil
Kings and their Kingdoms, and decide their Fates.
Are they not here? Have I delay'd too long?

> [*he espies them asleep.*

Yes, in a Posture too beyond my Hopes,   10
Asleep! This is the Providence of Fate,
And proves she patronizes my Design,
And I'll shew her that *Philip* is no coward.

> [*taking up his Hatchet in one Hand, and Scalping Knife in
> the other, towards them.*

A Moment now is more than Years to come:
Intrepid as I am, the Work is shocking.   15

> [*he retreats from them.*

Is it their Innocence that shakes my Purpose?
No; I can tear the Suckling from the Breast,
And drink their Blood who never knew a Crime.
Is it because my Brother's Charmer dies?
That cannot be, for that is my Revenge.   20
Is it because *Monelia* is a Woman?
I've long been blind and deaf to their Enchantments.
Is it because I take them thus unguarded?
No; though I act the Coward, it's a Secret.
What is it shakes my firm and fix'd Resolve?   25
'Tis childish Weakness: I'll not be unman'd.

> [*approaches and retreats again.*

There's something awful[140] in the Face of Princes,

---

140 Awe-inspiring.

And he that sheds their Blood, assaults the Gods:
But I'm a Prince, and 'tis by me they die;

> [*advances arm'd as before.*

Each Hand contains the Fate of future Kings,   30
And, were they Gods, I would not balk my Purpose.

> [*stabs* Monelia *with the Knife.*

Torax. Hah, *Philip*, are you come? What can you mean?

> [Torax *starts and cries out.*

Philip. Go learn my Meaning in the World of Spirits;

> [*knocks him down with his Hatchet,* &c.

'Tis now too late to make a question of it.
The Play is ended *(looking upon the Bodies)* now succeeds the Farce.[141]   35
Hullo! Help! Haste! the Enemy is here.

> [*calling at one of the Doors, and returning.*

Help is at hand—But I must first be wounded:

> [*wounds himself.*

Now let the Gods themselves detect the Fraud.

Enter an Indian.

What means your Cry? Is any Mischief here?

Philip. Behold this flowing Blood; a desperate Wound!   40

> [*shewing his Wound.*

And there's a Deed that shakes the Root of Empires.

2ᵈ Ind. O fatal Sight! the *Mohawk* Prince is murder'd.

3ᵈ Ind. The Princess too is weltering in her Blood.

Philip. Both, both are gone; 'tis well that I escap'd.

Enter Ponteach.

What means this Outcry, Noise, and Tumult here?   45

Philip. O see, my Father! see the Blood of Princes,
A Sight that might provoke the Gods to weep,

---

141   In the eighteenth century, shorter five-act plays would often be followed by an afterpiece, a short,
often farcical play to fill out the expected four- to five-hour length of an evening a the theatre.

And drown the Country in a Flood of Tears.
Great was my Haste, but could not stop the Deed;
I rush'd among their Numbers for Revenge,   50
They frighted fled; there I receiv'd this Wound.

                          [*shewing his Wound to* Ponteach.

Ponteach. Who, what were they? or where did they escape?

Philip. A Band of *English* Warriors, bloody Dogs![142]
This Way they ran from my vindictive Arm,

                                              [*pointing,* &c.
Which but for this base Wound would sure have stopp'd them.   55

Ponteach. Pursue, pursue, with utmost Speed pursue,
                          [*to the Warriors present.*
Outfly the Wind till you revenge this Blood;
'Tis royal Blood, we count it as our own.

                          [*Exeunt Warriors in haste.*

This Scene is dark, and doubtful[143] the Event;
Some great Decree of Fate depends upon it,   60
And mighty Good or Ill awaits Mankind.
The Blood of Princes cannot flow in Vain,
The Gods must be in Council to permit it:
It is the Harbinger of their Designs,
To change, new-mould, and alter Things on Earth: 65
And much I fear, 'tis ominous of Ill
To me and mine; it happen'd in my Kingdom.
Their Father's Rage will swell into a Torrent—
They were my Guests—His Wrath will centre here;
Our guilty Land hath drunk his Children's Blood.   70

Philip. Had I not seen the flying Murderers,
Myself been wounded to revenge their Crime,
Had you not hasten'd to pursue the Assassins,
He might have thought us treacherous and false,
Or wanting in our hospitable Care: 75

---

142 General Amherst was reportedly known for referring to Indigenous people as dogs, so this
     reversal is informative.
143 Ambiguous in implication, rather than suspicious.

But now it cannot but engage his Friendship,
Rouse him to Arms, and with a Father's Rage
He'll point his Vengeance where it ought to fall;
And thus this Deed, though vile and dark as Night,
In its Events will open Day upon us, 80
And prove of great Advantage to our State.

Ponteach. Haste then; declare our Innocence and Grief;
Tell the old King we mourn as for our own,
And are determin'd to revenge his Wrongs;
Assure him that our Enemies are his, 85
And rouse him like a Tyger to the Prey.

Philip. I will with Speed; but first this bleeding Wound
Demands my Care, lest you lament me too.
[*Exit, to have his Wound dress'd.*
Ponteach, solus.
Pale breathless Youths! your Dignity still lives:
[*viewing the Bodies.*
Your Murderers were blind, or they'd have trembled, 90
Nor dar'd to wound such Majesty and Worth;
It would have tam'd the savage running Bear,
And made the raging Tyger fondly fawn;
But your more savage Murderers were Christians.
Oh the distress'd good King! I feel for him, 95
And wish to comfort his desponding Heart;
But your last Rites require my present Care. [*Exit.*

SCENE II.

The Senate-House.

Ponteach, Tenesco, *and others.*

Ponteach.
Let all be worthy of the royal Dead;
Spare no Expence to grace th' unhappy Scene,
And aggrandize the solemn gloomy Pomp

With all our mournful melancholy Rites.

Tenesco. It shall be done; all Things are now preparing.   5

Ponteach. Never were Funeral Rites bestow'd more just;
Who knew them living, must lament them dead;
Who sees them dead, must wish to grace their Tombs
With all the sad Respect of Grief and Tears.

Tenesco. The Mourning is as general as the News;   10
Grief sits on every Face, in every Eye,
And gloomy Melancholy in Silence reigns:
Nothing is heard but Sighs and sad Complaints,
As if the First-born of the Realm were slain.

Ponteach. Thus would I have it; let no Eye be dry,   15
No Heart unmov'd, let every Bosom swell
With Sighs and Groans. What Shouting do I hear?
                    [*a Shouting without, repeated several Times.*

Tenesco. It is the Shout of Warriors from the Battle;
The Sound of Victory and great Success.
                              [*he goes to listen to it.*

Ponteach. Such is the State of Men and human Things;   20
We weep, we smile, we mourn, and laugh thro' Life,
Here falls a Blessing, there alights a Curse,
As the good Genius or the evil reigns.
It's right it should be so. Should either conquer,
The World would cease, and Mankind be undone   25
By constant Frowns or Flatteries from Fate;[144]
This constant Mixture makes the Potion safe,
And keeps the sickly Mind of Man in Health.

Enter Chekitan.

---

144 Ponteach's speech on the necessary balance of good and evil alludes to both Christian
    iconography of God and Satan, and to contemporary Ottawa and larger Algonquin ideas of the
    good manifested in the Manitou and Nanabush and the evil of malevolent spirits such as the
    Windigos.

It is my Son. What has been your Success?

Chekitan. We've fought the Enemy, broke thro' their Ranks,   30
Slain many on the Spot, pursu'd the rest
Till Night conceal'd and sav'd them from our Arms.

Ponteach. 'Tis bravely done, and shall be duely honour'd
With all the Signs and Marks of public Joy.

Chekitan. What means this Gloom I see in every Face?   35
These smother'd Groans and stifled half-drawn Sighs;
Does it offend that I've return'd in Triumph?

Ponteach. I fear to name—And yet it must be known.   [*aside.*
Be not alarm'd, my Son, the Laws of Fate
Must be obey'd: She will not hear our Dictates.   40
I'm not a Stranger to your youthful Passion,
And fear the Disappointment will confound you.

Chekitan. Has he not sped? Has ill befel my Brother?

Ponteach. Yes, he is wounded but—*Monelia*'s slain,
And *Torax* both. Slain by the cowardly *English*,   45
Who 'scap'd your Brother's wounded threatning Arm,
But are pursued by such as will revenge it.—

Chekitan. Oh wretched, wretched, wretched *Chekitan*!   [*aside.*

Ponteach. I know you're shock'd—The Scene hath shock'd us all,
And from what we could, we've done to wipe the Stain   50
From us, our Family, our Land and State;
And now prepare due Honours for the Dead,
With all the solemn Pomp of public Grief,
To shew Respect as if they were our own.[145]

---

145 Gi-be wiikonge (Feast of the Dead) was an Ottawa ritual, performed in spring or early summer to honour the dead. The women prepared the bodies for burial, and deep pits, large
enough to accommodate bodies and mourners, were prepared for the ceremony. Mourners
feasted through the night until sunrise, while tobacco burned as an offering to the spirits

Chekitan. Is this my Triumph after Victory?   55
A solemn dreadful pompous Shew:
Why have I scap'd their Swords and liv'd to see it?   [*aside.*
Monelia dead! aught else I cou'd have borne:
I'm stupify'd: I can't believe it true;
Shew me the Dead; I will believe my Eyes,   60
But cannot mourn or drop a Tear till then.

Tenesco. I will conduct you to them—Follow me—
[*Exeunt Tenesco and Chekitan.*

Ponteach. This is a sad Reception from a Conquest,
And puts an awful Gloom upon our Joy;
I fear his Grief will over-top his Reason;   65
A Lover weeps with more than common Pain.
Nor flows his greatest Sorrow at his Eyes:
His Grief is inward, and his Heart sheds Tears,
And in his Soul he feels the pointed Woe,
When he beholds the lovely Object lost.   70
The deep-felt Wound admits no sudden Cure;
The festering Humor will not be dispers'd,
It gathers on the Mind, and Time alone,
That buries all Things, puts an End to this.   [*Exuent omnes.*

SCENE III.

The Grove, with the dead Bodies; Tenesco *pointing* Chekitan *to them.*

Tenesco.

There lie the Bodies, Prince, a wretched Sight!
Breathless and Pale.

Chekitan.   A wretched Sight indeed;

[*going towards them.*

O my *Monelia*; has thy Spirit fled?

---

who were present. At the end of the gi-be wiikonge, the pit was filled, and the dead no
longer spoken of.

Art thou no more? a bloody breathless Corpse!   5
Am I return'd full flush'd with Hopes of Joy,
With all the Honours Victory can give,
To see thee thus? Is this, is this my Welcome?
Is this our Wedding? Wilt thou not return?
O charming Princess, art thou gone for ever?   10
Is this the fatal Period of our Love?
O! had I never seen thy Beauty bloom,
I had not now been griev'd to see it pale:
Had I not known such Excellence had liv'd,
I shou'd not now be curs'd to see it dead: 15
Had not my Heart been melted by thy Charms,
It would not now have bled to see them lost.
O wherefore, wherefore, wherefore do I live:
Monelia is not—What's the World to me?
All dark and gloomy, horrid, waste, and void;   20
The Light of the Creation is put out!—
The Blessings of the Gods are all withdrawn!
Nothing remains but Wretchedness and Woe;
Monelia's gone; *Monelia* is no more.
The Heavens are veil'd because she don't behold them: 25
The Earth is curs'd, for it hath drunk her Blood;
The Air is Poison, for she breathes no more:
Why fell I not by the bale *Briton*'s Sword?
Why press'd I not upon the fatal Point?
Then had I never seen this worse than Death,   30
But dying said, 'tis well—*Monelia* lives.

Tenesco. Comfort, my Prince, nor let your Passion swell
To such a Torrent, it o'erwhelms your Reason,
And preys upon the Vitals of your Soul.
You do but feed the Viper by this View;   35
Retire, and drive the Image from your Thought,
And Time will soon replace you every Joy.

Chekitan. O my *Tenesco*, had you ever felt
The gilded Sweets, or pointed Pains of Love,
You'd not attempt to sooth a Grief like mine.   40
Why did you point me to the painful Sight?
Why have you shewn this Shipwreck of my Hopes,

And plac'd me in this beating Storm of Woe.
Why was I told of my *Monelia*'s Fate?
Why wa'n't the wretched Ruin all conceal'd   45
Under some fair Pretence—That she had fled—
Was made a Captive, or had chang'd her Love—
Why wa'n't I left to guess her wretched End?
Or have some slender Hope that she still liv'd?
You've all been cruel; she died to torment me;   50
To raise my Pain, and blot out every Joy.—

Tenesco. I fear'd as much: His Passion makes him wild—   [*aside.*
I wish it may not end in perfect Phrensy.

Chekitan. Who were the Murderers? Where did they fly?
Where was my Brother, not to take Revenge?   55
Shew me their Tracks, I'll trace them round the Globe;
I'll fly like Lightning, ravage the whole Earth—
Kill every thing I meet, or hear, or see.
Depopulate the World of Men and Beasts,
'Tis all too little for that single Death.   60
                    [*pointing to* Monelia's *Corpse.*
I'll tear the Earth that dar'd to drink her Blood;
Kill Trees, and Plants, and every springing Flower:
Nothing shall grow, nothing shall be alive,
Nothing shall move; I'll try to stop the Sun,
And make all dark and barren, dead and sad;   65
From his tall Sphere down to the lowest Centre,
There I'll descend, and hide my wretched Self,
And reign sole Monarch in a World of Ruin.

Tenesco. This is deep Madness, it hath seiz'd his Brain.   [*aside.*

Chekitan. But first I'll snatch a parting last Embrace.   70
                    [*he touches and goes to embrace the Corpse.*
Thou dear cold Clay! forgive the daring Touch;
It is thy *Chekitan*, thy wounded Lover.
'Tis; and he hastens to revenge thy Death.
                    [Torax *groans and attempts to speak.*

Torax. Oh, oh, I did not—Philip—Philip—Oh.
                    [Chekitan *starts.*

Chekitan. What—did I not hear a Groan? and *Philip* call'd? 75

Tenesco. It was, it was, and there is Motion too.
                    [*approaches* Torax, *who groans and speaks again.*

Torax. Oh! Oh! Oh! Oh! Oh! *Philip*—help. Oh! Oh!

Tenesco. He is alive—We'll raise him from the Ground.
                              [*they lift him up, and speak to him.*
Torie, are you alive? or are our Ears deceiv'd?

Torax. Oh *Philip*, do not—do not—be so cruel. 80

Chekitan. He is bewilder'd, and not yet himself.
Pour this into his Lips—it will revive him.
                              [*they give him something.*

Tenesco. This is a Joy unhop'd for in Distress.
                              [Torax *revives more.*

Torax. Oh! *Philip, Philip!*—Where is *Philip* gone?

Tenesco. The Murderers are pursued—He will go soon. 85
And now can carry Tidings of your Life.

Torax. He carry Tidings! he's the Murderer.

Tenesco. He is not murder'd; he was slightly wounded,
And hastens now to see the King your Father.

Torax. He is a false, a barbarous bloody Man, 90
A Murderer, a base disguis'd Assassin.

Chekitan. He still is maz'd,[146] and knows not whom he's with.

Torax. Yes, you are *Chekitan*, and that's *Monelia*,
                              [*pointing to the Corpse.*
This is *Tenesco*—*Philip* stabb'd my Sister,

---

146 Confused.

And struck at me; here was the stunning Blow: 95
                                        [*pointing to his Head.*
He took us sleeping in this silent Grove;
There by Appointment from himself we waited.
I saw him draw the bloody Knife from her,
And, starting, ask'd him, Why, or what he meant?
He answered with the Hatchet on my Skull,   100
And doubtless thought me dead and bound in Silence.
I am myself, and what I say is Fact.

Tenesco. The *English* 'twas beset you; *Philip* ran
To your Assistance, and himself is wounded.

Torax. He may be wounded, but he wounded me;   105
No *Englishman* was there, he was alone.
I dare confront him with his Villainy:
Depend upon't, he's treacherous, false, and bloody.

Chekitan. May we believe, or is this all a Dream?
Are we awake? Is *Torax* yet alive?   110
Or is it Juggling, Fascination all? [147]

Tenesco. 'Tis most surprising! What to judge I know not.
I'll lead him hence; perhaps he's still confus'd.

Torax. I gladly will go hence for some Relief,
But shall not change, from what I've now aver'd.   115

Tenesco. Then this sad Storm of Ruin's but begun.   [*aside.*
Philip must fly, or next it lights on him.
                            [*Exeunt* Tenesco *and* Torax *led by him.*

Chekitan. And can this be—Can *Philip* be so false?
Dwells there such Baseness in a Brother's Heart?
So much Dissimilation in the Earth?   120
Is there such Perfidy among Mankind?
It shocks my Faith—But yet it must be so—

---

147 A trick or enchantment. Several accounts, including Rogers' *Concise Account* refer to
    Indigenous shamans and medicine men as 'jugglers.'

Yes, it was he, *Monelia*, shed thy Blood.
This made him forward to commence our Friend,
And with unusual Warmth engage to help us;   125
It was for this so chearful he resign'd
To me the Honour of Command in War;
The *English* Troops would never come so near;
The Wounds were not inflicted by their Arms.
All, all confirms the Guilt on *Philip*'s Head,   130
You died, *Monelia*, by my Brother's Hand;
A Brother too intrusted with our Love.
I'm stupify'd and senseless at the Thought;
My Head, my very Heart is petrify'd.
This adds a Mountain to my Weight of Woe.   135
It now is swell'd too high to be lamented;
Complaints, and Sighs, and Tears are thrown away,
Revenge is all the Remedy that's left;
But what Revenge is equal to the Crime?
His Life for her's! An Atom for the Earth—   140
A Single Fly—a Mite for the Creation:
Turn where I will I find myself confounded:
But I must seek and study out new Means.
Help me, ye Powers of Vengeance! grant your Aid,
Ye that delight in Blood, and Death, and Pain!   145
Teach me the Arts of Cruelty and Wrath,
Till I have Vengeance equal to my Love,
And my *Monelia*'s Shade[148] is satisfied.   [*Exit.*

SCENE IV.

Philip solus.

His Grief no Doubt will rise into a Rage,
To see his Charmer rolling in her Blood,
I chuse to see him not till my Return;
By then the Fierceness of the Flame may cease;
Nay, he'll grow cool, and quite forget his Love,   5
When I report her Father's kindled Wrath,

---

148 Spirit.

And all the Vengeance he intends to take.

[Chekitan *come in sight.*

But this is he, I cannot now avoid him;
How shall I sooth his Grief—He looks distracted—
I'm such a Stranger grown to Tears and Pity,   10
I fear he will not think I sympathize.

Enter Chekitan.

Chekitan. Have I then found thee, thou false hearted Traitor?
Thou Tyger, Viper, Snake, thou worse than Christian;
Blood thirsty Butcher, more than Murderer!
Thou every Thing but what Men ought to love!   15
Do you still live to breathe and see the Sun?
And face me with your savage guilty Eye?

Philip. I fear'd, alas, you would run mad and rave.
Why do you blame me that I am not dead?
I risk'd my Life, was wounded for your Sake,   20
Did all I could for your *Monelia*'s Safety,
And to revenge you on her Murderers.
Your Grief distracts you, or you'd thank me for 't.

Chekitan. Would you still tempt my Rage, and fire my Soul,
Already bent to spill your treacherous Blood?   25
You base Dissembler! know you are detected,
Torax still lives, and has discover'd all.

[Philip *starts and trembles.*

Philip. Torax alive!—It cannot—must not be   [*aside.*

Chekitan. Well may you shake—You cannot mend your Blow.
He lived to see, what none but you could think of,   30
The bloody Knife drawn from *Monelia*'s Breast.
Had you a thousand Lives, they'd be too few;
Had you a Sea of Blood, 'twould be too small
To wash away your deep-dy'd Stain of Guilt.
Now you shall die; and O if there be Powers   35
That after Death take Vengeace on such Crimes,
May they pursue you with their Flames of Wrath,

Till all their Magazines of Pain are spent.

> [*he attacks* Philip *with his Hatchet.*

Philip. I must defend myself *(drawing his Hatchet)* the Case is
  desperate.

> [*Fight,* Philip *falls.*
>   40

Fate is too hard; and I'm oblig'd to yield.
'Twas well begun—but has a wretched End—
Yet I'm reveng'd—She cannot live again.
You cannot boast to've shed more Blood than I—
Oh had I—had I—struck but one Blow more!   [*dies.*

Chekitan. What have I done! this is my Brother's Blood!   45
A guilty Murderer's Blood! He was no Brother.
All Nature's Laws and Ties are hence dissolv'd;
There is no Kindred, Friendship, Faith, or Love
Among Mankind—*Monelia*'s dead—The World
Is all unhing'd—There's universal War—   50
She was the Tie, the Centre of the Whole;
And she remov'd, all is one general Jar.[149]
Where next, *Monelia*, shall I bend my Arm[150]
To heal this Discord, this Disorder still,
And bring the Chaos Universe to Form?   55
Blood still must flow and float the scatter'd Limbs
Till thy much injur'd love in Peace subsides.
Then every jarring Discord once will cease,
And a new World from these rude Ruins rise.   [*pauses.*
Here then I point the Edge, from hence shall flow   60

> [*pointing his Knife to his Heart.*

The raging crimson Flood, this is the Fountain
Whose swift Day's Stream shall waft me to thy Arms.
Lest *Philip*'s Ghost should injure thy Repose.   [*Stabs himself.*
I come, I come—*Monelia*, now I come—
Philip—away—She's mine in spite of Death.   [*dies.* 65

Enter Tenesco.

---

149 A state of discord. Jar also refers to discordant sound, making this speech plausible also as a
     reference to the music of the spheres, a tradition whereby harmonious music was believed
     produced by the movement of heavenly bodies.
150 Raise a weapon.

Oh! I'm too late, the fatal Work is done.
Unhappy Princes; this your wretched End;
Your Country's Hopes and your fond Father's Joy;
Are you no more? Slain by each other's Hands.
Or what is worse; or by the Air you breath'd?   70
For all is Murder, Death, and Blood about us:
Nothing is safe; it is contagious all:
The Earth, and Air, and Skies are full of Treason!
The Evil Genius rules the Universe,
And on Mankind rains Tempests of Destruction.   75
Where will the Slaughter of the Species end?
When it begins with Kings and with their Sons,
A general Ruin threatens all below.
How will the good King hear the sad Report.
I fear th' Event; but as it can't be hid,   80
I'll bear it to him in the softest Terms,
And summon every Power to sooth his Grief,
And slack the Torrent of his Royal Passion.   [*Exit.*

SCENE V.

Senate House.

Ponteach, solus.

The Torrent rises, and the Tempest blows;
Where will this rough rude Storm of Ruin end?
What crimson Floods are yet to drench the Earth?
What new-form'd Mischiefs hover in the Air,
And point their Stings at this devoted Head?   5
Has Fate exhausted all her Stores of Wrath,
Or has she other Vengeance in reserve?
What can she more? My Sons, my Name is gone;
My Hopes all blasted, my Delights all fled;
Nothing remains but an afflicted King,   10
That might be pitied by Earth's greatest Wretch.
My Friends; my Sons, ignobly, basely slain,
Are more than murder'd, more than lost by Death.
Had they died fighting in their Country's Cause,
I should have smil'd and gloried in their Fall;   15

Yes, boasting that I had such Sons to lose,
I would have rode in Triumph o'er their Tombs.
But thus to die, the Martyrs of their Folly,
Involv'd in all the complicated Guilt
Of Treason, Murder, Falshood, and Deceit,   20
Unbridled Passion, Cowardice, Revenge,
And every Thing that can debase a Man,
And render him the just Contempt of all,
And fix the foulest Stain of Infamy,
Beyond the Power of Time to blot it out;   25
This is too much; and my griev'd Spirit sinks
Beneath the Weight of such gigantic Woe.
Ye that would see a piteous wretched King,
Look on a Father griev'd and curs'd like me;
Look on a King whose Sons have died like mine!   30
Then you'll confess that these are dangerous Names,
And put it in the Power of Fate to curse us;
It is on such she shews her highest Spite.
But I'm too far—'Tis not a Time to grieve
For private Losses, when the Public calls.   35

Enter Tenesco, *looking sorrowful.*

What are your Tidings?—I have no more Sons.

Tenesco. But you have Subjects, and regard their Safety.
The treacherous Priest, intrusted with your Councils,
Has publish'd all, and added his own Falshoods;
The Chiefs have all revolted from your Cause,   40
Patch'd up a Peace, and lend their Help no more.[151]

Ponteach. And this is all? we must defend ourselves,
Supply the Place of Numbers with our Courage,
And learn to conquer with our very Looks:
This is a Time that tries the Truth of Valour;   45
He shews his Courage that dares stem the Storm,
And live in spite of Violence and Fate.

---

151 The Potawattomis and Hurons involved in the Siege of Detroit reached a peace agreement
      with the English over the course of negotiations and prisoner exchanges between 7 and
      12 July.

Shall holy Perfidy[152] and seeming Lyes
Destroy our Purpose, sink us into Cowards?

Tenesco. May your Hopes prosper! I'll excite the Troops   50
By your Example still to keep the Field.   [*Exit.*

Ponteach. 'Tis coming on. Thus Wave succeeds to Wave,
Till the Storm's spent, then all subsides again—
The Chiefs revolted:— My Design betray'd:—
May he that trusts a Christian meet the same!   55
They have no Faith, no Honesty, no God,
And cannot merit Confidence from Men.
Were I alone the boist'rous Tempest's Sport,
I'd quickly move my shatter'd trembling Bark,
And follow my departed Sons to Rest.   60
But my brave Countrymen, my Friends, my Subjects,
Demand my Care: I'll not desert the Helm,
Nor leave a dang'rous Station in Distress:
Yes, I will live, in spite of Fate I'll live;
Was I not *Ponteach*, was I not a King,   65
Such Giant Mischiefs would not gather round me.[153]
And since I'm *Ponteach*, since I am a King,
I'll shew myself Superior to them all;
I'll rise above this Hurricane of Fate,
And shew my Courage to the Gods themselves.   70

Enter Tenesco, *surprised and pausing.*

I am prepar'd, be not afraid to tell;
You cannot speak what *Ponteach* dare not hear.

Tenesco. Our bravest Troops are slain, the rest pursu'd;
All is Disorder, Tumult, and Rebellion.
Those that remain insist on speedy Flight;   75
You must attend them, or be left alone
Unto the Fury of a conquering Foe,

---

152 Untrustworthiness or breach of faith.
153 Perhaps an attempt to lay claim to the greatness of stature conventionally demanded by
    classical tragedy.

Nor will they long expect your Royal Pleasure.

Ponteach. Will they desert their King in such an Hour,
When Pity might induce them to protect him?   80
Kings like the Gods are valued and ador'd,
When Men expect their Bounties in Return,
Place them in Want, destroy the giving Power,
All Sacrifices and Regards will cease.
Go, tell my Friends that I'll attend their Call.   85
              [*rising.* Exit Tenesco.

I will not fear—but must obey my Stars:
              [*looking round.*

Ye fertile Fields and glad'ning Streams, adieu;
Ye Fountains that have quench'd my scorching Thirst,
Ye Shades that hid the Sun-beams from my Head,
Ye Groves and Hills that yielded me the Chace,   90
Ye flow'ry Meads, and Banks, and bending Trees,
And thou proud Earth, made drunk with Royal Blood,
I am no more your Owner and your King.
But witness for me to your new base Lords,
That my unconquer'd Mind defies them still;   95
And though I fly, 'tis on the Wings of Hope.
Yes, I will hence where there's no *British* Foe,
And wait a Respite from this Storm of Woe;
Beget more Sons, fresh Troops collect and arm,
And other Schemes of future Greatness form;   100
Britons may boast, the Gods may have their Will,
Ponteach I am, and shall be *Ponteach* still.   [*Exit.*

FINIS.

APPENDIX A: EXCERPT FROM ROBERT ROGERS' *CONCISE ACCOUNT OF NORTH AMERICA*

Rogers' *Concise Account* was popular and well reviewed (see Appendix C), but was far from the only publication of its type. Published accounts of travels were common in England between the sixteenth and nineteenth centuries, and generally included some mix of geographical details (including bodies of water, animal life, vegetation, and agricultural possibility); tales of individual adventure and misadventure; reports of European settlements and communities; and descriptions of the lives and persons of Indigenous North Americans. The most widely referenced of these accounts from the eighteenth century include Cadwallader Colden's *History of the Five Indian Nations* (1747) and James Adair's *History of the American Indians* (1775). Along with the French *Jesuit Relations* (1610–73; ed. Thwaites, 1901) and Pierre Charlevoix's *Journal of a Voyage to North America* (1744; trans. 1761), these texts offer descriptions from knowledgeable reporters who travelled in North America and had extensive first-person experience with several Indigenous nations and communities. Rogers' account purports to be of this group, but though he certainly fought side by side with many Native men and he certainly did travel extensively, his account fits more closely with publications like that of his sometimes protégé Jonathan Carver. Carver's (also popular and widely referenced) *Travels to the Interior Parts of America* (1778), combines first-person knowledge gained in his extensive travels with information gathered from other sources. Like the most accurate sources of eighteenth-century ethnography and geography, Rogers' account is important for its consciousness of the distinct natures of the different Indigenous nations and of individual communities within those nations, and his information is generally accurate, but it is essential to note that it is only one account among hundreds, and perhaps middling in its degree of originality of information. It is, however, an excellent example of Rogers' general perceptions of Indigenous North Americans and their environment, and thus offers important illumination for *Ponteach*.

A CONCISE

ACCOUNT

OF

NORTH AMERICA:

CONTAINING

A Defcription of the feveral BRITISH COLONIES
on that Continent, including the Iflands of
NEWFOUNDLAND, CAPE BRETON, &c.

AS TO

Their Situation, Extent, Climate, Soil, Produce, Rife,
Government, Religion, Prefent Boundaries, and
the Number of Inhabitants fuppofed to be in each.

ALSO OF

The Interior, or Wefterly Parts of the Country, upon the
Rivers ST. LAURENCE, the MISSISSIPI, CHRISTINO, and
the Great Lakes.

To which is fubjoined,

An Account of the feveral Nations and Tribes of Indians
refiding in thofe Parts, as to their Cuftoms, Manners, Government, Numbers, &c.

Containing many Ufeful and Entertaining Facts, never before
treated of.

By Major ROBERT ROGERS.

LONDON:
Printed for the AUTHOR,
And fold by J. MILLAN, Bookfeller, near Whitehall.
MDCCLXV.

Title page: Robert Rogers, *Concise Account of North America*. London: 1765 (McGill
University Library, Lande Canadiana Collection 761).

CUSTOMS, MANNERS, &C. *OF THE* INDIANS.

Having thus endeavoured to give a sketch of the interior country of North America, so far as I have any knowledge or intelligence concerning it, I will now more particularly, but briefly, mention the customs, manners, and connections of the Indians who inhabit there.

Those of them who have any concerns or commerce with the English, as such as inhabit from the east-side of the Mississippi to the south-side of the River Christino; and among all the nations and tribes in this vast extent of country, those called the Five Nation Indians stand distinguished, and are deserving of the first notice. They are dreaded and revered by all the others for their superior understanding, activity and valour in war, in which constant practice renders them expert, they being in almost continual wars with one nation or other, and sometimes with several together. Their customs, manners, and modes of dress, are adopted by many of the other tribes as near as possible. In short, those Indians are generally among the other nations esteemed the politest and best bred who the nearest resemble these. Their most northern settlement is a town called Chockonawago, on the south of the River St. Lawrence, opposite to Montreal; but their largest settlements are between Lake Ontario and the provinces of New York and Pensylvania, or the heads of the Mohock, Tanesee, Oneoida and Onondaga Rivers. They claim all the country south of the River St. Lawrence to the Ohio, and down the Ohio to the Wabach, from the mouth of the Wabach to the bounds of Virginia; westerly, to the Lakes Ontario and Erie, and the River Miamee; their eastern boundaries are Lake Champlain, and the British colonies. When the English first settled in America, they could raise 15,000 fighting men; but now, including the Delawares and Shawanees, they do not amount to more than between three or four thousand, having been thus reduced by the incessant wars they have maintained with the other Indians, and with the French, in Canada.

The Mohocks were formerly the most numerous tribe amongst them, but now they are the smallest; however, they still preserve a superiority and authority over the rest, as the most honourable nation, and are consulted and appealed to by the others in all great emergencies. About 100 years ago they destroyed the greatest part of the Hurons, who then lived on the south-side of Lake Ontario, and the remains fled to the French in Canada for protection; but the greatest part have since returned to their own country again, and live, by permission from the Five Nations, on the lands at the west-end of Lake Erie. They also took prisoners the whole nation of the Sawanees, who lived upon the Wabach, and afterwards, by the mediation of Mr. Penn, at the first settlement of Pensylvania, gave them liberty to settle in the westerly parts of that province; but obliged them, as a badge of their cowardice, to wear petticoats for a long time: they gave them, however, the appellation of cousins, and allowed them to claim kindred with the Five Nations, as their uncles. They conquered the Delawares about the same time, and brought them into the like subjection; and also the Mickanders, or Mohegons, that lived on the banks of Hudson's River. They suffered the two last mentioned nations to live in any uninhabited part of their southern territory but the latter, upon condition of paying them an annual tribute. They also conquered several tribes upon the frontiers of New England. Some nations to this day are not allowed to appear ornamented with paint at any general meeting or congress where the Five Nations attend, that being an express article in the capitulations. They have been inveterate enemies to the French ever since their first settling in Canada, and are almost the only Indians within many hundred miles, that have been proof against the solicitations of the French to turn against us; but the greatest part of them have maintained their integrity, and been our stedfast friends and faithful allies.

They once burnt great part of the city of Montreal, and put the French into great consternation; they have also conquered most of the Abnaques,or eastern Indians. They now maintain a constant war with the Cherokees, Creeks, and Chickesaws, and many of their young men are annually employed that way; others of them go against the Misauri; and in short, they sometimes carry their hostilities almost as far south as the isthmus of Darien; but they have long lived in peace with the Indians on the lakes, and with the Tweeghtwees, those two nations being too near, and well provided to retaliate any affront they may offer them.

The Indians do not want for natural good sense and ingenuity, many of them discovering a great capacity for art or science, liberal or mechanical. Their imaginations are so strong, and their memories so retentive, that when they have once been at a place, let it be ever so distant, or obscure, they will readily find it again. The Indians about Nova Scotia and the Gulf of St. Lawrence have frequently passed over to the Labrador, which is thirty or forty leagues, without a compass, and have landed at the very spot they at first intended: and even in dark cloudy weather they will direct their course by land with great exactness; but this they do by observing the bark and boughs of trees, the north-side, in this country, being always mossy, and the boughs on the south-side the largest.

It is also observable, that you will rarely find among the Indians a person that is in any way deformed, or that is deprived of any sense, or decrepid in any limb, notwithstanding the little care taken about the mother in the time of her pregnancy, the neglect the infant is treated with when born, and the fatigues the youth is obliged to suffer; yet generally they are of a hale, robust, and firm

constitution; but spiritous liquors, of which they are insatiably fond, and the
women as well as the men, have already surprizingly lessened their numbers,
and will, in all probability, in one century more nearly clear the country of them.

Indeed the mothers, in their way, take great care of their children, and are
extremely fond of them. They seldom wean them till they are two years old, or
more, and carry them on their backs till the burden grows quite insupportable
to them. When they leave the cradle they are very much at liberty to go when
and where they please; they are however careful to instruct them early in the
use of arms, especially the bow, and are often recounting to them the exploits
and great atchievements of their ancestors, in order to inspire them with great
and noble sentiments, and lead them on to brave and heroic actions. They intro-
duce them very young into their public councils, and make them acquainted
with the most important affairs and transactions, which accustoms them to
secresy, gives them a composed and manly air, inspires them with emulation,
and makes them bold and enterprising. They seldom chastise their children;
when they are young, they say, because they are not endued with reason to
guide them right, otherwise they would not do wrong; when they are more
advanced in life, they say, because they are capable of judging, and ought to be
masters of their own actions, and are not accountable to any one. These max-
ims are carried so far that parents sometimes suffer themselves to be abused by
their children; and in the same way they will excuse any ill treatment they meet
with from a drunken man: Should we blame or punish him, say they, when he
does not know what he does, or has not his reason? When a mother sees her
daughter act amiss, she falls into tears, and upon the other's taking notice of it,
and enquiring the cause, she replies, because you so and so dishonour me;
which kind of admonition seldom fails of the desired effect. The Indians do not
always enter into a formal obligation of marriage, but take companions for a
longer or shorter time, as they please; the children which spring from hence lie
under no disgrace, but enjoy all the privileges of lawfully begotten children.

The Indian men are remarkable for their idleness, upon which they seem to
value themselves, saying, that to labour would be degrading them, and belongs only to the women; that they are formed only for war, hunting, and
fishing; tho' it is their province to make and prepare every thing requisite for
these exercises, as their arms for hunting, lines for fishing, and to make canoes, to build and repair their houses; but so profoundly lazy are they, that
they often make their women assist even in these, besides attending all domestic affairs, and agriculture.

Most of the Indians are possessed of a surprising patience and equanimity of
mind, and a command of every passion, except revenge, beyond what philoso-
phers or Christian usually attain to. You may see them bearing the most sudden

and unexpected misfortunes with calmness and composure of mind, without a word, or change of countenance; even a prisoner, who knows not where his captivity may end, or whether he may not in a few hours be put to a most cruel death, never loses a moment's sleep on this account, and eats and drinks with as much chearfulness as those into whose hands he has fallen.

Their resolution and courage under sickness and pain is truly surprising. A young woman will be in labour a whole day without uttering one groan or cry; should she betray such a weakness, they would immediately say, that she was unworthy to be a mother, and that her offspring could not fail of being cowards. Nothing is more common that to see persons, young and old of both sexes, supporting themselves with such constancy even under the greatest pains and calamities, that even when under those shocking tortures which prisoners are frequently put to, they will not only make themselves chearful, but provoke and irritate their tormentors with most cutting reproaches.

Another thing remarkable among these people, who put on at all times a savage, cruel appearance, is, that those of the same nation, or that are in alliance, behave to each other with an high degree of complaisance and good nature.

Those advanced in years are rarely treated disrespectfully by the younger; and if any quarrels happen, they never make use of oaths, or any indecent expressions, or call one another by hard names; but, at the same time, no duration can put a period to their revenge; it is often a legacy transferred from generation to generation, and left as a bequest from father to son, till an opportunity offers of taking ample satisfaction, perhaps in the third or fourth generation from those who first did the injury. They are not, however, strangers to the utility and pleasures of friendship, for each of them, at a certain age, makes choice of some one near about their own age, to be their most intimate and bosom friend; and these two enter into mutual engagements, and are obliged to brave any danger, and run any risk to assist and support each other; and this attachment is carried so far, as even to overcome the fears of death, as they look upon it to be only a temporary separation, and that they shall meet and be united in friendship in the other world, never to be separated more, and imagine they shall need one another's assistance there as well as here.

There is no nation of Indian but seem to have some sense of a Deity, and a kind of religion among them; but this is so various, so perplexed and confused, that it is difficult to describe it very minutely. Their ideas of the nature and attributes of the Deity are very obscure, and some of them absurd; but they all acknowledge him to be the creator and master of the world; but how the world was created they know not, and of course have various conjectures about it. Some of them imagine that men were first rained down from the clouds, and that brute animals descended with them. They seem to have some idea of angels, or spirits of an higher and more excellent nature than man; to these they attribute a kind of immensity, supposing them to be every where present, and are frequently invoking them, imagining they hear them, and act, or endeavour to act, agreeable to their desires. They likewise hold of an evil spirit, or demon, who, say they, is always inclined to mischief, and bears great sway in the creation; and it is this latter that is the principal objects of their adorations and devotions; they generally address him by way of deprecation, most heartily beseeching him to do them no harm, but avert evils from them: the other they address by way of petition, supposing him to be propitious, and ever inclined to do them good; that he would bestow blessings upon them, and prevent the demon or evil spirit from hurting them; and to merit or procure the protection of the good spirit, they imagine it necessary to distinguish themselves; and that, in the first place, they must become good warriors, expert hunters, and steady marksmen.

The Indians depend much upon their dreams, and really believe that they dream the whole history of their future life, or what it may be collected from their youth, for which reason they make dreaming a kind of religious ceremony when they come to sufficient years, which is thus performed: They besmear their faces all over with black paint, and fast for several days, in which time they expect the good genius, or propitious spirit, will appear, or manifest himself to him in some shape or other in his dreams. The effect which this long fast must naturally occasion in the brain of a young person, must without doubt be considerable; and the parents, and other old people, take care, during the operation, that the dreams they have in the night be faithfully reported next morning. In favour to particular constitutions, they sometimes curtail this fast to a shorter term than is generally judged necessary; and this good genius, or propitious spirit, being the subject of the person's waking thoughts, becomes also the subject of his dreams, and every phantom of their sleep is regarded as a figure of the genius, whether it be bird, beast, fish, or tree, or any thing else, animate of inanimate, and is particularly respected by them all their lives after. When any person of more distinguished parts than ordinary rises up among them, they suppose him naturally inspired, or actuated by this propitious spirit, and have an uncommon regard and veneration for him on that account, supposing him to receive intimations and intelligences from the good genius, or some of his agents. Religious impostures are not less frequent among the Indians of America, than among the Christians of Europe; and some of them are very successful in persuading the multitude that they are filled with a divine enthusiasm, and a kind of inspiration, few knowing better how to act their part in this sacred juggle than they. They often persuade the people that they have revelations of future events, and that they are authorised to command them to pursue such and such measures. They not only prescribe laws and rules, and persuade the populace to believe them; but undertake to unfold the mysteries of religion and a future state, to solve and interpret all their dreams and visions, &c. They represent the other world as a place abounding with an inexhaustible plenty of every thing desirable, and that they shall enjoy the most full and exquisite gratification of all their senses: and hence it is, no doubt, that the Indians meet death with such indifference and composure of mind, no Indian being in the least dismayed at the news that he has but a few hours or minutes to live; but with the greatest intrepidity sees himself upon the brink of being separated from terrestrial things, and with spirit and composure harangues those who are round him; and thus a father leaves his dying advice to his children, and takes a formal leave of all his friends.

The Indians generally bury their dead with great decency, and erect monuments over their graves. They deposit in the grave such things as the deceased had made the greatest use of, and been most attached to; as pipes, tobacco, bows, arrows, &c. that he may not be in want of any thing when he comes to the other country. The mothers mourn for their children a long time; and the neighbours make presents to the bereaved father, which he retaliates by giving them a feast.

The Indian feasts, whether at a funeral, a triumph, a visit, or whatever the occasion be, are very simple and inartful. The savage does not mortify his friend with a splendid appearance, but makes him chearful by dividing his riches with him, and values not spending the fruits of a whole season's toil, to convince him that he is welcome; nay, thinks himself happy in having such an opportunity to oblige him. The guest is sure to be treated with an unaffected gravity and complaisance, and that he shall not be the subject of whispering ridicule and banter while present, nor of cruel remarks when departed; which certainly is a privilege they do not always enjoy among more civilized nations. Nor is a servile regard paid to the distinctions of high and low, rich and poor, noble and ignoble, so as to lessen the spirit and pleasure of conversation, when the company happens to be made up of a mixture of these.

The Indians being both of a very active and revengeful disposition, they are easily induced at any time to make wars, and seldom refuse to engage when solicited by their allies; very often the most trifling provocations rouse them to arms, and prove the occasions of bloodshed and murder; their petty private quarrels being often decided this way, and expeditions of this kind may be undertaken without the knowledge or consent of a general council, or any formal declarations of war. These private excursions are winked at, excused, and encouraged, as a means of keeping their young men alert, and of acquainting them with the discipline and exercises of war. And indeed these petty wars seem necessary, since their laws and penalties are insufficient to restrain them within the bounds of reason and common justice, and are a poor security of private property against the insults and depredations of any one; but when war becomes a national affair, it is entered upon with great deliberation and solemnity, and prosecuted with the utmost secrecy, diligence and attention, both in making preparations and in carrying their schemes into execution. Their method of declaring war is very solemn and pompous, attended with many ceremonies of terror. In the first place, they call an assembly of the Sachems and Chief Warriors, to deliberate upon the affair, and determine upon matters, how, when, and in what manner it shall be entered upon and prosecuted, &c. In which general congress, among the northern Indians and the Five Nations, the women have a voice as well as the men. When they are assembled, the President or chief Sachem proposes the affair they have met to consult upon, and, taking up the hatchet (which lies by him) says, Who among you will go and fight against such a nation? Who among you will go and bring captives from thence, to replace our deceased friends, that our wrongs may be avenged, and our name and honour maintained as long as rivers flow, grass grows, or the sun and moon endure? He having thus said, one of the principal warriors rises, and harangues the whole assembly; and then addresses himself to the young men, and inquires, who among them will go along with him and fight their enemies? when they generally rise, one after another, and fall in behind him, while he walks round the circle or parade, till he is joined by a sufficient number. Generally at such a congress they have a deer or some beast roasted whole; and each of them, as they consent to go to war, cuts off a piece and eats, saying, this way will I devour our enemies, naming the nation they are going to attack. All that chuse, having performed this ceremony, and thereby solemnly engaged to behave with fidelity and as a good warrior, the dance begins, and they sing the war-song; the matter of which relates to their intended expedition and conquest, or to their own skill, courage and dexterity in fighting, and to the manner in which they will vanquish and extirpate their enemies; all which is expressed in the strongest and most pathetic manner, and with a tone of terror. So great is the eloquence or influence of their women in these consultations, that the final result very much depends upon them. If any one of these nations, in conjunction with the Chiefs, has a mind to excite one, who docs not immediately depend upon them, to take part in the war, either to appease the names of her husband, son, or near relations, or to take prisoners, to supply the place of such as have died in her family, or are in captivity, she presents, by the hands of some trusty young warrior, a string of wampum to the person whose help she solicits; which invitation seldom fails of its desired effect. And when they solicit the alliance, offensive or defensive, of a whole nation, the send an embassy with a large belt of wampum, and a bloody hatchet, inviting them to come and drink the blood of their enemies. The wampum made use of upon these and other occasions, before their acquaintance with the Europeans, was nothing but small shells, which they picked up by the sea-coasts and on the banks of the lakes; and now it is nothing but a kind of cylindrical beads, made of shells white and black, which are esteemed among them as silver and gold are among us. The black they call the most valuable, and both together are their greatest riches and ornaments; these among them answering all the ends that money does among us. They have the art of stringing, twisting, and interweaving these into their belts, collars, blankets, mogasons, &c. in ten thousand different sizes, forms and figures, so as to be ornaments for every part of dress, and expressive to them of all their important transactions. They dye the wampum of various colours and shades, and mix and dispose them with great ingenuity and order, and so as to be significant among themselves of almost any thing they please; so that by these their records are kept, and their thoughts communicated to one another, as our's are by writing. The belts that pass from one nation to another, in all treaties, declarations, and important transactions, are carefully preserved in the palaces or cabbins of their Chiefs, and serve, not only as a kind of record or history, but as a public treasure. It must, however, be an affair of national importance in which they use collars or belts, it being looked upon as a very great abuse and absurdity to use them on trifling occasions. Nor is the calumet or pipe of peace of less importance, or less revered among them in many trans-actions, relative both to war and peace. The bowl of this pipe is made of a kind of soft red stone, which is easily wrought and hollowed out; the stem is of cane, elder, or some kind of light wood, painted with different colours, and decorated with the heads, tails, and feathers of the most beautiful birds, &c. The use of the calumet is, to smoak either tobacco, or some bark-leaf, or herb, which they often use instead of it, when they enter into an allegiance, or on any serious occasion, or solemn engagement; this being among them the most sacred oath that can be taken, the violation of which is esteemed most infamous, and de-serving of severe punishment from heaven. When they treat of war, the whole pipe and all its ornaments are red; sometimes it is red only on one side, and by the disposition of the feathers, &c. one acquainted with their customs will know, at first sight, what the nation who presents it intends or desires. Smoking the calumet is also a religious ceremony upon some occasions, and in all treat-ies is considered as a witness between the parties; or rather as an instrument by which they invoke the sun and moon to witness their sincerity, and to be, as it were, guarantees of the treaty between them. This custom of the Indians, tho' to appearance somewhat ridiculous, is not without its reasons; for, they finding smoaking tended to disperse the vapours of the brain, to raise the spirits and qualify them for thinking and judging properly, introduced it into their councils, where, after their resolves, the pipe was considered as a seal of their decrees, and, as a pledge of their performance thereof, it was sent to those they were consulting an alliance or treaty with: so that smoking among them in the same pipe is equivalent to our drinking together and out of the same cup.

The size and decorations of their calumets are commonly proportioned to the quality of the personas they are presented to, and the esteem or regard they have for them, and also to the importance of the occasion.

Another instrument of great esteem and importance among them is the tomahawk. This is an ancient weapon universally used by them in war, before they were taught the use of iron and steel; since which hatchets have been substituted in lieu of them. But this instrument still retains its use and importance in public transactions, and, like the pipe, is often very significant. This weapon is formed much like an hatchet, having a long stem or handle; the head is a round ball or knob of solid wood well enough calculated to knock men's brains out, which on the other side of the stem terminates in a point where the edge would be, if made an hatchet, which point is set a little hooking or coming towards the stem; and near the center, where the stem or handle pierces the head, another point projects forward of a considerable length, which serves to trust with like a spear, or pike-pole.

The tomahawk likewise is ornamented with feathers and paintings, disposed and variegated in many significant forms, according to the occasion and end for which it is used; and on it they keep journals of their marches, and most important and noted occurrences, in a kind of hieroglyphics. When the council is called to deliberate on war, the tomahawk is painted all over red, and when the council sits it is laid down by the chief; and if war is concluded upon, the captain of the young warriors takes it up, and with it in his hands dances and sings the war-song, as before-mentioned; when the council is over, this hatchet, or some other of the kind, is sent by the hands of some warrior to every tribe concerned, and with it he presents a belt of wampum, and delivers his message, throwing the hatchet on the ground, which is taken up by one of their most expert warriors, if they chuse to join; if not, they return it, and with a belt of their wampum suitable to the occasion.

Every nation or tribe have their distinguishing ensigns or coats of arms, which is generally some beast, bird, or fish. Thus among the Five Nation are the bear, otter, wolf, tortoise and eagle; and by these names the tribes are generally distinguished, and they have the shapes of these animals curiously pricked and painted on several parts of their bodies; and when they march through the woods, generally at every encampment they cut the figure of their arms on trees, especially if it be from a successful campaign, that travellers that way may know they have been there, recording also, in their way, the number of scalps or prisoners they have taken.

Their military dress has something in it very romantic and terrible, especially the cut of their hair, and the paintings and decorations they make use of. They cut off, or pull our all their hair, excepting a spot about the size of two English crowns near the crown of their heads, their beards and eye-brows they totally destroy. The lock left upon their head is divided into several parcels, each of which is stiffened and adorned with wampum, beads, and feathers of various shapes and hues, and the whole twisted, turned, and connected together, till it takes a form much resembling the modern Pompadour upon the top of their heads. Their heads are painted red down to the eyebrows, and sprinkled over with white down. The gristles of their ears are split almost quite round, and then distended with wire or splinters, so as to meet and tie together in the knap of their necks. These also are hung with ornaments, and have generally the figure of some bird or beast drawn upon them. Their noses are likewise bored, and hung with trinkets of beads, and their faces painted with divers colours, which are so disposed as to make an aweful appearance. Their breasts are adorned with a gorget, or medal of brass, copper, or some other metal; and that horrid weapon the scalping-knife hangs by a string which goes round their necks.

Thus attired, and equipped with the other armour they make use of, and warlike stores, they march forth, singing the war-song, till they lose sight of the castle or village from which they marched, and are generally followed by their women for some considerable space, who assist them in carrying their baggage, whether by land or water, but commonly return before they proceed to any action.

When a small party goes out, they seldom have more than one commander, i.e. if the number does not exceed ten, which is one of their companies; if there by twenty, they have two commanders; if forty, four, &c. and when it comes to 100 or upwards, a general is appointed over the others, not properly to command, but to give his opinion and advice, which they make no scruple to disregard, if it does not happen to tally with their own; however, it is very rare that the directions of the general is disregarded, especially if countenanced and supported by the advice of the old men, which seems to be the highest authority both in the state and army amongst them.

The generalissimo, or commander in chief, as well civil as military, among all the Indians to the northward, who speak the Roundock dialect, is elective, which election is attended with many ceremonies of singing and dancing; and the chief, when chose, never fails making a panegyric upon the person to whom he succeeds.

The Indians have no stated rules of discipline, or fixed methods of prosecuting a war; they make their attacks in as many different ways as there are occasions on which they make them, but generally in a very secret, skulking, underhand manner, in flying parties that are equipped for the purpose, with a thin light dress, generally consisting of nothing more than a shirt, stocking, and mogasons, and sometimes almost naked.

The weapons used by those who have commerce with the English and French, are commonly a firelock, hatchet, and scalping-knife; the others use bows, tomahawks, pikes, &c.

In any considerable party of Indians, you will generally find a great number of headmen, or chiefs, because they give that title to all whoever commanded; but all these are subordinate to the commander of the party, who, after all, is a general without any real authority, and governs by advice only, not by orders; for he can neither reward nor punish, and every private man has a right to return home when he pleases, without assigning any reason for it; or any number may leave the main body, and carry on a private expedition, when, how, and where they please, and are never called to account for so doing.

The commander every morning harangues the detachment under his command, and gives his advice for the conduct of affairs during the day. If he wants to detach a party for reconnoitering, or on any occasion, he proposes the matter, and gives his opinion how, when, where, what number, &c. and it seldom happens that he is opposed in any of his measures. So greatly are the savages influenced by a sense of honour, and the love of their country, that coercive penal laws are needless to restrain and govern them upon these occasions; but then it should be observed, that the qualifications indispensibly necessary to recommend a person to the chief command among them, are, that he must be fortunate, brave, and disinterested; and no wonder that they chearfully obey a person in whom they firmly believe that all these qualifications are united; to which may be added, that of secrecy in all his operations; in which art they greatly excell, their designs being seldom known to any but themselves, till they are upon the point of being executed.

The chiefs seldom speak much themselves at general meetings, or in public assemblies, counting it beneath their dignity to utter their own sentiments upon these occasions in an audible manner; they therefore intrust them with a person to declare for them, who is called their speaker or orator, there being one of this profession in every tribe and town; and their manner of speaking is generally natural and easy, their words strong and expressive, their stile truly laconic, nothing being said but what is to the purpose, either to inform the judgment, or raise such passions as the subject-matter naturally excites.

Those who profess oratory, make it their business to be thoroughly acquainted with the subject they are to speak upon, and have the whole matter and method well fixed in their memories beforehand, that they may be at no loss what to say, or how to express themselves; tho' they hold no regular parliaments, or courts of justice, yet they have frequent opportunities to display their talents this way, they being almost constantly busied in making fresh, or renewing former treaties, in tenders of their services, in solicitations, in addresses on the birth, death, or advancement of some great person, &c.

In their private petty debates, not only the orators, but every person is heard who chuses to intermiddle in it; and generally, if one has given a present to a sachem for his vote one way or another, he is pretty sure to have it, for they seldom fail of performing engagements of this kind, which renders justice in the redress of private grievances very precarious.

But this is not attended with so bad consequences as one would imagine, for their contentions of a private nature are few, and are generally compromised by the interposition of friends.

Avarice, and a desire to accumulate those great disturbers of the peace of society, are unknown to them; they are neither prompted by ambition, nor actuated by the love of gold; and the distinctions of rich and poor, high and low, noble and ignoble, do not so far take place among them as to create the least uneasiness to, or excite the resentment of any individual; the brave and deserving, let their families or circumstances be what they will, are sure to be esteemed and rewarded.

In short, the great and fundamental principles of their policy are, that every man is naturally free and independent; that no one or more on earth has any right to deprive him of his freedom and independency, and that nothing can be a compensation for the loss of it.

When the Indians return from a successful campaign, they manage their march so as not to approach their village till towards the evening. When night comes on, they send two or three forwards to acquaint their chief, and the whole village, with the most material circumstances of the campaign. At daylight next morning they cloathe their prisoners with new cloaths, adorn their heads with feathers, paint their faces with various colours, and put into their hands a white staff or want, tosseled round with the tails of deer. When this is done, the war-captain or commander in this expedition sets up a cry, and gives as many holloos or yells as he has taken scalps and prisoners, and the whole village assemble at the water-side, if there be one near. As soon as the warriors appear, four or five of their young men, well cloathed, get into a canoe, if they came by water, or otherwise march by land: the two first carry each a calumet, and go singing to search the prisoners, whom they lead in triumph to the cabin where they are to receive their doom. It is the prerogative of the owner of this cabin to determine their fate, tho' very often it is left to some woman, who has lost her husband, brother, or son, in the war; and, when this is the case, she generally adopts him into the place of the deceased, and saves his life. The prisoner, after having been presented, has victuals immediately given him to eat, and while he is at this repast a consultation is held; and if it be resolved to save the prisoner's life, two young men untie him, and, taking him by the hands, lead him directly to the cabin of the person into whose family he is to be adopted. But if the sentence be death, the whole village set up the death holloo or cry, and the execution is no longer deferred than till they can make the necessary preparations for it. They first strip the person who is to suffer from head to foot, and, fixing two posts in the ground, they fasten to them two pieces crossways, one about two feet from the ground, the other about five or six feet higher; they then oblige the unhappy victim to mount upon the lower cross piece, to which they tie his legs a little asunder. His hands are extended, and tied to the angles formed by the upper cross piece; and in this posture they burn him all over the body, sometimes first daubing him with pitch. The whole village, men, women, and children, assemble round him, and every one has a right to torture him in what manner they please, and as long as there is life in him. If none of the bystanders are in-clined to lengthen out his torments, he is not long kept in pain, but is either shot to death with arrows, or inclosed with dry bark, to which they set fire: they then leave him on the frame, and in the evening run from cabin to cabin, and strike with small twigs their furniture, the walls and roofs of their cabins, to prevent his spirit from remaining there to take vengeance for the evils committed on his body; the remainder of the day, and the night following, is spent in rejoicings.

The above is their most usual method of executing prisoners; but sometimes they fasten them to a single stake, and build a fire round them; at other times they gash and cut off the fingers, toes, &c. of their prisoners joint by joint; and at other times they scald them to death. They often kill their prisoners on the spot where they take them, or in their way home, when they have any fear of their escaping, or when they find it inconvenient to carry them further.

But if they have been unsuccessful, things wear quite a different face; they then return, and enter the village without ceremony by day, with grief and mel-ancholy in their countenances, keeping a profound silence: or if they have sus-tained any loss, they enter in the evening, giving the death hoop, and naming those they have lost, either by sickness or by the enemy. The village being as-sembled, they sit down with their heads covered, and all weep together, with-out speaking a single word for some considerable time. When this silence is over, they begin to lament aloud for their companions, and every thing wears the face of mourning among them for several days.

Such in general are the manners and customs of the Indians called the Five Nations, which in the main agree to those of all the Indians with whom we have any connexions or commerce, as they all endeavour to imitate these. But all the tribes have some things peculiar to themselves. Among the Hurons (who are called fathers by the Five Nations, and who are doubtless of the same nation) the dignity of Chief is heredity, and the succession is in the female line: so that, on the death of the Chief, it is not his son, but his sister's son, that succeeds him, and, in default of him, his nearest relation in the female line; and in case this whole line should be extinct, the most noble matron of the tribe or town makes choice of any one she pleases for a Chief. If the person who succeeds is not arrived to years sufficient to take the charge of the government, a regent is appointed, who has the whole authority, but acts in the name of the minor.

The Delawares and Shawanees are remarked for their deceit and perfidy, paying little or no regard to their word and most solemn engagements.

The Tweeghtwees and Yeahtanees are remarkably mild and sedate, and seem to have subdued their passions beyond any other Indians on the continent. They have always been steady friends to the English, and are fond of having them in their country; they might no doubt be made very useful subjects, were proper steps taken to christianize and civilize them.

The Cherokees are governed by several Sachems or Chiefs (something like the United Provinces or States of Holland) which are elected by their different tribes or villages. The Creeks and Chictaws are governed in the same manner. The Chickesaws have a King, and a Council for his assistance, and are esteemed a brave people; they are generally at war with all the other Indians east of the Mississipi; the Chictaws, Creeks, and Cherokees, and these Southern Indians, often fight pitched battles with them on the plains of their country; having horses in plenty, they ride to the field of battle, and there dismount, where the women fight as well as the men, if they are hardly pushed.

It is supposed that the Chickesaws came from South America, and introduced horses into the North. The Creeks and Chictaws punish their women when they prove disloyal to their husbands, by cutting off their hair, which they will not suffer to grow again until the corn is ripe the next season. The Chickesaws, their neighbours, are not at all troubled with a spirit of jealousy, as say it demeans a man to suspect a woman's chastity. They are tall, well-shaped, and handsome featured, especially their women, far exceeding in beauty any other nation to the southward; but even these are exceeded by the Huron women upon Lake Erie, who are allowed to be the best shaped and most beautiful savages on the continent, and are universally esteemed by the other nations. They dress much neater than any others, and curiously adorn their heads, necks, wrists, &c. notwithstanding which you will seldom find a jealous husband, either among the Hurons or the Five Nation Indians.

The men of the Ottawawas, or Souties, are lusty, square, and strait limb'd. The women short, thick, and but very indifferent for beauty, yet their husbands are very prone to be jealous of them; and whenever this whim comes in their heads, they cut off the tip of the suspected wife's nose, that she may for ever after be distinguished by a mark of infamy.

The Indians on the lakes are generally at peace with one another, having a wide extended and fruitful country in their possession. They are formed into a sort of empire, and the Emperor is elected from the eldest tribe, which is the Ottawawas, some of whom inhabit near our fort at Detroit, but are mostly further westward towards the Mississipi. Ponteack is their present King or Emperor, who has certainly the largest empire and greatest authority of any Indian Chief that has appeared on the continent since our acquaintance with it. He puts on an air of majesty and princely grandeur, and is greatly honoured and revered by his subjects. He not long since formed a design of uniting all the Indian nations together under his authority, but miscarried in the attempt.

In the year 1760, when I commanded and marched the first detachment into this country that was ever sent there by the English, I was met in my way by an embassy from him, of some of his warriors, and some of the chiefs of the tribes that are under him; the purport of which was, to let me know, that Ponteack was at a small distance, coming peacably, and that he desired me to halt my detachment till such time as he could see me with his own eyes. His ambassadors had also orders to inform me, that he was Ponteack, the King and Lord of the country I was in.

At first salutation when we met, he demanded my business into his country, and how it happened that I dared to enter it without his leave? When I informed him that it was not with any design against the Indians that I came, but to remove the French out of his country, who had been an obstacle in our way to mutual peace and commerce, and acquainted him with my instructions for that purpose. I at the same time delivered him several friendly messages, or belts of wampum, which he received, but gave me no other answer, than that he stood in the path I travelled in till next morning, giving me a small string of wampum, as much as to say, I must not march further without his leave. When he departed for the night, he enquired whether I wanted any thing that his country afforded, and he would send his warrior to fetch it? I assured him that any provisions they brought should be paid for; and the next day we were supplied by them with several bags of parched corn, and some other necessaries. At our second meeting he gave me the pipe of peace, and both of us by turns smoaked with it; and he assured me he had made peace with me and my detachment; that I might pass thro' his country unmolested, and relieve the French garrison; and that he would protect me and my party from any insults that might be offered or intended by the Indians; and, as an earnest of his friendship, he sent 100 warriors to protect and assist us in driving 100 fat cattle, which we had brought for the use of the detachment from Pittsburg, by way of Presque Isle. He likewise sent to the several Indian towns on the south-side and west-end of Lake Erie, to inform them that I had his consent to come into the country. He attended me constantly after this interview till I arrived at Detroit, and while I remained in the country, and was the means of preserving the detachment from the fury of the Indians, who had assembled at the mouth of the strait with an intent to cut us off.

I had several conferences with him, in which he discovered great strength of judgment, and a thirst after knowledge. He endeavoured to inform himself of our military order and discipline. He often intimated to me, that he could be content to reign in his country in subordination to the King of Great Britain, and was willing to pay him such annual acknowledgment as he was able in furs, and to call him his uncle. He was curious to know our methods of manufacturing cloth, iron, &c. and expressed a great desire to see England, and offered me part of his country if I would conduct him there. He assured me, that he was inclined to live peaceably with the English while they used him as he deserved, and to encourage their settling in his country; but intimated, that, if they treated him with neglect, he should shut up the way, and exclude them from it; in short, his whole conversation sufficiently indicated that he was far from considering himself as a conquered Prince, and that he expected to be treated with the respect and honour due to a King or Emperor, by all who came into his country, or treated with him.

In 1763, this Indian had the art and address to draw a number of tribes into a confederacy, with a design first to reduce the English forts upon the lakes, and then make a peace to his mind, by which he intended to establish himself in his Imperial authority; and so wisely were his measures taken, that, in fifteen days time, he reduced or took ten of our garrisons, which were all we had in his country, except Detroit; and had he carried this garrison also, nothing was in the way to complete his scheme. Some of the Indians left him, and by his consent made a separate peace; but he would not be active or personally concerned in it, saying, that when he made a peace, it should be such an one as would be useful and honourable to himself, and to the King of Great Britain: but he has not as yet proposed his terms.

In 1763, when I went to throw provisions into the garrison at Detroit, I sent this Indian a bottle of brandy by a Frenchman. His counsellors advised him not to taste it, insinuating that it was poisoned, and sent with a design to kill him; but Ponteack, with a nobleness of mind, laughed at their suspicions, saying it was not in my power to kill him, who had so lately saved my life.

In the late war of his, he appointed a commissary, and began to make money, or bills of credit, which he hath since punctually redeemed. His money was the figure of what he wanted in exchange for it, drawn upon bark, and the shape of an otter (his arms) drawn under it. Were proper measures taken, this Indian might be rendered very serviceable to the British trade and settlements in this country, more extensively so than any one that hath ever been in alliance with us on the continent.

In travelling northward from Montreal, towards the Ottawawas river, you meet with some few villages belonging to the Round Heads, and the Ottawawas. The Round Heads are so called from the shape of their heads, there being all possible pains taken by their mothers to make their heads round in their infancy, this being esteemed a great beauty.

On the banks of the river St. Joseph, that flows into Lake Meshigan, are two towns settled not long since by the Pottawatamees and Yeahtanees. The Miamee Indians were formerly settled upon this river, but are now dispersed into several parts of the country, upon the Miamee and the Wabach that empties into the Ohio; the last are now known by the name of the Yeahtanees; they are remarkably good-humoured and well-disposed, and always treat their prisoners with kindness, contrary to the practice of most other Indians.

The language of almost all the Indians to the northward, is undoubtedly derived either from that of the Five Nations or the Ottawawas; and any one who is master of these two tongues, may make himself thoroughly understood by upwards of 100 tribes of Indians; for though each tribe has some peculiarities in their language, no great difficulty arises therefrom in conversation.

The Ottawawas, of the two, is understood and spoke by the greatest number. Indeed the Five Nations speak five distinct dialects, tho' they perfectly understand each other.

The Mohock dialect is the most copious, pathetic, and noble. Their discourses run like a gentle flowing stream, without noise or tumult. Their lips scarcely move through a whole speech. The Ottawawas is spoke quicker, and with greater emotion; but both languages are strong and expressive; and, what is more remarkable, they are observed universally to utter themselves with great propriety; a false syntax, or wrong pronunciation, is seldom known among them. Their language is in many respects very deficient, as they have few words expressive of our abstracted ideas, for before their acquaintance with us they talked about few things that were not present as sensible; so that we are obliged, in order to communicate some of our ideas to them, to make use of numberless circumlocutions, which are tedious and perplexing both to speaker and hearer.

The Indians, especially to the southward, do not neglect to fortify themselves, many of their towns being well stockadoed, so as to stand a long siege against an enemy unacquainted with the arts of war. The Five Nations were formerly accounted the best architects on the continent, and are now inferior to those only near Lake Superior, and some nations to the westward. The Indian hunting houses are generally but the work of half an hour at the most, and sometimes they range through the woods for months together, without any house at all, or covering but a skin or blanket.

It is very disagreeable travelling with them, on account of their being enemies to conversation; for they not only never speak themselves but when necessity obliges them, but are displeased with their company if they talk or converse upon a march by land, or a voyage by water. Among the Chickesaws, Creeks, Cherokees, and others to the southward, you will find a conjuror in almost every village, who pretends to great things, both in politicks and physick, undertaking to reveal the most hidden secrets, and to tell what passes in the most secret cabinets, and cause the most difficult negotiations to succeed, to procure good fortune to their warriors and hunters, &c. The conjuror, to prepare himself for these exploits, takes a sound sweat in a stove, and directly after it plunges into a river or lake, be it ever so cold. But the principal employment of these artists, is the practice of physick and surgery. The Indians have few distempers among them, in comparison of what we have. The gout, gravel, bilious cholic, apoplexy, and many other disorders common to us, are unknown to them; nor was the small pox among them till we gave them the infection, since which it hath greatly thinned the numbers of several tribes. They make use of simples in wounds, fractures, dislocations, &c. pouring in the juice or infusion of roots, herbs, &c. into the wound, or into an incision made for the purpose. They likewise make frequent use of bathing, and, during the course of the means, the patient has very little nourishment allowed him; and when these simple means (which almost every one among them knows how to apply) prove ineffectual, the conjuror is called, who exercises his legerdemain over the patient; and whether the patient lives or dies, the worthy doctor is sure to save his credit; for when he sees all hope of recovery past, he never fails to prescribe something that cannot be procured or performed, pretending it to indispensibly necessary, and its efficacy in the present case infallible.

The Indians certainly have remedies that seldom fail in many disorders of their desired effect, particularly in the palsy, dropsy, and the venereal disorder. They frequently make use of cupping and phlebotomy; but their most universal remedy is sweating, and the cold bath immediately after it. They very often take a sweat by way of refreshment, to compose their minds, and to enable them to speak with greater fluency in publick.

They never think a person very dangerously sick till he refuses all kinds of nourishment; and, when this is the case, frequently attribute the disorder to witchcraft, and then the conjurer is sure to be called, who, after sweating, crying, and beating himself, and invoking his genius, confidently assigns the cause of the disorder and a remedy.

The savages who inhabit, or rather wander upon the coasts of Labrador, about the Gulf of St. Lawrence, and the straits of Belleisle, bear very little resemblance to any of the other Indians in America. They wander in large parties, are great cowards; their horrid appearance is the chief thing to be feared from them; they muffle themselves up in such manner as almost conceals their faces, their shirts terminating in a kind of hood about their head, and at top comes out a tuft of hair that hangs over their foreheads; their coat hangs behind as low as their thighs, and terminates before in a point a little below their girdle; from their girdle dangle a border of trinkets, shells, bones, &c. Their chief cloathing are skins and furs, which they put on one over another, to a great number; notwithstanding which heavy dress they appear to be suple and active. They are governed by the old men of each tribe, who form a kind of a senate. Our acquaintance with the Siaux Nippissongs, and other northern Indians, is yet but very slender; but, by the accounts we have, they are idle, savage, cruel, and beastly, beyond any other nations on the continent.

The Seguntacooks, or the Abnaques, settled in New England, were formerly very numerous, as were the Mimaux in Nova Scotia. Of the Penobscots, Narigeewalks, the Saint John Indian, and many others to the eastward and southward of the Gulf of St. Lawrence, there are now scarce any footsteps to be found, except a few families dispersed up and down.

The bark-canoes, used by the Indians, seem for their curious workmanship to deserve particular notice. They are made of two kinds of bark, viz. elm and birch. Those made of elm are generally shorter than the others, and not so neatly constructed. The birch-canoes are used by the English as well as the Indian upon the inland lakes and rivers; they distend the bark, which is very thick, upon a frame of cedar or pine; between the bark and the frame they put small splinters, which help to stiffen and strengthen the canoe. The two ends rise gradually, and terminate in sharp points exactly alike. He that sits behind steers, and he that is forward looks out to prevent their running foul of any thing that might damage the vessel. They sit flat on the bottom, or kneel upon it; their paddles are five or six feet in length, and are in general made of maple. When they go against a current, they use setting poles; but in doing this great care must be taken to preserve an equilibrium; the canoes being very light, are easily overset.

The bark ribs and bars are sewed together with spruce or pine roots, split to a suitable size, which are more pliant, and do not dry so quick as the elm-bark. All the seams are besmeared with gum, inside and out, and every day they examine them. A large canoe will carry twelve men, and some of them more. Among all the savages the Ottawawas are the best builders.

The Indians, in the months of February and March, extract the juice from the maple-tree, which is wholesome and delicious to the palate. The way they extract it is by cutting a notch in the body of the tree, and, by means of a piece of wood or quill, convey the juice from the tree to a vessel placed to receive it. The same tree may be tapped for several years successively. The liquor is as clear as spring-water, and is very refreshing. It is accounted a very good pectoral, and was never known to hurt any one, tho' he drank ever so freely of it. The liquor will not freeze, but, when kept any time, becomes excellent vinegar. The Indians, by boiling it, make from it a kind of sugar, which has a taste very much like honey, but is milder, and answers all the ends of sugar for sweetening; and, no doubt, was it properly manufactured, might be rendered equal to that extracted from sugar-cane. A manufactory of this kind is begun in the Province of New York, near South Bay, which I am told answers very well, and produces considerable quantities of powder and loaf sugar.

There have been many conjectures concerning the different nations of Indians in America, as who, what, and from whence they are, it being taken for granted that they are emigrants from some other country. But as the Indians are very solicitous and careful to hand down their own story from father to son, perhaps the account they give of themselves is most deserving of credit. The Hurons and Five Nation Indians, and all the other nations to the southward (except the Chickesaws) agree that they came from the setting of the sun into this country. The Chickesaws came from South America since the Spaniards took possession of it. The Indians on the great lakes north of the River St. Lawrence, and those between that river and the Bay of Fundy, and quite to Hudson's Bay northward (except the Eskimaux) tell us that they came from the northward.

It will perhaps be agreeable to some to subjoin here an account of the most remarkable animals in America, and of the manner in which the savages take them. And among these the *Beaver* is deserving of the first notice. This animal was not unknown in Europe before the discovery of America. It is an amphibious quadrupede, that continues not long at a time in the water, but yet cannot live without frequently bathing in it. A large beaver will weigh 60 or 70 lb. Their colour is different, according to the country they are taken in. To the northward they are quite black, and to the southward they are almost white, and in the country of the Illinois they are almost the colour of the deer, and some have been seen of a yellowish or straw colour; but it is observed, that the lighter their colour, the less valuable is their fur.

The beaver lives to a great age; the females generally bring forth four young ones at a time. Its jaws are furnished with two cutters and eight grinders; the upper cutter is two inches and a half long, and the lower something longer. The upper jaw projects over the lower one; the head is shaped like the head of a rat, and is small in proportion to the body; its snout is long, its eyes are small and short, and round and shaggy on the outside, but have no hair within. Its fore-feet are not more than five or six inches long, the nails are indented, and hollow like a quill; the hind-feet are flat, and webbed between the toes like those of a duck; they walk very slow, but swim fast; the tail is shaped like the blade of a paddle, is four inches broad where it joins the body, five or six in the middle, and three at the extremity, about an inch thick, and a foot long; and there is no flesh, fowl, or fish, that is more agreeable to the palate and the stomach than this part of the beaver; it is covered with a scaly skin, the scales being near a quarter of an inch long, and fold over each other like those of a fish.

The musk bags or castor taken from these animals is of great use among druggists, but it is said are not so good in America as in Russia. The Indians also use them in many disorders. They dress themselves in mantles made of their skins, which after they have worn for some time become more valuable, for the long hair drops off, and the fur remains more fit for the hat-makers use than when raw or fresh taken.

The industry, foresight, and good management among these animals is very surprizing, and scarcely credible to those who never saw them. When they want to make a settlement, three, four, or more assemble together, and first agree, or pitch upon a place where they may have provisions (which is the bark of trees, lilly-roots, or grass) and every thing necessary for erecting their edifices, which must be surrounded with water; and if there is neither lake nor pond convenient, they make one by stopping the course of some river or brook with a dam. For this end, they cut down trees above the place they are resolved to build it; and they always take their measures so well, as to make the tree fall towards the water, that they may have less distance to roll it when cut to pieces. This done, they float them down to the place appointed, and these pieces they cut bigger or less, longer or shorter, as the case requires. Sometimes they use the trunks of large trees, which they lay flat in the water; at others, they fasten stakes in the bottom of the channel, and then interweave small branches, and fill up the vacancies with clay, mud and moss, in such manner as renders it very tight and secure. The construction of their houses is no less artful and ingenious; they are generally built upon piles in their ponds at some distance from the shore, but sometimes upon the banks of rivers; their form is sound, with a flat roof; the walls are two feet thick, and sometimes more, and they are built of the same materials as their dams; every part is so well finished that no air can possibly enter; about two-thirds of the edifice is raised above the water, and in this they lodge, having the floor strewed with splinters, &c. to render the lodging comfortable, and they are very careful to keep it clean. They have generally three or four different avenues to each house, but all their doors are under water. As fast as they peel off the bark from the billets of wood laid up for their subsistence, they convey them to their dam to strengthen that, or else pile them on the tops of their houses, and fasten them there with mud. You will sometimes find eight or ten beavers in one house, at others not more than three or four, and be the number what it will they all lodge upon one floor.

These animals are never found unprovided, by a sudden and unexpected approach of winter; all their business is completed by the end of September, and their stores laid in. They lay up their provisions in piles near their houses in such a manner that it keeps under the water fit for their use, the but-ends being fastened in the mud or clay at the bottom, so that the current cannot carry it away. When the snows melt and raise the stream, they leave their houses, and every one goes his own way till the season returns for repairing them, or for building new ones, which is the month of July, when they re-assemble, or else form new associations.

The *Ground-Beaver*, as they are called, conduct their affairs in a different manner; all the care they take is, to make a kind of covered way to the water. They are easily known from the others by their hair, which is much shorter. They are always poor, the natural consequence of their idleness. The Indians never hunt these but out of mere necessity.

The manner of hunting beaver is very simple and easy, for this animal has not strength enough to defend itself. The Indians hunt them from November to April, in which season their fur is the best. They either decoy them into traps, or shoot them; but the latter is very difficult, by reason of the quickness of their sight and motion; and should they happen to wound them mortally in the water, it is chance if they ever get them out.

They lay their traps in the paths frequented by the beaver, and bait them with fresh cut poplar boughs, which they are very fond of, and ramble abroad for, notwithstanding their winter-store. Sometimes the Indians open the ice near the beaver-houses, at which opening one stands, while another disturbs the house; the beaver hastens upon this to make his escape at the opening, and seldom fails of having his brains beat out the moment he raises his head above water.

The beaver which frequent the lakes, besides their houses in the water, have a kind of country-house, two or three hundred yards from it, and the Indians here hunt them from one to the other. When these animals discover an enemy of any kind, they hasten into the water, and give warning to their companions, by slapping the water with their tails, which may be heard at a considerable distance.

The *Musk-Rat* resembles the beaver in every part, except its tail, which is round like a rat's. One of these animals weighs about five or six pounds; during the summer season the male and female keep together, but separate at the approach of winter, and each seek a shelter in some hollow tree, without laying up any provision.

Scarce any thing among the Indians is undertaken with greater solemnity than hunting the *Bear*; and an alliance with a noted bearhunter, who has killed several in one day, is more eagerly sought after, than that of one who has rendered himself famous in war; the reason is, because the chace supplies the family with both food and rayment. So expert are some of the Indians at passing thro' the woods and thickets, that they have run down the bears in autumn when they are fat, and then drove them with switches to their towns.

The bears lodge, during the winter, either in hollow trees, or caves; they lay up no provision, and have no nourishment during this season, but what they suck from their own claws, yet they retain both their strength and fat without any sensible diminution.

The bear is not naturally fierce, unless when wounded, or oppressed with hunger. They run themselves very poor in the month of July, and it is somewhat dangerous to meet them till this appetite is satisfied, and they recover their flesh, which they do very suddenly. These animals are very fond of grapes and most kinds of fruit. When provisions are scarce in the woods, they venture out among the settlements, and make great havock of the Indian corn, and sometimes kill the swine. Their chief weapons are their fore-paws, with which they will hug any animal they get into them immediately to death.

The *Elk* is near as large as a horse, but resembles the deer, and, like it, annually renews its horns. The Indians have a great veneration for this animal, and imagine that to dream of it portends good fortune and long life.

The elk delights in cold countries, feeding upon grass in summer, and moss buds &c. in winter, when they herd together. It is dangerous to approch very near this animal when he is hunted, as he sometimes springs furiously on his pursuers, and tramples them to pieces. To prevent this, the hunter throws his cloaths to him, and while the deluded animal spends his fury on these, he takes proper measure to dispatch him.

The *Catamounts* and *Wild-Cats* are great enemies to the elk, and often make a prey of him. He has no other way to disengage himself from these, but by plunging into the water.

On the south and west parts of the great lakes, and on both sides of the Mississipi, the most noted hunt is that of the buffalo.

The hunters encompass as large a tract as they can, where they suppose the buffaloes are, and begin by setting fire to the grass and leaves, and so as the fire advances toward the center, they close up nearer and nearer, by which means they generally slaughter all that happen to be thus inclosed. The buffalo is a large heavy animal, has short, thick, crooked, black horns, and a large beard hanging from his muzzle and head, a part of which falls down by his eyes, and gives him a disagreeable appearance; the back is rounding, covered with hair; on the other parts of the body is a kind of wool. Those to the northward about Hudson's Bay have the best wool upon them, and in the greatest abundance.

There are in this country some *Panthers*, which prey upon almost every living thing that comes in their way. Their flesh is white like veal, and agreeable to the palate, and their fur is valuable.

Here are likewise *Foxes* of various colours, black, grey, red, and white, who by their craft and cunning make great havock among the water-fowl by a thousand deceitful capers, which they cut upon the banks of lakes and rivers.

The *Skunck* or *Pole-Cat* is very common, and is called by the Indians the *Stinking Beast*, on account of its emitting a disagreeable savour to a considerable distance when pursued or disturbed. It is about the size of a small cat, has shining hair of a grey colour, with two white lines, that form an oval, on its back. The fur of this animal, with that of the Ermin, Otter, and Martin, make up what they call the small peltry. The Ermin is about the size of a squirrel, its fur is extremely white, its tail long, and the tip of it as black as jet.

The *Martin*, or *Sable*, lives principally among the mountains, is as long as a common cat, but very slender; the fur is very fine and valuable.

The *Opposum* is a remarkable animal in this country, having under its belly a bag or false belly, in which they breed their young. The young ones proceed from the teats to which they stick, as a part thereof, till they take life, and issue forth, or rather drop off. And to this false belly they fly for shelter and protection in case of any alarm.

The *Porcupine* is as large as a small dog. Its quills are about two inches and a half long, white, and hollow, and very strong, especially on its back; they are exceeding sharp, and bearded in such manner, that if they once enter the flesh of a person, they quickly bury themselves, and occasion great pain.

The savages make great use of these quills for ornamenting their cloaths, belts, arms, &c.

The *Moose* is larger than a large horse, and is one of the deer-kind, every year changing his horns; the colour of this animal is a dark brown, the hair coarse. He has a mane like a horse, a dulap like a cow, a very large head, and a short tail. During the summer he frequents bogs and swamps; in the winter, the north sides of hills and mountains, where the sun will not melt the snow. Their common pace of travelling is a trott, but when hunted are very swift.

It hath been sufficiently remarked, as we have travelled through this extensive country, that it every where abounds with fish, fowl, and variety of game, that in its forests are most kinds of useful timber, and a variety of wild fruit; and, no doubt, every kind of European fruit might be cultivated and raised here in great perfection. In a word, this country wants nothing but that culture an improvement, which can only be the effect of time and industry, to render it equal, if not superior, to any in the world.

FINIS.

APPENDIX B: EXCERPTS FROM *THE JOURNAL OF PONTIAC'S CONSPIRACY* (1763), ATTRIBUTED TO ROBERT NAVARRE

Despite critics' concerns about its process of composition (discussed in the introduction to this volume), *The Journal of Pontiac's Conspiracy* is the surviving document that appears to reflect the most intimate access to Pontiac during the events of Pontiac's Rebellion. The first excerpt printed here is the *Journal*-writer's account of Wolf prophet Neolin, framed as a summary of Pontiac's use of Neolin's dream vision in his war council of 27 April 1763. The two speeches reprinted here represent the best available reporting of Pontiac's efforts to motivate his fellow war sachems and the local French citizenry to war against the British, using Neolin's vision as a central rhetorical foundation.

The original text is in French. I have reprinted the standard translation of the document by R. Clyde Ford from the 1912 edition published by Clyde M Burton and Mary Agnes Burton.

THE VISION OF NEOLIN, THE DELAWARE PROPHET, RELATED BY PONTIAC AT WAR COUNCIL (*JOURNAL*-WRITER'S SUMMARY) 27 APRIL 1763

An Indian of the Wolf nation, eager to make the acquaintance of the Master of Life, – this is the name for God among all the Indians – resolved to undertake the journey to Paradise, where he knew He resided, without the knowledge of any of his tribe or village. But the question was how to succeed in his purpose and find the way thither. Not knowing anyone who had been there and was thus able to teach him the road, he had recourse to incantation in the hope of deriving some good augury from his trance. As a rule all the Indians, even those who are enlightened, are subject to superstition, and put a good deal of credence in their dreams and those things which one has a good deal of trouble to wean them from. This episode will be proof of what I say.

This Wolf Indian in his dream imagined that he had only to set out and by dint of travelling would arrive at the celestial dwelling. This he did the next day. Early in the morning he arose and equipped himself for a hunting journey, not forgetting to take provisions and ammunition, and a big kettle. Behold him then setting out like that on his journey to Heaven to see the Master of Life.

The first seven days of his journey were quite favorable to his plans; he walked on without growing discouraged, always with a firm belief that he would arrive at his destination, and eight days went by without his encountering anything which could hinder him in his desire. On the evening of the eighth day he halted at sunset as usual, at the opening to a little prairie upon the bank of a stream which seemed to him a suitable camping place. As he was preparing his shelter for the night he beheld at the other end of this prairie where he camped, three roads, wide and plainly marked. This struck him as singular, nevertheless, he went on working his shelter so as to be protected from the weather, and made a fire. While doing his cooking he thought he noticed that the three roads became all the brighter the darker it grew, a thing which surprised him to the point of fear. He hesitated for some time over what he should do, whether to remain in his present camp, or move and camp elsewhere; but as he pondered he recalled his incantations, or rather his dream, and that he had undertaken this journey from no other reason than to see the Master of Life. This led him to believe that one of the roads was the one he must take to reach the spot he desired. He concluded to remain where he was until the next day, when he would choose one of the three routes at random. However, his curiosity hardly allowed him time to reflect upon it before he abandoned his camp and set out along the road which seemed to him the widest. He continued in it for half a day without seeing anything to stop him, but, pausing a little to take breath, he saw suddenly a great fire coming out of the earth. This aroused his curiosity. He drew nearer to see what this fire was, but the closer he approached the more the fire appeared to increase. This frightened him and caused him to retrace his steps and take another road which was narrower than the first one.

After following this road the same length of time as the other he beheld the same spectacle, and his fear which had been quieted by the change of route was again aroused. He was once more obliged to turn about and take the third road which he followed for a day without discovering anything. Suddenly he saw before him what appeared to be a mountain of marvelous whiteness, and he stopped, overcome with astonishment. Nevertheless, he again advanced, firmly determined to see what this mountain could be, but when he arrived at the foot of it he no longer saw any road and was sad. At this juncture, not knowing what to do to continue his way, he looked around in all directions and finally saw a woman of this mountain, of radiant beauty, whose garments dimmed the whiteness of the snow. And she was seated.

This woman addressed him in his own tongue: 'Thou appearest to me surprised not to find any road to lead thee where thou wishest to go. I know that for a long while thou hast been desirous of seeing the Master of Life and of speaking with him; and that is why thou hast undertaken this journey to see him. The road which leads to his abode is over the mountain, and to ascend it thou must forsake all that thou has with thee, and disrobe completely, and leave all thy trappings and clothing at the foot of the mountain. No one shall harm thee; go and bathe thyself in a river which I shall show thee, and then thou shalt ascend.'

The Wolf was careful to obey the words of the woman, but one difficulty yet confronted him, namely, to know how to reach the top of the mountain which was perpendicular, pathless, and smooth as ice. He questioned this woman how one should go about climbing up, and she replied that if he was really anxious to see the Master of Life he would have to ascend, helping himself only with his hand and his left foot. This appeared to him impossible, but encouraged by the woman he set about it and succeeded by dint of effort.

When he reached the top he was greatly astonished not to see anyone; the woman had disappeared, and he found himself alone without a guide. At his right were three villages which confronted him; he did not know them for they seemed of different construction from his own, prettier and more orderly in appearance. After he had pondered some time over what he ought to do, he set out toward the village which seemed to him the most attractive, and covered half the distance from the top of the mountain before he remembered that he was naked. He was afraid to go further, but he heard a voice telling him to continue and that he ought not to fear, because, having bathed as he had, he could go on in assurance. He had no more difficulty in continuing up to a spot which seemed to him to be the gate of the village, and here he stopped, waiting for it to open so he could enter. While he was observing the outward beauty of this village the gate opened, and he saw coming toward him a handsome man, clothed all in white, who took him by the hand and told him that he was going to satisfy him and let him talk with the Master of Life. The Wolf permitted the man to conduct him, and both came to a place of surpassing beauty which the Indian could not admire enough. Here he saw the Master of Life who took him by the hand and gave him a hat all bordered with gold to sit down upon. The Wolf hesitated to do this for fear of spoiling the hat, but he was ordered to do so, and obeyed without reply.

After the Indian was seated the Lord said to him: 'I am the Master of Life, and since I know what thou desirest to know, and to whom thou wishest to speak, listen well to what I am going to say to thee and to all the Indians:

'I am He who hath created the heavens and the earth, the trees, lakes, rivers, all men, and all that thou seest and hast seen upon the earth. Because I love you, ye must do what I say and love, and not do what I hate. I do not love that ye should drink to the point of madness, as ye do; and I do not like that ye should fight one another. Ye take two wives, or run after the wives of others; ye do not well, and I hate that. Ye ought to have but one wife, and keep her till death. When ye wish to go to war, ye conjure and resort to the medicine dance, believing that ye speak to me; ye are mistaken, – it is to Manitou that ye speak, an evil spirit who prompts you to nothing but wrong, and who listens to you out of ignorance of me.

'This land where ye dwell I have made for you and not for others. Whence comes it that ye permit the Whites upon your lands? Can ye not live without them? I know that those whom ye call the children of your Great Father supply your needs, but if ye were not evil, as ye are, ye could surely do without them. Ye could live as ye did live before knowing them, – before those whom ye call your brothers had come upon your lands. Did ye not live by the bow and arrow? Ye had no need of gun or powder, or anything else, and nevertheless ye caught animals to live upon and to dress yourselves with their skins. But when I saw that ye were given up to evil, I led the wild animals to the depths of the forests so that ye had to depend upon your brothers to feed and shelter you. Ye have only to become good again and do what I wish, and I will send back the animals for your food. I do not forbid you to permit among you the children of your Father; I love them. They know me and pray to me, and I supply their wants and all they give you. But as to those who come to trouble your lands – drive them out, make war upon them. I do not love them at all; they know me not, and are my enemies, and the enemies of your brothers. Send them back to the lands which I have created for them and let them stay there. Here is a prayer which I give thee in writing to learn by heart and to teach to the Indians and their children.'

The Wolf replied that he did not know how to read. He was told that when he should have returned to earth he would have only to give the prayer to the chief of his village who would read it and teach him and all the Indians to know it by heart; and he must say it night and morning without fail, and do what he has just been told to do; and he was to tell all the Indians for and in the name of the Master of Life.

'Do not drink more than once, or at most twice in a day; have only one wife and do not run after the wives of others nor after the girls; do not fight among yourselves; do not "make medicine," but pray, because in "making medicine" one talks with the evil spirit; drive off your lands those dogs clothed in red who will do you nothing but harm. And when ye shall have need of anything address yourselves to me; and as to your brothers, I shall give to you as to them; do not sell to your brothers what I have put on earth for food. In short, become good and ye shall receive your needs. When ye meet one another exchange greeting and proffer the left hand which is nearest the heart.

'In all things I command thee to repeat every morning and night the prayer which I have given thee.'

The Wolf promised to do faithfully what the Master of Life told him, and that he would recommend it well to the Indians, and that the Master of Life would be pleased with them. Then the same man who had led him by the hand came to get him and conducted him to the foot of the mountain where he told him to take his outfit again and return to his village. The Wolf did this, and upon his arrival the members of his tribe and village were greatly surprised, for they did not know what had become of him, and they asked where he had been. As he was enjoined not to speak to anybody before he had talked with the chief of his village, he made a sign with his hand that he had come from on high. Upon entering the village he went straight to the cabin of the chief to whom he gave what had been given to him, – namely, the prayer and the law which the Master of Life had given him.

This adventure was soon noised about among the people of the whole village who came to hear the message of the Master of Life, and then went to carry it to the neighboring villages. The members of these villages came to see the pretended traveller, and the news was spread from village to village and finally reached Pontiac. He believed all this, as we believe an article of faith, and instilled it into the minds of all those in his council. They listened to him as to an oracle, and told him that he had only to speak and they were all ready to do what he demanded of them.

PONTIAC'S SPEECH TO ASSEMBLED OTTAWAS, HURONS, AND POTAWATOMIES
5 MAY 1763

It is important for us, my brothers, that we exterminate from our lands this nation which seeks only to destroy us. You see as well as I that we can no longer supply our needs, as we have done, from our brothers, the French. The English sell us goods twice as dear as the French do, and their goods do not last. Scarcely have we bought a blanket or something else to cover ourselves with before we must think of getting another; and when we wish to set out for our winter camps, they do not want to give us any credit as our brothers, the French do.

When I go to see the English commander and say to him that some of our comrades are dead, instead of bewailing their death, as the French brothers do, he laughs at me and at you. If I ask anything for our sick, he refuses with the reply that he has not use for us. From all this you can well see that they are seeking our ruin. Therefore, my brothers, we must all swear their destruction and wait no longer. Nothing prevents us; they are few in numbers, and we can accomplish it. All the nations who are our brothers attack them, – why should we not attack? Are we not men like them? Have I not shown you the wampum belts which I received from our Great Father, the Frenchman? He tells us to strike them, – why do we not listen to his words? What do we fear? It is time. Do we fear that our brothers, the French, who are here among us will prevent us? They do not know our plans, and they could not hinder anyway, if they would. You all know as well as I that when the English came upon our lands to drive out our Father, Belestre, they took away all the Frenchmen's guns and that they now have no arms to protect themselves with. Therefore, it is time for us to strike. If there are any French who side with them, let us strike them as well as the English. Remember what the Master of Life told our brother, the Wolf, to do. That concerns us all as well as others. I have sent wampum belts and messengers to our brothers, the Chippewas of Saginaw, and to our brothers, the Ottawas of Michillimackinac, and to those of the Thames River to join us. They will not be slow in coming, but while we wait let us strike anyway. There is no more time to lose. When the English are defeated we shall then see what there is left to do, and we shall stop us the ways hither so that they may never come again upon our lands.

PONTIAC'S SPEECH TO FRENCH SETTLERS NEAR DETROIT
25 MAY 1763

My brothers, we have never intended to do you any injury or harm, neither have we pretended that any should be done you, but among my young men there are some, as among you, who are always doing harm in spite of all precautions that one can take. Moreover, it is not for personal vengeance merely that I am making war upon the English; it is for you, my brothers, as well as for us. When the English have insulted us in the councils which we have held with them, they have insulted you, too, without your knowing it. And since I and all my brothers, also, know that the English have taken away from you all means to avenge yourselves by disarming you and making you sign a paper which they have sent to their own country, – a thing they could not do to us, – for this reason we wish to avenge you equally with ourselves, and I swear the destruction of all that may be upon our lands.

What is more, you do not know all the reasons which oblige me to act as I do. I have told you only what concerns you, but you will know the rest in time. I know very well that many of you, my brothers, consider me a fool, but you will see in the future if I am what people say I am, and if I am wrong. I know very well, also, that there are some among you, my brothers, who side with the English in making war upon us and that grieves me. As for them, I shall know them well and when our Great Father returns I shall name and point them out to him and they will see whether they or we will be most satisfied with the results in the end.

I do not doubt, my brothers, that his war causes you annoyance because of the movements of our brothers who are coming and going in your homes constantly; I am chagrined at it, but do not think, my brothers, that I inspire the harm which is being done you. As a proof that I do not desire it just call to mind the war with the Foxes, and the way I behaved as regards you seventeen years ago. Now when the Chippewas and Ottawas of Michillimackinac, and all the northern nations, came with the Sacs and Foxes to destroy you, who was it that defended you? Was it not I and my men?

When Mackinaw, the great chief of all these nations, said in his council that he would carry the head of your commander to his village, and devour his heart, and drink his blood, did I not take up your cause, and go to his village, and tell him that if he wanted to kill the French he would have to begin first with me and my men? Did I not help you rid yourselves of them and drive them away? How does it come then, my brothers, that you would think me today ready to turn my weapons against you? No, my brothers, I am the same French Pontiac who helped you seventeen years ago; I am French, and I want to die French, and I repeat that it is altogether your interests and mine that I avenge. Let me carry out my plan. I do not demand your assistance, because I know you could not give it; I only ask you for provisions for myself and all my followers. If, however, you should like to help me I would not refuse; you would please me and get out of trouble the quicker, for I promise when the English shall be driven away from here, or killed, we shall all withdraw to our villages, following our custom, to await the coming of our French Father.

Thus you see, my brothers, what my sentiments are. Do not worry. I shall see to it that neither my followers nor any other Indians harm you any further, but I ask that our women may have permission to raise our corn upon your fields and fallow lands. By allowing this you will oblige us greatly.

And the French replied that they were very willing.

APPENDIX C: CONTEMPORARY REVIEWS OF THE WORKS OF ROBERT ROGERS

REVIEWS OF *PONTEACH*

The Gentleman's Magazine
February 1766

1. Ponteach. or, The Savages of *America*, a tragedy; by Major *Rogers*. 2s 6d. *Millan*.

The characters of this piece are, *Ponteach*, the *Indian* emperor on the great lakes; *Philip* and *Chekitan* his sons; *Tenesco* his counsellor and generalissimo; *Astinaco*, the Bear, and the Wolf, *Indian* kings in alliance with *Ponteach*; *Torax* and *Monelia*, son and daughter of *Hendrick*, emperor of the *Mohawks*; an *Indian* conjurer; a *French* priest; *Sharp, Gripe*, and *Catchum, English* governors; Colonel *Cockum* and Capt. *Frisk*, commanders of a garrison in *Ponteach's* country; *M'Dole* and *Murphey*, two *Indian* traders; *Honnyman* and *Orsbourne*, two *English* hunters; and Mrs *Honnyman, Honnyman's* wife.

The *English* traders are represented as practising every species of fraud to circumvent and over-reach the *Indians*; the *English* hunters, as way-laying and shooting them at their return from the chace, and carrying off the peltry they were bringing home; the colonel and captain as treating their just complaints with derision and insult; and the governors as embezzling three-fourths of a present sent from his Majesty to the *Indian* chiefs, and converting the returns wholly to their own use.

Ponteach, justly incens'd at these villanies, forms a project of destroying the *English*, and to effect his purpose finds it necessary to gain *Hendrick*, the Chief of the *Mohawks*, who is a friend to the *English*. The indignation which the reader feels at the villainies of our traders, hunters, officers, and governors, at first creates an interest for *Ponteach*; but this interest is immediately destroyed, by representing *Ponteach* as equally cruel and perfidious. He engages the other *Indian* chiefs to join him in opposing the *English*, under the specious pretence of procuring for them freedom & independance, and at the same time intends as soon as they have served his purpose, to throw them off the mark, and assume an universal tyranny himself.

The same unskillful management destroys the effect of the under plot. *Philip*, one of the sons of *Ponteach*, in order to induce *Hendrick* to join his father against the *English*, forms a scheme of murdering *Monelia* and *Torax*, his son and daughter, and persuading him that the *English* were the assassins. We are struck with horror at a project so diabolically cruel, but we abhor the projector yet more, when we find that *Monelia* is beloved by his brother *Chekitan*, with the utmost tenderness and ardour. *Chekitan*, however, ceases to be an object of pity, when we find that he had some time before taken a captive with whom *Philip* was equally enamoured, and obstinately refused to deliver her to him, at his earnest entreaty, at the same time gratifying his own sordid avarice, by selling her for a slave. All the personages of the play may be considered as devils incarnate, mutually employed in tormenting one another; as their character excite no kindness, their distress moves no pity. The dialogue, however adapted to the characters, is so much below the dignity of tragedy, that it cannot be read without disgust; *damning* and *sinking*, and calling *bitch*, can scarcely be endured in any composition, much less in a composition of this kind: The manners, too, are liable to the same exception, for who but would turn with abhorrence and disgust, from a scene in which *Indian* savages are represented as tossing the scalps of murdered *Englishmen* from one to the other.

Ponteach is finally disappointed of his project, but the perfidy of some whom he trusted; and the piece concludes with the following speech, which he is supposed to utter as he is retiring to some unknown desart, whither his enemies cannot pursue.

[reprints the play's final 22 lines, beginning with 'Kings like Gods are valued & ador'd']

The Monthly Review, or Literary Journal
March 1766

Art. 41. *Ponteach; or the Savages of America. A Tragedy.* 8vo. 2s. 6d. Millan. Major Rogers, of whose Military Journal, and Description of North America, we gave some account in our Review for January last, is the reputed author of this Indian tragedy; which is one of the most absurd productions of the kind that we have seen. It is great pity that so brave and judicious an officer should thus run the hazard of exposing himself to ridicule, by an unsuccessful attempt to entwine the poet's bays with the soldier's laurel. His journal, and account of our western acquisitions, were not foreign to his profession and opportunities; but in turning bard, and writing a tragedy, he makes just as good a figure as would a Grubstreet rhymester at the head of our Author's corps of North American Rangers.

REVIEWS OF *A CONCISE ACCOUNT OF NORTH AMERICA*

The Gentleman's Magazine
November 1765

22. A concise account of *North-America* ... By Major *Rogers, Millan.* 5*s.*
This is an account very different from the compilations which are undertaken for booksellers, by persons wholly unacquainted with the subject, and who generally have neither sufficient diligence nor skill to regulate the mulitfarious materials which lie scattered before them, perhaps in an hundred volumes, nor even to reject, much less reconcile the inconsistencies and contradictions with which such materials always abound.

Major *Rogers* has travelled through great part of the country he has described, in the course of his duty as an officer in his majesty's army, and has received accounts of other parts immediately from the inhabitants, or from persons who had been carried prisoners thither, and afterwards released.

The author gives an account of every province separately, and of its first discovery and settlement; he describes its situation as to latitude and longitude, and to the countries and seas by which it is bounded; its extent; its rivers; its climate; its commodities, buildings, and number of inhabitants: With a particular attention to such facts and circumstances as appeared most interesting in a political or commercial view.

In this work there is also an account of the interiour part of *America*, a territory much larger than the whole continent of *Europe*, and hitherto almost wholly unknown. This territory he has considered under three several divisions, marked out by three great rivers that rise near the center of it, St. *Lawrence*, the *Christino*, and the *Mississippi*.

The river St. *Lawrence* he has traced, and is pretty well acquainted with the country adjacent to it, as far up as lake *Superiour*; and with the country from the *Green Bay* westward, to the *Mississippi* at the Gulph of *Mexico*: He has also travelled the country adjacent to the *Ohio* and the lakes *Erie* and *Meshigan*, and his situation gave him opportunities of gaining accounts of the other parts, more particular and authentic than any other.

He has subjoined such an account of the *Indians*, their customs and manners, as gives a just idea of the genius and policy of the people, and of the method in which they are to be treated by those who wish to preserve a safe and advantageous commerce with them. This is a very entertaining as well as useful part of the work, for which the Major was particularly qualified, by a long and experimental acquaintance with their several tribes and nations, both in peace and war.

It is proposed to continue this History in a second volume, containing maps of the colonies and the interiour country, in which the faults and deficiencies of those already extant will be corrected and supplied; by subscription; the price one guinea.

[Some extracts from this work shall be occasionally given in the future numbers of this miscellany.]

The Critical Review
November 1765

11. *A concise Account of* North-America; *containing a Description of the Several* British *Colonies on that Continent, including the Islands of* Newfoundland, Cape-Breton, &c. *By Major* Robert Rogers. *8vo. Pr. 3s.* Millan.

Works of this nature may be considered as a kind of almanac; and indeed, when we consider the particular circumstances of our American provinces at this time, we wish that some more authentic account of them than has yet appeared, was published; and that the alterations to which the several governments are subject, were authenticated as occasion may offer. The relations we have from Charlevoix, La Hontan, and other French writers, concerning the American Indians, may have been faithful at the time those authors wrote; but the change of the possessors must undoubtedly give North-America a new face.

The work before us is very properly called *concise*. The historical part of it, we apprehend, is extracted chiefly from former publications. The descriptive part is valuable, because it exhibits a view of the country and its savages, at the time that Mr. Rogers had occasion to be well acquainted with it. The credibility of his accounts, however, rests upon the moral character of the author, of whose person we know nothing; tho' we are rather pre-possessed in his favour, by the air of openness with which he writes, unmixed with the marvellous. We own the perusal of his book has given us pleasure, and till one better authenticated appears, we shall hold it in esteem. The picture which Mr. Rogers has exhibited of the emperor Ponteack, is new and curious, and his character would appear to vast advantage in the hands of a great dramatic genius.

The Monthly Review, or Literary Journal
January 1766

A Concise Account of North America. ... By Major Robert Rogers. 8vo. 5s bound. Millan.

Few of our Readers, we apprehend, are unacquainted with the name, or ignorant of the exploits, of Major Rogers; who, with so much reputation, headed the provincial troops called *Rangers*, during the whole course of our late successful wars in America. To this brave, active, judicious officer, it is, that the public are obliged for the most satisfactory account we have ever yet been favoured with, of the interior parts of that immense continent which victory hath so lately added to the British empire. – For, as to what Charlevoix, and other French writers, have related, experience hath shewn with what artful fallacy their accounts have been drawn up: – with the obvious design of concealing, from other nations, the true situation, and real circumstances of that country, of which we were, in many respects, totally ignorant, till the British lion, in revenge of repeated insults, tore away the veil, and opened to our view, the wide, extended, glorious prospect!

The present publication, however, as may be supposed, from the quantity and price above specified, contains but a part of the Major's intended work; the remainder being proposed to be printed by subscription; and to be illustrated with maps of the several colonies, and of the interior country of North America. These we are assured, in the Author's advertisement, will be 'more correct, and easier to be understood, than any yet published.'

Our Author was, happily for his country, the better qualified not only for the task he hath new enjoined his pen, but also for the atchievements in which his sword hath been employed, by the circumstances of his having received his 'early education in a frontier town in the province of New Hampshire, where he could hardly avoid obtaining some knowledge of the manners, customs, and language of the Indians, as many of them resided in the neighbourhood, and daily conversed with the English. – Between the years 1743 and 1755, his manner of life was such, as led him to a general acquaintance both with the British and French settlements in North America, and especially with the uncultivated desart, the mountains, valleys, rivers, lakes, and several passes that lay between and contiguous to the said settlements. Nor did he content himself with the accounts he received from the Indians, or the information of hunters, but travelled over large tracts of the country himself; which tended not more to gratify curiosity, than to inure him to hardships.' – And *hardships* enough he was destined to endure!

[Eight pages of excerpts from *Concise Account*]

Here we cannot help observing what a noble and consistent spirit of liberty prevails among these Indians, with respect to the method used by their chiefs of *inviting*, not *impressing*, the people to accompany them to the wars. What a striking contrast does this afford, to our tyrannical practice of *seizing* our fellow-subjects by brutal force, *imprisoning* and *transporting* them like felons and Newgate convicts; and after such base treatment, compelling them to go forth with our fleets and armies, to fight in defence of the RIGHTS and LIBERTIES of their country!

In short, says our Author, the great and fundamental principles 'of their policy are, that every man is natually free and independant; that no one or more on earth has any right to deprive him of his freedom and independancy, and that nothing can be a compensation for the loss of it.'

[Rogers' seven paragraphs on Pontiac from *Concise Account* (pages 180–2 this volume)]

As our Readers are, perhaps, by this time, fully satisfied with regard to these free-born sons of the vast American wilderness, we shall conclude the present article, with a remark or two, borrowed from Mr. Colden, in respect to the Five nations. 'They are called, says he, a barbarous people, bred under the darkest ignorance; and yet a bright and noble genius shines through these black clouds. None of the Roman heroes have discovered a greater love to their country, or a greater contempt of death, than these people called *barbarians* have done, when liberty came in competition. Indeed I think,' continues that learned and sensible historian, 'our Indians have out-done the Romans in this particular. Some of the greatest of those have murdered themselves to avoid shame or torments; but the Indians have refused to die meanly, or with but little pain, when they thought their country's honour would be at stake by it; but have given their bodies, willingly, to the most cruel torments of their enemies, to shew, as they said, that the Five Nations consisted of men whose courage and resolution could not be shaken. – They greatly sully, however, these noble virtues, by that cruel passion, *revenge*; this, they think, is not only lawful, but honourable; and for this only it is that they can deserve the name of barbarians. – But what, alas! have we *Christians* done, to make them *better?* We have, indeed, reason to be ashamed that these infidels, by our conversation and neighbourhood, are become *worse* than they were before they knew us. Instead of virtues, we have only taught them vices, which they were entirely free from before that time.' In another place he observes, on the same subject, that this cruelty of revenge, is not peculiar to the Five Nations, but is common to all the other Indians. To blunt, however, the keenness of that censure *we* might be apt to cast on them, upon this account, he hath the following just reflection: 'It is wonderful, how custom and education are able to soften the most horrid actions, even among a polite and learned people. Witness the Carthaginians and Phaenicians burning their own children alive in sacrifice; and several passages in the Jewish history; – and witness, in later times, the Christians burning one another for God's sake!'

REVIEW OF *THE JOURNALS OF MAJOR ROBERT ROGERS*

The Critical Review
November 1765

12. *Journals of Major* Robert Rogers: *containing an Account of the several Excursions he made under the Generals who commanded upon the Continent of* North-America, *during the late War. 8vo. Pr. 5s.* Millan.

Though these Journals, as we have observed in our last article, must, as to their credibility, depend greatly on the author's moral character, yet we perceive he has strengthened his relations by the military authorities to which he was subjected, and the communications which he sent to his superiors. The fatigues he underwent in the course of his duty, according to his own account, would be almost incredible, were they not confirmed by the unquestionable relations of persons in the like circumstances. If the author has obtained a government in the country he was so instrumental in reducing, we very heartily wish him joy.

APPENDIX D: CONTEMPORARY REPORTS ON THE LIFE OF ROBERT ROGERS

The social life and various military struggles of the colonies in America were topics of curiosity for English audiences, and Rogers was known to Londoners for his strategic prowess long before he published his own versions of events. The account reprinted here is fairly typical of the genre of the battle narrative, and suggests how Rogers' literary audience was created.

THE GENTLEMAN'S MAGAZINE
MAY 1759

Particulars of Major Robert Rogers*'s last Expedition against the Enemy*

On the 3rd of *March* he marched from *Fort Edward* for *Ticonderoga*, with Capt. *Lotteridge* and 52 *Indians*, and the following detachments, *viz.* of the Royal Regiment, Lieuts. *West* and *Cook*, 4 serjeants, 1 corporal, and 40 privates, *Royal Americans*, light infantry, Capt. *Wylliamos*, Lieut. *McKey*, Ensigns *Brown* and *Moony*, 4 serjeants, 4 corporals, and 110 privates. Volunteers, Lieut. *Trumbal*, 3 sergeants, 4 corporals, and 41 privates; and Lt *Brime*, engineer: And of the Rangers, Lieut. *Tute, Holmes, Brewer,* and *Stark*; 7 serjeants, and 79 privates; the whole, officers included, being 358: – They encamped the first night at half way brook, on the road to Fort *William Henry*: One *Indian* having hurt himself on the road, returned back, with another to take care of him: On the 4th, at ten o'clock they began their march towards Lake *George*, and within a mile of it, halted till the close of the evening, when they continued their march till two o'clock in the morning, at which time they halted again at the first narrows. In the morning, several being frost bitten, 23 of them were sent back to *Fort Edward*. On the evening of the 5th they began their march, and

reached *Sabbath Day Point* about 1 o'clock, and encamped till the morning of
the 7th; at which time they marched again, and arrived at the landing place
about 8 o'clock in the morning, and halted on a point of land on the east side,
where they intended to form an ambuscade, and endeavour to draw out a party
from the fort, by a few skulking persons, who were to return again to the main
body. – At nine o'clock they sent out 2 Rangers and 2 *Indians* to reconnoiter,
that the major might better effect his designs: – They returned again about 11,
and reported that there was no party out on the west side, but on the east there
were 2 parties cutting wood: – It then appearing a good time for the engineer
to make his observations, &c. Capt. *Wylliamos* was ordered to remain with the
regulars, and 30 Rangers, whilst the major, with the engineer and 49 Rangers;
and Capt. *Lotteridge*, with 45 *Indians*, should go up to the hill on the *Isthmus*
that overlooks the fort; where Major *Rogers* left Lieut. *Tute*, and 10 Rangers as
a guard, with an intent to cross the lake with the remainder to the east side, and
cut off the working party that night. – When he came near the lake, he found he
could not get over undiscovered, in the day-time, therefore returned to the engineer, who was left to make observations on the fort, &c. – and with him, and
the whole party, marched back to the point where Capt. *Wylliamos* was, first
leaving five *Indians* and one ranger to observe what numbers crossed the lake
in the evening, from the east side, to the fort. That about dark, the *Indians* and
Rangers returned with an account of their numbers, at which time the engineer
set out again with Lieut. *Tute*, and ten rangers, and went to the entrenchment,
from whence he returned about midnight, without any molestation, and said,
he had accomplished his business to his satisfaction. Upon this, the major
ordered Capt. *Wylliamos*, with the regulars, back to *Sabbath-Day Point*; as
the weather was excessive cold, and the party much fatigued, it did no appear
prudent to march them any further, therefore sent with them Lieut. *Tute*, and
30 rangers, as occasional pilots, or flanking parties. At 3 o'clock the major
marched, with Capt. *Lotteridge* and 46 of his *Indians*, with Lieutenants *Holmes,
Stark,* and *Brewer*, and 40 of his rangers, and one regular, in order to attack the
working party on the east side early in the morning, and crossed *South Bay*
eight miles south of the fort, from thence bore down the same, till they were
opposite the fort on the east side, where they halted, within half a mile of the
lake, from whence they sent out two *Indians* to reconnoitre, who returned in
a few minutes, and brought intelligence that the working party was close to
the bank of the lake, opposite the fort; upon which they stripped off their
blankets, and ran down upon them, took 7 prisoners, 4 scalps, and killed several others as they were retreating to the fort. Whereupon 80 *Indians* and
Canadians rushed out of the fort, and pursued our men closely, being backed
by about 150 *French* regulars. In about one mile's march the *Indians* and

Canadians overtook them, and began to play upon their rear. As they marched in a line abreast, their front was easily made, so they halted on a rising ground, and engaged the enemy, who at first behaved with great bravery, but soon found they could not stand before our marksmen; so scattered and ran. After this the major began his march again in a line abreast, when, in about half a mile, the enemy appeared again, but he did not chuse to engage them there, so went a little further, and halted on a long ridge on that side, opposite to the enemy, when the *Canadians*[1] and *Indians* came up very close; but their pursuit was soon stopped by a volley from the Mohawks and Rangers, which broke them immediately, when part of *Roger*'s detachment pursued them till they were in sight of the *French* regulars, where the *French* made a stand. Afterwards the major marched off without any opposition, the enemy not daring to pursue them any farther. In these several skirmishes 2 Rangers and 1 regular were killed, & 1 *Indian* badly wounded; and the major judges there were killed of the enemy about thirty.

We can further assure the public that Major *Rogers*'s party in general, both officers and men, behaved well; especially Capt. *Lotteridge* and Lieut. *Holmes*, who strove to exceed each other, both of whom behaved with great bravery and coolness during the whole affair. That he continued his retreat till 12 o'clock at night; and at the end of 50 miles march from where he set out in the morning, joined Capt. *Wylliamos*, at Sabbath-day point, who had kindled fires for his reception, which were, no doubt, very acceptable to the party. And that next morning he marched as far as *Long-Island*, on the lake, with the whole detachment where he encamped; from which place he sent an express to Col. *Handiman* at Fort *Edward*, and was met at Lake *George*, by Capt. *M'Bein*, with a detachment, who brought some sleighs to carry the disabled men to Fort *Edward*, where they all arrived the evening of the tenth past.

We hear the Mohawks carried 4 of the *French* prisoners home with them.

---

1 Corrected from *Canaans*.

BIBLIOGRAPHY

Adair, James. *The History of the American Indians; particularly those nations adjoining to the Missisippi, East and West Florida, Georgia, South and North Carolina, and Virginia.* London, 1775.

Anderson, Fred. *Crucible of War: The Seven Years' War and the Fate of Empire in British North America, 1754–1766.* New York: Knopf, 2000.

Anderson, Marilyn J. '*Ponteach*: The First American Problem Play.' *American Indian Quarterly* 3 (1977): 225–41.

Appiah, K. Anthony. 'Identity, Authenticity, Survival: Multicultural Societies and Social Reproduction.' In *Multiculturalism: Examining 'The Politics of Recognition.'* Ed. Amy Gutmann. Princeton: Princeton University Press, 1994, 149–64.

Augstein, Hannah. 'Introduction.' In *Race: The Origins of an Idea, 1760–1860.* Bristol: Thoemmes Press, 1996.

Axtell, James, and William C. Sturtevant. 'The Unkindest Cut, or Who Invented Scalping.' *William and Mary Quarterly*, 3rd Ser., 37/3 (1980): 451–72.

Behn, Aphra. *Oroonoko, or The Royal Slave.* London, 1688.

Bell, Vicki. 'On Speech, Race, and Melancholia: An Interview with Judith Butler.' *Theory, Culture and Society* 16 (1999): 163–74.

Bellin, Joshua David. *The Demon of the Continent: Indians and the Shaping of American Literature.* Philadelphia: University of Pennsylvania Press, 2001.

Berhkofer, Robert F. *The White Man's Indian: Images of the American Indian from Columbus to the Present.* New York: Knopf, 1978.

– 'White Conceptions of Indians.' In *Handbook of North American Indians,* vol 4. Ed. Wilcomb E. Washburn. Washington: Smithsonian, 1988, 522–47.

Bevis, Richard. *Eighteenth-Century Drama 1660–1789.* London and New York: Longman, 1988.

Bhabha, Homi. 'Of Mimicry and Man: The Ambivalence of Colonial Discourse.' *October* 28 (1984): 125–33.

– 'Remembering Fanon: Self, Psyche, and the Colonial Condition.' In *Colonial Discourse and Postcolonial Theory*. Ed. P. Williams and L. Chrisman. New York: Columbia University Press, 1994, 112–23.

Bickham, Troy. *Savages within the Empire: Representations of American Indians in Eighteenth-Century Britain*. Oxford: Oxford University Press, 2006.

Bieder, Robert E. *Science Encounters the Indian, 1820–1880: The Early Years of American Ethnology*. Norman: University of Oklahoma Press, 1986.

Bissell, Benjamin. *The American Indian in English Literature of the Eighteenth Century*. Hamden: Archon Books, 1968 [1925].

Block, Sharon. *Rape and Sexual Power in Early America*. Chapel Hill: University of North Carolina Press, 2006.

Brooke, Frances. *The History of Emily Montague*. London, 1769.

Burton, Clyde M., and Mary Agnes Burton. 'Preface.' In *The Journal of Pontiac's Conspiracy*. 1763. Trans. R.Clyde Ford. Detroit: 1912.

Butler, Judith. 'Performative Acts and Gender Constitution: An Essay in Phenomenology and Feminist Theory.' *Theater Journal* 40 (1988): 519–31.

Calloway, Colin. *The Scratch of a Pen: 1763 and the Transformation of North America*. Oxford: Oxford University Press, 2006.

Calloway, Colin, and Neal Salisbury, eds. *Reinterpreting New England Indians and the Colonial Experience*. Boston: Colonial Society of Massachusetts, 2003.

Carver, Jonathan. *Travels to the Interior Parts of America, in the Years 1766, 1767, and 1768*. London, 1778.

Castillo, Susan. *Performing America: Colonial Encounters in New World Writing 1500–1786*. New York and London: Routledge, 2006.

Cave, Alfred A. *Prophets of the Great Spirit: Native American Revitalization Movements in Eastern North America*. Lincoln: University of Nebraska Press, 2006.

Charlevoix, Pierre F.X. *Journal of a Voyage to North America*. London, 1761 [1744].

Chevrette, Louis. 'Pontiac.' In *Dictionary of Canadian Biography Online*. Accessed 10 Sept. 2008 at www.biographie.ca.

Choudhury, Mita. *Interculturalism and Resistance in the London Theater, 1660–1800: Identity, Performance, Empire*. Lewisburg: Bucknell University Press, 2000.

Colden, Cadwallader. *History of the Five Indian Nations*. London, 1747.

Colley, Linda. *Britons: Forging the Nation 1707–1837*. New Haven: Yale University Press, 1992.

– *Captives: Britain, Empire and the World: 1600–1850*. London: J. Cape, 2002.

Critical Review. London, Nov. 1765.

Cuneo, John R. *Robert Rogers of the Rangers*. New York: Oxford University Press, 1959.

Davies, Robertson. 'Playwrights and Plays.' In *The Revels History of Drama in English*, 6 vols. Ed. Michael Booth et al. London: Methuen, 1975, vol. 6, 145–269.

Deloria, Philip. *Playing Indian*. New Haven: Yale University Press, 1998.

Derounian-Stodola, Kathryn, and James Levernier. *The Indian Captivity Narrative 1550–1900*. New York: Twayne, 1993.

Dillon, John Brown. *Oddities of Colonial Legislation in America*. Indianapolis: R. Douglass, 1879.

Dixon, David. *Never Come to Peace Again: Pontiac's Uprising and the Fate of the British Empire in North America*. Norman: University of Oklahoma Press, 2005.

Dobson, Michael. *The Making of the National Poet: Shakespeare, Adaptation and Authorship, 1660–1769*. Oxford: Clarendon Press, 1992.

Dowd, Gregory Evans. *War under Heaven: Pontiac, the Indian Nations and the British Empire*. Baltimore: Johns Hopkins University Press, 2002.

Eastman, Charles A. *From the Deep Woods to Civilization*. Boston: Little Brown, 1916.

Ellison, Julie. *Cato's Tears and the Making of Anglo-American Emotion*. Chicago: University of Chicago Press, 1999.

Feest, Johanna E., and Christian F. Feest. 'Ottawa.' In *Handbook of North American Indians*, vol. 15. Ed. Bruce Trigger. Washington: Smithsonian, 1978, 772–86.

Fulford, Tim. *Romantic Indians: Native Americans, British Literature and Transatlantic Culture, 1756–1830*. Oxford: Oxford University Press, 2006.

Gale Encyclopedia of Native American Tribes, vol. 1. Detroit: Gale Group, 1998.

Gentleman's Magazine. London, May, 1759; Nov. and Dec. 1760: Dec. 1765; Mar. 1766.

Glover, Susan. 'Battling the Elements: Reconstructing the Heroic in Robert Rogers.' *Journal of American Culture* 26/2 (2003): 180–7.

Greenblatt, Stephen. 'Introduction: New World Encounters.' In *New World Encounters*. Berkeley and Los Angeles: University of California Press, 1993, vii–xviii.

Henry, Alexander. *Travels and Adventures in Canada and the Indian Territories between the years 1760 and 1776*. New York: I. Riley, 1809.

Hiller, Lejaren. *Ponteach: A Melodrama for Narrator and Piano*. Philadelphia: Kallisti Music Press, 1992.

Hinderaker, Eric. *Elusive Empires: Constructing Colonialism in the Ohio Valley, 1763–1800*. Cambridge: Cambridge University Press, 1997.

'Historical Chronicle.' *Gentleman's Magazine*. London. June, July, Aug. 1672.

Hoffer, Peter Charles. *Law and People in Colonial America*. London: Johns Hopkins University Press, 1992.

Hogan, Charles Beecher. *Shakespeare in the Theatre, 1701–1800,* 2 vols. Oxford: Clarendon Press, 1952–7.

Homer. *Odyssey*. Trans. Alexander Pope. London, 1726.

Hough, Franklin B. *Diary of the Siege of Detroit in the War with Pontiac. Also a Narrative of the Principal Events of the Siege by Major Robert Rogers*. Albany, 1860.

Hudson, Nicholas. 'From "Nation" to "Race": The Origin of Racial Classification in Eighteenth-Century Thought.' *Eighteenth-Century Studies* 29/3 (1996): 247–64.

– 'The Vexed Question: Shakespeare and the Nature of Middle Class Appropriation.' In *Shakespeare and the Eighteenth Century*. Ed. Peter Sabor and Paul Yachnin. Aldershot: Ashgate Press, 2008, 43–54.

Hulme, Peter. *Colonial Encounters, Europe and the Native Caribbean 1492–1797*. London: Methuen, 1986.

Hume, Robert D. 'Before the Bard: "Shakespeare" in Early Eighteenth-Century London.' *ELH* 64 (1997): 41–75.

Jennings, Francis. *Empire of Fortune: Crowns, Colonies, and Tribes in the Seven Years' War in America*. New York: Norton, 1988.

Johnson, Odai, and William J. Burling. *The Colonial American Stage, 1765–1774: A Documentary Calendar*. London: Associated University Presses, 2001.

Johnston, Charles. *Chrysal: or the Adventures of a Guinea*. London, 1760.

Jones, Eugene H. *Native Americans as Shown on the Stage 1753–1916*. Metuchen NJ and London: Scarecrow Press, 1988.

Kolodny, Annette. *The Lay of the Land: Metaphor as Experience in History in American Life and Letters*. Chapel Hill: University of North Carolina Press, 1975.

Komlos, John. 'A Malthusian Episode Revisited: The Height of British and Irish Servants in North America.' *Economic History Review* 46 (1993): 768–82.

Loomba, Ania. *Colonialsim/Postcolonialism,* 2nd ed. London and New York: Routledge, 2005.

Manning, Susan. *The Last of the Race: The Growth of a Myth from Milton to Darwin*. Oxford: Clarendon Press, 1994.

Marsden, Jean. 'Shakespeare and Sympathy.' In *Shakespeare and the Eighteenth Century*. Ed. Peter Sabor and Paul Yachnin. Aldershot: Ashgate Press, 2008.

Maxwell, Thomas J. Jr. 'Pontiac before 1763.' *Ethnohistory* 4/1 (1957): 41–6.

McCulloch, Ian. 'Buckskin Soldier: The Rise and Fall of Major Robert Rogers.' *The Beaver* 73/2 (1993): 17–26.

Merchant, Carol. *The Death of Nature: Women, Ecology, and the Scientific Revolution*. San Francisco: Harper, 1990.

Middleton, Richard. *Pontiac's War: Its Causes, Courses, and Consequences*. New York: Routledge, 2007.

Monthly Review. London, Jan. 1766.

Morsberger, Robert E. 'The Tragedy of Ponteach and the Northwest Passage.' *Old Northwest: A Journal of Regional Life and Letters* 4 (1978): 241–57.

Moses, Montrose J. *Representative Plays by American Dramatists: 1765–1819*. New York: Dutton, 1918.

Murray, David. *Forked Tongues: Speech, Writing and Representation in North American Indian Texts*. London: Pinter, 1991.

Navarre, Robert. *The Journal of Pontiac's Conspiracy*. 1763. Ed. Clyde M. Burton and Mary Agnes Burton. Trans. R.Clyde Ford. Detroit, 1912.

Nester, William R. *Haughty Conquerors: Amherst and the Great Indian Uprising of 1763*. Westport: Praeger, 2000.

Nevins, Allan. 'Life of Robert Rogers.' *Ponteach, or the Savages of America: A Tragedy*. New York: Burt Franklin, 1914.

Nussbaum, Felicity. *The Limits of the Human: Fictions of Anomaly, Race, and Gender in the Long Eighteenth Century*. Cambridge: Cambridge University Press, 2003.

O'Toole, Fintan. *White Savage: William Johnson and the Invention of America*. London: Faber and Faber, 2005.

Parkman, Francis. *The Conspiracy of Pontiac and the Indian War after the Conquest of Canada*. 6th ed., 2 vols. Boston, 1870 [1851].

Paterek, Josephine. *Encyclopedia of American Indian Costume*. Santa Barbara: ABC-CLIO, 1994.

Peckham, Howard H. *Pontiac and the Indian Uprising*. Chicago: University of Chicago Press, 1947.

Perdue, Theda. 'Native Women in the Early Republic: Old World Perceptions, New World Realities.' In *Native Americans and the Early Republic*. Ed. Frederick E. Hoxie, Ronald Hoffman, and Peter J. Albert. Charlottesville: University Press of Virginia, 1999, 85–122.

Rankin, Hugh F. *The Theater in Colonial America*. Chapel Hill: University of North Carolina Press, 1965.

Richards, Jeffrey H. *Drama, Theatre, and Identity in the American New Republic*. Cambridge: Cambridge University Press, 2005.

Richter, Daniel K., and James H. Merrell, eds. *Beyond the Covenant Chain: The Iroquois and Their Neighbors in Indian North America 1600–1800*. Syracuse: Syracuse University Press, 1987.

– *Facing East from Indian Country: A Native History of Early America*. Cambridge: Harvard University Press, 2001.

Ritchie, Leslie. '"Expectations of Grease and Provisions": The Circulation and Regulation of Fur Trade Foodstuffs.' *Eighteenth-Century Life* 23/2 (1999): 124–42.

Roach, Joseph R. *Cities of the Dead: Circum-Atlantic Performance*. New York: Columbia University Press, 1996.

Rogers, Robert. *A Concise Account of North America*. London: J. Millan, 1765.

– *The Diary of the Siege of Detroit in the War with Pontiac: also a narrative of the principal events of the siege*. Ed. Franklin B. Hough. Albany: J. Munsell, 1860.

– *Journals of Major Robert Rogers*. 1765. Ed. Howard H. Peckham. New York: Corinth Books, 1961.

– *Ponteach: or the Savages of America. A Tragedy*. London: J. Millan, 1766.

Rowlandson, Mary. *A True History of the Captivity and Restoration of Mrs Mary Rowlandson*. London: Joseph Poole, 1682.

Sabor, Peter, and Paul Yachnin, eds. *Shakespeare and the Eighteenth Century*. Aldershot: Ashgate Press, 2008.

Sayre, Gordon. *The Indian Chief as Tragic Hero: Native Resistance and the Literatures of America from Moctezuma to Tecumseh*. Chapel Hill: University of North Carolina Press, 2005.

– *Les Sauvages Americains: Representations of Native Americans in French and English Colonial Literature*. Chapel Hill: University of North Carolina Press, 1997.

Shaffer, Jason. *Performing Patriotism: National Identity in the Colonial and Revolutionary American Theater*. Philadelphia: University of Pennsylvania Press, 2007.

Sivertsen, Barbara J. *Turtles, Wolves, and Bears: A Mohawk Family History*. Bowie: Heritage Books, 1996.

Slotkin, Richard. *Regeneration through Violence: The Mythology of the American Frontier 1600–1860*. Middletown: Wesleyan University Press, 1973.

Smith, Henry Nash. *Virgin Land: The American West as Symbol and Myth*. Cambridge: Harvard University Press, 1950.

Snow, Dean R.. 'Searching for Hendrick: Correction of a Historic Conflation.' *New York History* 88/3 (2007): 229–53.

Southerne, Thomas. *Oroonoko*. London, 1695.

Spivak, Gayatri. 'Can the Subaltern Speak?' In *Marxism and the Interpretation of Culture*. Basingstoke: Macmillan, 1988, 271–315.

Stacey, C.P. 'Rogers, Robert.' In *Dictionary of Canadian Biography Online*. Accessed 10 Sept. 2008 at www.biographie.ca.

Staves, Susan. 'Tragedy.' In *The Cambridge Companion to British Theatre 1730–1830*. Ed. Jane Moody and Daniel O'Quinn. Cambridge: Cambridge University Press, 2007, 87–102.

Sugden, John. *Tecumseh: A Life*. New York: Henry Holt, 1998.

Tanner, Laura E., and James N. Krasner. 'Exposing the "Sacred Juggle": Revolutionary Rhetoric in Robert Rogers' *Ponteach*.' *Early American Literature* 24 (1989): 4–19.

Taylor, Alan. *The Divided Ground: Indians, Settlers and the Northern Borderland of the American Revolution*. New York: Knopf, 2006.

Tedlock, Dennis. *Rabinal Achi: A Mayan Drama of War and Sacrifice*. Oxford: Oxford University Press, 2003.

Thomas, David Hurst. *Skull Wars: Kennewick Man, Archeology, and the Battle for Native American Identity*. New York: Basic Books, 2000.

Thwaites, Reuben Gold, ed. *The Jesuit Relations and Allied Documents: Travels and Explorations of the Jesuit Missionaries in New France, 1610–1791*, 73 vols. Cleveland: Burrows Bros., 1896–1901.

Thwaites, Reuben Gold, and Louise Phelps Kellogg. *The Revolution on the Upper Ohio, 1775–1777: Compiled from the Draper Manuscripts in the Library of the Wisconsin Historical Society*. Madison: Wisconsin Historical Society, 1908.

Tuhiwai Smith, Linda. *Decolonizing Methodologies: Research and Indigenous Peoples*. Dunedin: University of Otago Press, 1999.

van Kirk, Sylvia. *Many Tender Ties: Women in Fur Trade Society, 1670–1870*. Norman: University of Oklahoma Press, 1983.

– *Toward a Feminist Perspective in Native History*. Toronto: Centre for Women's Studies in Education, 1987.

Vaughan, Alden T. *Roots of American Racism: Essays on the Colonial Experience*. Oxford: Oxford University Press, 1995.

Virgil. *Aeneid*. Ed. K.W. Gransden. Cambridge: Cambridge University Press, 1990.

Wallace, Anthony F.C. *The Death and Rebirth of the Seneca*. New York: Knopf, 1970.

Ward, Edward. *A Trip to New England*. London, 1699.

Warrior, Robert Allen. *Tribal Secrets: Recovering American Indian Intellectual Traditions*. Minneapolis: University of Minnesota Press, 1995.

Wheeler, Roxanne. *The Complexion of Race: Categories of Difference in Eighteenth-Century English Culture*. Philadelphia: University of Pennsylvania Press, 2000.

White, Hayden. *Tropics of Discourses: Essays in Cultural Criticism*. Baltimore: Johns Hopkins University Press, 1987.

White, Richard. *The Middle Ground: Indians, Empires, and Republics in the Great Lakes Region, 1650–1815*. Cambridge: Cambridge University Press, 1991.

– 'Pontiac.' In *Encyclopedia of North American Indians*. Ed. Frederick E. Hoxie. Boston: Houghton Mifflin, 1996, 496–7.

– 'The Fictions of Patriarchy: Indians and Whites in the Early Republic.' In *Native Americans and the Early Republic*. Ed. Frederick E. Hoxie, Ronald Hoffman, and Peter J. Albert. Charlottesville: University Press of Virginia, 1999, 62–84.

Williamson, Peter. *French and Indian Cruelty, Exemplified in the Life and Various Vicissitudes of Peter Williamson*. London, 1757.

Winkfield, Unca Eliza. *The Female American*. Ed. Michelle Burnham. Peterborough: Broadview Press, 2001.

Wrong, George M. *Canada and the American Revolution: The Disruption of the First British Empire*. New York: Macmillan, 1935.

Young, Robert J.C. *Colonial Desire: Hybridity in Theory, Culture, and Race*. London and New York: Routledge, 1995.

INDEX